Unwin Critical Library
GENERAL EDITOR: CLAUDE RAWSON

MONTAIGNE'S *ESSAIS*

Montaigne's
Essais

DOROTHY GABE COLEMAN

*Reader in French Literature in the
University of Cambridge and Fellow
of New Hall*

London
ALLEN & UNWIN
Boston Sydney Wellington

Allen & Unwin, the academic imprint of
Unwin Hyman Ltd
PO Box 18, Park Lane, Hemel Hempstead, Herts HP2 4TE, UK
40 Museum Street, London WC1A 1LU, UK
37/39 Queen Elizabeth Street, London SE1 2QB

Allen & Unwin Inc.,
8 Winchester Place, Winchester, Mass. 01890, USA

Allen & Unwin (Australia) Ltd,
8 Napier Street, North Sydney, NSW 2060, Australia

Allen & Unwin (New Zealand) Ltd in association with the Port Nicholson Press Ltd,
Private Bag, Wellington, New Zealand

First published in 1987

British Library Cataloguing in Publication Data

Coleman, Dorothy Gabe
Montaigne's Essais.
1. Montaigne, Michel de ——Criticism and
interpretation
I. Title
844'.3   PQ1643
ISBN 0–04–800072–8

Library of Congress Cataloging-in-Publication Data

Coleman, Dorothy Gabe.
Montaigne's Essais.
(Unwin critical library)
Bibliography: p.
Includes index.
1. Montaigne, Michel de, 1533–1592. Essais. I. Title.
II. Series.
PQ1643.C57 1987   844'.3   86–28669
ISBN 0–04–800072–8 (alk. paper)

Typeset in 10 on 12 point Plantin Light by Columns, Caversham, Reading
and printed in Great Britain by
Billing and Sons Limited, London and Worcester

For Odette
with love

GENERAL EDITOR'S PREFACE

Each volume in this series is devoted to a single major text. It is intended for serious students and teachers of literature, and for knowledgeable non-academic readers. It aims to provide a scholarly introduction and a stimulus to critical thought and discussion.

Individual volumes will naturally differ from one another in arrangement and emphasis, but each will normally begin with information on a work's literary and intellectual background, and other guidance designed to help the reader to an informed understanding. This is followed by an extended critical discussion of the work itself, and each contributor in the series has been encouraged to present in these sections his own reading of the work, whether or not this is controversial, rather than to attempt a mere consensus. Some volumes, including those on *Paradise Lost* and *Ulysses*, vary somewhat from the more usual pattern by entering into substantive critical discussion at the outset, and allowing the necessary background material to emerge at the points where it is felt to arise from the argument in the most useful and relevant way. Each volume also contains a historical survey of the work's critical reputation, including an account of the principal lines of approach and areas of controversy, and a selective (but detailed) bibliography.

The hope is that the volumes in this series will be among those which a university teacher would normally recommend for any serious study of a particular text, and that they will also be among the essential secondary texts to be consulted in some scholarly investigations. But the experienced and informed non-academic reader has also been in our minds, and one of our aims has been to provide him with reliable and stimulating works of reference and guidance, embodying the present state of knowledge and opinion in a conveniently accessible form.

C.J.R.
University of Warwick,
December 1979

ACKNOWLEDGEMENTS

Acknowledgements are due, for permission to quote copyright material, to Guy Lee, John Murray and Oxford University Press.

CONTENTS

PREFACE

Montaigne is a difficult author but a fascinating, stimulating and imaginative one. Unlike many writers on the *Essais* I do not find him easy to read, not do I find interpreting him easy. Writers 'explain' his thought and technique, and by so doing fail to observe how much better Montaigne is than they. My aim echoes Emerson's remark, ' 'Tis the good reader that makes the good book', and the perfect reader realizes that his own experience of life and literature not only helps his understanding of Montaigne but actually is itself enhanced intellectually, emotionally and sensitively through reading Montaigne.

Every great work is difficult, and in every true critic there is a disciple. My remarks are inevitably subjective but they are pushing all the while towards objectivity. I 'sense' Montaigne standing at my shoulder, teasing, humorous and inscrutable; a civilized gentleman, with a sense of human absurdity, but aware, too, of human dignity, founded precisely on our awareness and acceptance of absurdity. Montaigne is perfectly aware of distortion and ambiguity in all human communication – nothing but commentary after commentary in order to try to speak intelligibly – 'nous ne faisons que nous entregloser'(III.13).

I quote Cotgrave, whose dictionary has great historical value for the study of French and English, when I am 'trying out' the meaning of a particular word, and Florio, who wrote not a literal translation but who can make Montaigne live in English just as Rabelais lives through the prism of Urquhart, since I think his rendering is particularly apt.

ABBREVIATIONS

Cotgrave	Randle Cotgrave, *A Dictionarie of the French and English Tongues* (London: Adam Islip, 1611)
EP	*Reproduction en phototypie de l'exemplaire avec notes manuscrites marginales des Essais de Montaigne appartenant à la ville de Bordeaux*, ed. Ferdinand Strowski, 3 vols (Paris: Librairie Hachette, 1912)
exemplaire	*L'Exemplaire de Bordeaux* (Paris: Chez Abel L'Angelier, 1588). Montaigne's own copy with manuscript alterations by the author himself
Florio	*The Essayes of Michael Lord of Montaigne*, trans. John Florio (London: Routledge, n.d.)
Villey-Saulnier	*Les Essais de Montaigne*, ed. Pierre Villey with a preface by V.-L. Saulnier, 2 vols (Paris: Presses Universitaires de France, 1978)

Note

The letters (A), (B) and (C), inserted where the information is relevant, refer to the 1580 edition of the *Essais*, the 1588 edition and the *exemplaire* version as it appears in Villey and Saulnier's edition.

Classical authors are in general quoted from modern editions, but where the quotation is Montaigne's the text of the *exemplaire* is retained, even when it is at variance with modern editions.

The English version used throughout is that of Florio (1553?–1625). Occasionally, the version is my own, and this is followed by the initials 'DGC'.

CHAPTER 1
Introduction

(i) BIOGRAPHY

We are all perhaps familiar with the personality of Montaigne as 'fictionalized' by Montaigne in the *Essais*: a convivial country gentleman with an atrocious memory, a soft and lazy disposition, a slow mind, a tardy faculty of invention and a sluggish apprehensive power (I.26). He paints a picture of an extremely sensitive man, both as regards poetry ('Elle ne pratique nostre jugement; elle le ravit et ravage': I.21) and as regards cruelty (III.8) and the suffering of other human beings ('La veue des angoisses d'autruy m'angoisse materielle-ment': I.21). He relishes telling us that radishes were good for him at one period, that they disagreed with his stomach at another and that today they agree with him again (III.13); that his eating habits are 'indecents' because he eats 'goulement' (III.13) and spoil his health and pleasure; that he prefers dinner to lunch, although it is not the meal itself that matters but the company he eats in (III.13). He delights our fondness for the picturesque with his thick moustache – 'Les estroits baisers de la jeunesse, savoureux, gloutons et gluans, s'y colloyent autresfois, et s'y tenoient plusieurs heures apres' (I.55: 'The close-smacking, sweetnesse-moving, love-alluring, and greedi-smirking kisses of youth, were heretofore wont to sticke on them [mostachoes] many houres after'); with his being a man who, because of his lack of height, preferred to be on horseback; who hated lying and dissimulation; who was rather stubborn and reactionary (III.1 and 4); and who did not suffer fools gladly. He savours giving us an account of his sexual capacity (III.5) or incapacity (I.2), of his gallstones, his old age and the presence within him of two personalities – the mayor of Bordeaux and Michel de Montaigne (III.10) – whom he keeps clearly separate.

We are attracted to the portrait and become fascinated by the 'autobiography'. We are like Sainte-Beuve, who said 'Il y a du Montaigne en chacun de nous'. But very soon we can find 'untruths' in this 'autobiography': for instance, there seems to be a contradiction between a statement like 'Je n'ay eu guere en maniement que mes affaires' (II.17) and 'En ce peu j'ay eu à negotier entre nos Princes' (III.1). After all, the real Montaigne was indeed an important political figure negotiating with Henri de Navarre, Henri de Guise, Catherine de Medici and Henri III; this suggests that the public facts of his life are peripheral to what he wants to do in the *Essais*. He is not concerned with being a historian of his life in a two-dimensional way. The *Essais* is neither his *Journal* nor his *Mémoires*; he never published his own *Journal de voyage en Italie*, and it was only in 1774 that it appeared and shocked the world of the Enlightenment by its *sympathique* attitude towards the church. The *Essais* is unique: a combination of fiction and experience which disorients the reader completely. And Montaigne is aware of its uniqueness: at the beginning of 'De l'affection des peres aux enfans' (II.8) some time between 1588 and his death in 1592 he adds the words 'Le seul livre au monde de son espece'.

Before tasting the 'fictional' Montaigne we shall briefly sum up the factual events of his life. He was born on 28 February 1533 at the château of Montaigne in the small hamlet known today as Saint-Michel de Montaigne, about fifty miles east of Bordeaux. The round tower still stands with the library (now empty of books) on the second floor where Montaigne wrote his *Essais*. From the library windows he could view the gently sloping hills and plains covered with vineyards. His father, back from fighting in Italy, sent his son to be brought up for about twenty-three months with a humble peasant family, where the first words he spoke would be in a dialect of Périgord; but once home in the château they disappeared (as any language or scraps of it will with a very young child, if there is no one speaking it around him). Thanks to a father who had been enlightened on education by Erasmus' treatise *De pueris* Montaigne learned Latin before French by the direct method under a German tutor.

At the age of 6 he was sent to the Collège de Guyenne in Bordeaux where his teachers – the Scotsman Buchanan, the fine literary critic Muret, Grouchy, Guillaume Guerente and others – were all Erasmianists. Montaigne's spoken Latin got worse in the college, but – and this is crucial if we are to understand the bi-literariness of his writing – he never lost the ability to read Latin or to love the literature of ancient Rome. At Guyenne, he says, he read Ovid first (I.26) because the *Metamorphoses* was 'most agreeing with my young age' (Florio). May I be allowed to disagree? The solitary reading of Ovid, Virgil, Horace, and so on, was bound to awaken his sensualism, his eroticism, his pagan leanings and his passionate nature: he would read in them that no man can win over passions and would discover the physiological nature of sensations around lust, the alternation between fire and ice and the sheer immobility that love creates. Montaigne hated the sempiternal Cicero that he had at school, and this hatred was to last throughout his life.[1]

Elie Vinet (1509–87), a humanist of Bordeaux, who became the principal of the Collège de Guyenne in 1562 and who kept up a close correspondence with Buchanan until his death (letters delivered by Scotsmen who came to Bordeaux for the wine trade), sets out the programme of schooling in the college in the sixteenth century.[2] Montaigne, having been taught Latin before he entered the school, skipped the tenth form where the children were called *alphabétaires* and the ninth (*les aulani*) and joined the seventh form where the pupils were taught 'l'art de versifier ainsi que les figures'.[3] In the fourth form he was treated to a discourse of Cicero and read the *Tristia* and the *Epistulae ex ponto* of Ovid: in the third form he learned of rhetoric, and in the second form he read Virgil and the *Pharsalia* of Lucan, 'dans les quatre classes supérieures et surtout dans la première on traite de la rhétorique . . . A trois heures, la Poétique, surtout d'après Virgile, Lucain et Perse, sans oublier Juvénal, Horace et Ovide, *mais dans les endroits où ils respectent les moeurs*.'[4] On 25 August every year the Bordeaux college held a great fête – the *Ludovicales* – where all the educational work of the year was shown off to the Bordelais people: 'de tous les quartiers de la ville on accourt en foule à ce spectacle' and after 20 September 'on donne congé aux enfants pour les vendanges jusqu'au 1er octobre!' This was the school system that Montaigne knew from 1539 until he left in 1546 or 1547.

For the following eleven years of his life we do not have any archival documentation as to his activity, and Montaigne does not tell us of anything in the *Essais*. The hypothesis of Trinquet that he went to Paris is singularly attractive: the enthusiasm that Montaigne had for the capital city is well known.

Je ne veux pas oublier cecy, que je ne me mutine jamais tant contre la France que je ne regarde Paris de bon œil: *elle a mon cœur des mon enfance*. Et m'en est advenu comme des choses excellentes: plus j'ay veu depuis d'autres villes belles, plus la beauté de cette-cy peut et gaigne sur mon affection. Je l'ayme par elle mesme, et plus en son estre seul que rechargée de pompe estrangiere. *Je l'ayme tendrement, jusques à ses verrues et à ses taches. Je ne suis françois que par cette grande cité*: grande en peuples, grande en felicité de son assiette, mais sur tout grande et incomparable en variété et diversité de commoditez, la gloire de la France, et l'un des plus nobles ornemens du monde.[5]

('De la vanité', III.9; Villey-Saulnier, p. 972: my italics)

I will not forget this, that I can never mutinie so much against Paris but I must needes looke on Paris with a favourable eye: it hath my hart from my infancy, whereof it hath befalne me as of excellent things: the more other faire and stately cities I have seene since, the more hir beauty hath power and doth still usurpingly gaine upon my affection. I love that citie for her own sake, and more in her onely subsisting and owne being then when it is full fraught and embellished with forraine pompe and borrowed garish ornaments: I love so tenderly that even hir spotts, her blemishes and hir warts are deare unto me. I am no perfect Frenchman, but by this great matchlesse citie, great in people, great in regard of the felicitie of her situation; but above al, great and incomparable in varietie and diversitie of commodities: the glory of France, and one of the noblest and chiefe ornaments of the world.

Trinquet has accumulated reasons for his conjecture – the presence of Turnebus, the illustrious Hellenist for whom Montaigne had enormous admiration, the lectures given by his old teachers, Buchanan and Muret (lectures attended by Ronsard and Du Bellay in 1553), the number of Greek books he owned suggesting a period of further education, and so on – but it is still only a conjecture.

We have a document dated October 1557 which supplies the first date of Montaigne as a magistrate in Bordeaux. And towards the end of the same year it is likely that he contracted with La Boëtie a friendship/love that was to illuminate his whole life. La Boëtie was a legal colleague, a classical scholar and neo-Latin poet, in touch with Ronsard and Du Bellay, Baïf and Saint-Gelais. His relationship with Montaigne until his death in 1563 was profound, and his influence on the *Essais* was important. We know for certain that Montaigne was in Paris for at least seventeen months from 1561 to 1562. This may have been when he knew Turnebus so well that he could say in the *Essais*:

comme j'ay veu Adrianus Turnebus, qui, n'ayant faict autre

profession que des lettres, en laquelle c'estoit, à mon opinion, *le plus grand homme qui fut il y a mil' ans*, n'avoit toutesfois rien de pedantesque que le port de sa robe, et quelque façon externe, qui pouvoit n'estre pas civilisée à la courtisane, qui sont choses de neant.

('Du pedantisme', I.25; Villey-Saulnier, p. 139.A: my italics)

as I have seene Adrianus Turnebus, who having never professed any thing but studie and letters, wherein he was, in mine opinion, the worthiest man that lived these thousand yeares, and who notwithstanding had no pedanticall thing about him but the wearing of his gowne, and some external fashions that could not well be reduced, and incivilized to the courtiers cut; things of no consequence.

Montaigne was 28 years old and could consult Turnebus more easily (for example, on the originality of Sebond's work: 'Apologie de Raimond Sebond', II.12, where he states that 'je m'enquis autrefois à Adrien Tournebu, qui sçavoit toutes choses, que ce pouvoit estre de ce livre') than he could have consulted him at 14 – the latest date if he sees him in Toulouse in 1547, the date Turnebus left to settle in Paris permanently.[6] He has several books from Turnebus' press in his library.[7] And we have one extra fact. There is in Libourne's Municipal Library (where there are at least three different books owned by Montaigne, signed with his autograph) a copy of Philibert de l'Orme's *Nouvelles inventions pour bien bastir et à petits fraiz*, with the autograph of Montaigne cut out. Presumably it was cut out after Montaigne's *Essais* had been put on the Index by a decree of 12 June 1676. The intriguing thing about this copy – apart from Montaigne's interest in a pioneering book of architecture – is the date and the publisher: *A Paris. De l'Imprimerie de Federic Morel, rue S. Jean de Beauuais au franc Meurier. M.D.LXI. Auec priuilege du Roy.* Federic Morel, surnamed the Elder (1523–83), set up in business in 1557 and was made printer to the king in 1571. Around him was a circle full of eminent Latinists such as Dorat, Macrin, Buchanan, Michel de l'Hospital, Lancelot de Carle, Guillaume Aubert, Sainte-Marthe and Turnebus. Turnebus had been the *lecteur royal* since Toussaint died in 1547; he taught in Latin; at first he had a dislike for everything in the vernacular but was soon won over by the Pléiade and was present at the production of Jodelle's *Cléopâtre* in 1553. He edited in 1552 and 1555 several works of Plutarch; in 1552 he published seven plays by

Aeschylus. The *cénacle* of Morel is going strongly in 1561: it still
counts Turnebus as a faithful client. It is likely that Montaigne entered
that *cénacle* and that he bought the Philibert de l'Orme book straight
from the Morel press. It is possible that he frequented the Morel
cénacle and, if so, he is much more of a scholar than he would like us
to think in the *Essais*.

In 1565 he married Françoise de la Chassaigne from an established
family in Bordeaux and from her he had six girls, of whom only one,
Leonor, survived. In the same year Turnebus died. In 1569 there
appeared, with no name of the translator, *La Theologie naturelle de
Raymond Sebon*,[8] translated from Latin into French. Montaigne had
started working on it at least four years earlier, for we have seen that
he consulted Turnebus about it (see above, page 5). This is a clue to
his real profession, that of a writer. And in fact he resigned from the
magistracy the following year and 'retired' to his library to read and
write. But he did not 'retire' really. He paid another trip to Paris in
1571–2 and went to Morel with works of La Boëtie that needed
publishing.[9] Altogether he paid many trips to Paris between 1557 and
1572, and there is no sense in regarding him as an inhibited country
gentleman. His friends included some of the most eminent people of
his time: the three Henris in the civil war that was raging in France
from 1562 to 1595 – Henri III, Henri, duc de Guise and Henri
de Navarre; the Queen Catherine de Medici and the Chancellor of
France, Michel de l'Hospital; Amyot, the translator of Plutarch; the poet
Jacques Peletier du Mans, Etienne Pasquier, and so on. On
9 September 1571, Charles IX named him 'gentilhomme ordinaire de
la chambre du roi' and, on 30 November 1577, Henri de Navarre
made him a 'gentilhomme de sa chambre'. On 1 March 1580 came the
publication in Bordeaux of the *Essais*, the first edition of books I and
II: *Essais de Messire Michel Seigneur de Montaigne, Chevalier de L'ordre
du Roy & Gentil-homme ordinaire de sa Chambre. Livre premier &
second. A Bourdeaus. Par S. Millanges Imprimeur ordinaire du Roy.
M.D.LXXX. Avec privilege du Roy.* After which he went to Paris
where Henri III told him how much he liked the *Essais* and
Montaigne answered: 'Sire, il faut donc que je plaise à Votre Majesté,
puisque mon livre lui est agreable, car il ne contient autre chose qu'un
discours de ma vie et de mes actions.'

He and a few friends then made the long journey to the spas of
France, Switzerland and Italy, spending seventeen months eight days
away from home. While away, he was elected mayor of Bordeaux and
served on his return for four years. We can gather from his letters (see

the Pléiade edition of his works) the kind of business he conducted: for the first two years it was mainly peaceful negotiating with Monseigneur de Matignon, marshal of France; with the king, Henri III; and with Henri de Navarre. In the last two years, from 1583 to 1585, the civil war became intense, and it was a question of holding the Bordelais to loyalty to the king of France. When Montaigne retired from this duty he was, none the less, still a negotiator and was in Paris on the day of the Barricades (12 May 1588); the Ligue forced Henri III to quit his own capital city and move to Chartres and then Rouen, accompanied by, among others, Montaigne and Pierre de Brach. The Paris edition of the *Essais* was published in June 1588, containing a new third book and over 600 additions to the Bordeaux edition. On 10 July, Montaigne came back from Rouen and was quickly put in the Bastille by the *Ligueurs*, only to be released in the evening by an order of Catherine de Medici. On his way home to Bordeaux he stopped in Blois for a couple of days when the Etats Généraux were taking place; he met there Pasquier and Thou, and left the town before the assassination of the two Guises. The last four years of his life are fascinating: he knows an intense period of creativity; the *Essais* is feverishly worked on as can be seen in the number of marginalia inserted by Montaigne's own hand in the *exemplaire* now in the public library of Bordeaux; and, too, his health declines. We can read in a letter to the new king, Henri IV (who as Henri de Navarre had twice been a guest in the château of Montaigne), the civilized intellectual gentleman declining, on health grounds, the request to come to Paris and advise the king on matters of controlling the affairs of France. For the last two years Montaigne was increasingly ill and had visitors to the château such as Florimond de Raemond and Pierre Charron. On 13 September 1592, Montaigne died and was buried in the church of the Feuillants in Bordeaux.[10]

(ii) THE 'LIVING' TEXT

In the act of literary communication two factors alone are present: the text and the reader. We 'speak' Montaigne's words in order to try at the thought they contain; we are rehearsing the verbal fabric in our own minds. In the essay 'De la vanité' (III.9) he makes it quite clear that he is *living* his biography. His work will be unfinished because he is writing down the thoughts he has just this very instant had, and he will only stop writing when his brain is dead. 'Qui ne voit que j'ay pris une route par laquelle, sans cesse et sans travail, j'iray autant qu'il y aura d'ancre et de papier au monde? Je ne puis tenir registre de ma vie par mes actions: fortune les met trop bas; je le tiens par mes fantasies' (Villey-Saulnier, p. 945: 'Who seeth not that I have entred so large a field, and undertaken so high a pitch, wherein so long as there is either inke or paper in the world, I may uncessantly wander and fly without encumbrance? I can keepe no register of my life by my actions: fortune placeth them too lowe: I hould them of my fantasies'). There is a long passage later on in this chapter on memory and the shape of his life:

> Encores en ces ravasseries icy crains-je la trahison de ma memoire que par inadvertance elle m'aye faict enregistrer une chose deux fois. Je hay à me reconnoistre, et ne retaste jamais qu'envis ce qui m'est une fois eschappé. Or je n'apporte icy rien de nouvel apprentissage. Ce sont imaginations communes: les ayant à l'avanture conceuës cent fois, j'ay peur de les avoir desjà enrollées.
>
> (ibid., p. 962)

And even in these fantasticall humors or dotings of mine, I feare the treason of my memory, least unwarily it have made me to register somethings twise. I hate to correct and agnize my selfe, and can never endure but grudgingly to review and repolish what once hath escaped my pen. I heere set downe nothing that is new or lately found out. They are vulgar imaginations, and which peradventure having beene conceived a hundred times, I feare to have already enrolled them.

It is as if memory were another person 'je me mets hors de moi'; it is memory which retains the shape of his life in this written form; it is memory which keeps him in slavery. The betrayal of memory would make him write a thing twice over. On rereading what he had written, he would – hatefully – recognize himself. His hatred of 'me gloser moymesme' is uppermost in this passage.

But where is the text that Montaigne left to posterity? Is it the *exemplaire* or is it the 1595 edition? I have elsewhere[11] reiterated the traditional argument that the *exemplaire* must be seen as the last copy that Montaigne possessed. It is possible that another copy was left in the château and that Madame de Montaigne, Pierre de Brach and Mademoiselle de Gournay (his adopted daughter) thought themselves to be his literary executors and produced the 1595 edition which was the 'sixth'[12] edition of the *Essais*. But this 'other' copy is not extant. The argument of Samuel de Sacy and Pierre Michel in their editions of the *Essais* – that Montaigne would have surely made clear in the final edition the pure text to be printed – is insoluble. For the fact is that *it would never be finished* by definition of what Montaigne was trying to record. David Maskell rightly says: 'Il [*exemplaire*] est le témoignage précieux des hésitations de Montaigne quand il rédigeait ses dernières additions et retouchait son texte entier.'[13] Strowski and others produced the Édition Municipale (based on the *exemplaire*) in Bordeaux from 1906 to 1933, and other editions take the decipherment from that edition: for example, Villey, Armaingaud, Plattard, Thibaudet and Rat. I propose to follow Villey and Saulnier's edition in this book. But in spite of Strowski's immense meticulousness there are defects in it, and the differences between this text and the original *exemplaire* are important.

In the first place, there is the question of different inks. Take, for example, the famous statement about love and friendship that comes in 'De l'amitié' (I.28): '(A) Si on me presse de dire pourquoy je l'aymois, je sens que cela ne se peut exprimer, (C) qu'en respondant: Par ce que c'estoit luy; par ce que c'estoit moy' (Villey-Saulnier, p. 188: 'If a man urge me to tell wherefore I loved him, I feele it cannot be expressed, but by answering; Because it was he, because it was my selfe'). Sayce makes the important remark: 'As often, the supreme statement comes in a late addition.'[14] In the *exemplaire*, however, there are very clearly two different inks: 'qu'en respondant: par ce que c'estoit luy, par ce que c'estoit moy' (*exemplaire*, p. 71v). This is crucial: the first correction stopping at 'luy' is followed by a full stop. In a different ink and maybe years later Montaigne moulds his statement. At the earlier stage it is incomplete as a definition of friendship. He seems to be hero-worshipping La Boëtie. The full force of his feeling is not considered. And so he added 'par ce que c'estoit moy', thus completing the correspondence between his friend and himself. In his own *exemplaire* you can just see the full stop cancelled with a little stroke of Montaigne's pen. Later on the same page he makes a correction, 'force inexplicable et fatale mediatrice' in the same ink as 'par ce que c'estoit moy', and one hazards a guess that the two corrections were made at the same time. In the whole essay 'De l'amitié' there is a mixture of inks, thus telling us that Montaigne came back to the task of defining feeling many times.

Another example which is equally crucial is on p. 3v in the essay 'De la tristesse' (I.2). It is a confession of his own sexual impotence.

He decides that this is too great a revelation for posterity to have and so he crosses it out: 'extreme, au girõ mesme de la ioüyssance ~~accident qui ne m'est pas incegnu~~'. The crossing-out is made twice and in different inks. Clearly, Montaigne came back to the passage and deliberately crossed it out again.

From these two examples it can be seen that recourse to Montaigne's own copy is vital. There are other instances: on page 56 of the *exemplaire* we find 'en doubte' followed by a full stop. Montaigne changes this to a comma and adds: 'Il n'y a que les fols certeins et resolus.' He makes the addition, then effaces it, and finally the effacement is erased. Clearly Montaigne came back to the phrase on at least three different occasions.[15]

He is not only writing marginal notes but also checking this 'fifth' edition for printer's errors. Though sixteenth-century authors did not always read the proofs of their books, Montaigne most certainly did. The early corrections like those of 'Au lecteur' are in a bolder, more aggressive style and the ink is darker. They are more legible. When a passage is removed from the marginalia the ink crossing them out is much lighter – the same colour as the later notes. We may hear him saying, as he did in the notes to the printer in his own *exemplaire*, 'Les uers a part et les placer selon leur nature pentemettres saphiques Les demi uers les comancemas au bout de la ligne la fin sur la fin en cet exemplere *il y a mille fautes en tout cela*' (my italics),[16] and we must feel some regret that the Edition Municipale has ignored this plea. It also ignores the original layout of the classical quotations, and thus very often gives the lines in a haphazard way – which is disturbing when we remember Montaigne writing 'plus en ça' when he wants to show clearly that a hemistich is at the end of a line. This is an exact instruction to the printer. His proof-correcting – whether it involves the insertion or rejection of a colon, a spelling change, an alteration to the words, or an indication of precisely where he wanted the words to appear in the next edition – was thorough, clear and sure.

Of course sixteenth-century punctuation practice was very different from that of today, and so in one sense I would agree with Strowski's modernizing of Montaigne's punctuation 'comme l'ont fait tous les éditeurs de Montaigne'.[17] On the other hand, it is surely misleading not to have the author's own punctuation in the text of the 'standard' edition. Strowski did not give sufficient thought to the fact that Montaigne went out of his way to instruct the printer in a clear manner. As Valéry Larbaud once said; 'La ponctuation d'un écrivain doué d'une forte personnalité sera personnelle et s'écartera plus ou moins des règles fixées par l'usage courant et les grammaires.' Surely Montaigne was a writer of this kind?

Strowski's aim was to produce a *ne varietur* edition, and he 'failed'. Until time brings another editor who has collated the *exemplaire* and the 1595 edition we shall have to stay with the 'standard' edition as regards the 'living' text, except that a few times in this book I shall refer specifically to EP.

A book is in some respects a pact between author and readers, and a good way to gain a 'feel' for Montaigne's *Essais* is to examine at the outset a particular passage that can illustrate his richness as a writer in concrete terms. This I shall do in the next chapter.

CHAPTER 2

How to Read a Page of Montaigne: Active Participation of the Reader

J'aimeray quelqu'un qui me sçache deplumer, je dy par clairté de jugement et par la seule distinction de la force et beauté des propos.

(Villey-Saulnier, p. 408)

Of course, there is no one true reading of the *Essais*. Active reading of literature means that 50 per cent of the text is the author's and 50 per cent what the reader/critic/scholar is making of it. There is no stable *Essais*: it has appeared and will always appear different according to the age or century, according to the individual critic, and according to the country it is being read in. 'The text becomes a blank cheque which the reader fills in for himself and its supposed "truth" remains hidden.'[1] This negative position is only true so long as we are concerned with Montaigne. But is it not always true that when an author publishes his work he has to say farewell to himself as its author? The Montaigne text is the only thing that we have to turn to. 'Works of literature . . . are only kept alive by being *possessed* by individuals as intimate parts of their own living experience.'[2]

Reading Montaigne is made ten times more difficult since he himself knows – far more so than most literary artists – that we have to 'hear' the text, to 'sing' the text and to 'musicalize' the text: 'Il faict besoing des oreilles bien fortes pour s'ouyr franchement juger . . . ' (Villey-Saulnier, p. 1077). The number of times Montaigne's synaesthetic views come out is frequent: for example, 's'il y eust escouté de près . . . il y eust senty quelque ton gauche de mixtion humaine, mais ton obscur et sensible seulement à soy' (ibid., p. 674). Or he is continually the person to 'pincer l'ouye' (ibid., p. 1078).[3] The kind of reader that Montaigne would like is a reader who is 'docile au texte, ce ne sera pas seulement s'abstenir de le corriger ou d'extrapoler, ce sera aussi ne fonder *l'explication* que sur les éléments dont la perceptibilité est obligatoire'[4] (my italics). The oblique approach, the darting back and forth, the heavy slowness with which a sentence winds itself out, the imagination working on the mind as a stimulus, the harmonious blending of two opposite ideas almost like a painting, the musical analogy – 'Elles portent souvent, hors de mon propos, la semence d'une matiere plus riche et plus hardie, et sonnent à gauche un ton plus delicat, et pour moy qui n'en veux exprimer d'avantage, et pour ceux qui rencontreront mon air . . . ' (ibid., p. 251: 'They often (beyond my purpose) produce the seed of a richer subject and bolder matter, and often, collaterally, a more harmonious tune, both for me, that will expresse no more in this place, and for them that shall hit upon my tune') – all draw the reader's attention to an aesthetic form, to a kind of meditation which is the centre of the *Essais*.[5] Montaigne knows that he is a 'difficult' author: look at the number of times he comes back to words like *obliquement*, *biais*, *consanguinité* and *consubstantialité*, *gloser* and *entregloser*. He knows that the format of his work is totally different from, say, that of Cicero, where the mind picks over the composition in its neat and tidy, brick-like framework, stops and perhaps admires the stylistic detail and the formulaic *esse uideatur* (noted by Quintilian)[6] and 'sinks' in his grandiose cadences. Montaigne's anti-rhetorical attitude is very clear: 'Je n'ayme point de tissure où les liaisons et les coutures paroissent, tout ainsi qu'en un beau corps, il ne faut qu'on y puisse compter les os et les veines' (ibid., p. 172: 'I like not a contexture, where the seames and pieces may be seen: As in a well compact bodie, what need a man distinguish and number all the bones and veines severally?'). But that does not mean that he has no rhetoric himself: rhetoric is the art of communicating and persuading, and communication is vital to Montaigne. The act of reading creates a reader who is in close conspiracy with the author; creative activity is involved in reading works of literature.

We can start to see the way Montaigne works by reading aloud to ourselves this passage:

(B) Moy, qui ne manie que terre à terre, hay cette inhumaine sapience qui nous veut rendre desdaigneux et ennemis de la culture du corps. J'estime pareille injustice prendre à contre cœur les voluptez naturelles que de les prendre trop à cœur. (C) Xerxes estoit un fat, qui, enveloppé en toutes les voluptez humaines, alloit proposer pris à qui luy en trouveroit d'autres. Mais non guere moins fat est celuy qui retranche celles que nature luy a trouvées. (B) Il ne les faut ny suyvre, ny fuir, il les faut recevoir. Je les reçois un peu plus grassement et gratieusement, et me laisse plus volontiers aller vers la pante naturelle. (C) Nous n'avons que faire d'exagerer leur inanité; elle se faict assez sentir et se produit assez. Mercy à nostre esprit maladif, rabat-joye, qui nous desgoute d'elles comme de soy-mesme: il traitte et soy et tout ce qu'il reçoit tantost avant tantost arriere, selon son estre insatiable, vagabond et versatile.

> Sincerum est nisi vas, quodcunque infundis, accessit.

Moy qui me vente d'embrasser si curieusement les commoditez de la vie, et si particulierement, n'y trouve, quand j'y regarde ainsi finement, à peu pres que du vent. Mais quoy, nous sommes par tout vent. Et le vent encore, plus sagement que nous, s'ayme à bruire, à s'agiter, et se contente en ses propres offices, sans desirer la stabilité, la solidité, qualitez non siennes.

Les plaisire purs de l'imagination, ainsi que les desplaisirs, disent aucuns, sont les plus grands, comme l'exprimoit la balance de Critolaüs. Ce n'est pas merveille: elle les compose à sa poste et se les taille en plein drap. J'en voy tous les jours des exemples insignes, et à l'adventure desirables. Mais moy, d'une condition mixte, grossier, ne puis mordre si à faict à ce seul objet; si simple que je ne me laisse tout lourdement aller aux plaisirs presents de la loy humaine et generale, intellectuellement sensibles, sensiblement intellectuels . . .

(B) Quand je dance, je dance; quand je dors, je dors; voyre et quand je me promeine solitairement en un beau vergier, si mes pensées se sont entretenues des occurences estrangieres quelque partie du temps, quelque autre partie je les rameine à la promenade, au vergier, à la douceur de cette solitude et à moy. Nature a maternellement observé cela, que les actions qu'elle nous a enjoinctes pour nostre besoing nous fussent aussi voluptueuses, et nous y convie non seulement par la raison mais aussi par l'appetit: c'est injustice de corrompre ses regles.

('De l'experience'; Villey-Saulnier, pp. 1106–8)[7]

My selfe, who but grovells on the ground, hates that kind of human wisdome which would make us disdainefull and enemies of the bodies reformation. I deeme it an equall injustice either to take natural sensualities against the hart, or to take them too neere the hart. Xerxes was a ninny-hammer, who, enwrapped and given to all humane voluptuousnesse, proposed rewards for those that should devise such as he had never heard of. And hee is not much behind him in sottishnesse that goeth about to abridge those which Nature hath devised for him. One should neither follow nor avoyd them, but receive them. I receive them somewhat more amply and graciously, and rather am contented to follow naturall inclination. We need not exaggerate their inanity, it will sufficiently be felt and doth sufficiently produce it selfe. Godamercy our weake, crazed, and joy-diminishing spirit, which makes us distaste both them and himselfe. Hee treateth both himselfe and whatsoever he receiveth, sometimes forward and othertimes backeward, according as himself is either insaciate, vagabond, new fangled, or variable,

> Sincerum est nisi vas, quodcumque infundis acescit.

> In no sweete vessell all you poure,
> In such a vessell soone will sowre.

My selfe, who brag so curiously to embrace and particularly to allow the commodities of life, whensoever I look precisely into it, finde nothing therein but winde. But what? We are nothing but winde. And the very winde also, more wisely then we loveth to bluster and to be in agitation, and is pleased with his owne offices, without desiring stability or solidity, qualities that be not his owne. The meere pleasures of imagination, as well as displeasures (say some) are the greatest, as the balance of Critolaus did expresse. It is no wonder she composeth them at her pleasure, and cuts them out of the whole cloath. I see dayly some notable presidents of it, and peradventure to be desired. But I, that am of a commixt condition, homely and plaine, cannot so thoroughly bite on that onely and so simple object, but shall grosely and carelessly give myselfe ever to the present delights of the generall and humane law, intellectually sensible and sensibly-intellectuall . . . When I dance, I dance; and when I sleepe, I sleepe; and when I am solitarie walking in a faire orchard, if my thoughts have a while entertained themselve with strange occurrences, I doe another while bring them to walke with mee in the orchard, and to be partakers of that solitarinesse and of my selfe. Nature hath like a kinde mother observed this, that such actions as shee for our necessities hath enjoyned unto us should also be voluptuous unto us, and doth not onely by reason but also by appetite envite us unto them; it were injustice to corrupt her rules.

The first word is, significantly, the first person singular: we saw in the last chapter that Montaigne was living his biography. The whole realm of self-discovery was new in sixteenth-century Europe, and the *Essais* is radically different from, say, Saint Augustine's *Confessions*:[8] whereas Saint Augustine used his own mind to establish the primacy of religious experience, Montaigne starts with the *moi* no longer placed in a framework of accepted knowledge. At the end of the 'Apologie de Raimond Sebond' he opts for experimental knowledge of his own mind, for:

> Nous n'avons aucune communication à l'estre . . . si . . . vous fichez vostre pensée à vouloir prendre son estre, ce sera ne plus ne moins que qui voudroit empoigner l'eau: car tant plus il serrera et pressera ce qui de sa nature coule par tout, tant plus il perdra ce qu'il vouloit tenir et empoigner . . .
>
> (Villey-Saulnier, p. 601)

> We have no communication with being . . . if . . . you fix your thought to take its being, it would be even as if one should go about to graspe the water; for, how much the more he shal close and presse that which by its owne nature is ever gliding, so much the more he shall loose what he would hold and fasten.

The angle of vision in the passage is direct centre: Montaigne has chosen the *I* or *moi* as the witness and protagonist. We may remember the great discovery he had made in I.8, 'De l'oysiveté': he had been there all the time without discovering himself. The shock of the discovery is like finding a sixth sense, for it changes the whole world; note the tone of triumph mingled with fear as he re-creates this *émerveillement*;

> je trouve, que au rebours, faisant le cheval eschappé, il [his mind] se donne cent fois plus d'affaire à soy mesmes, qu'il n'en prenoit pour autruy; et m'enfante tant de chimeres et monstres fantasques les uns sur les autres, sans ordre, sans propos, que pour en contempler à mon aise l'ineptie et l'estrangeté, j'ay commancé de les mettre en rolle, esperant avec le temps luy en faire honte à luy mesmes.
>
> (ibid., p. 33)

That contrariwise playing the skittish and loose-broken jade, he takes a hundred times more cariere and libertie unto himselfe, than hee did for others, and begets in me so many extravagant Chimeraes, and fantastical monsters, so orderlesse, and without any reason, one hudling upon another, that at leasure to view the foolishnesse and monstrous strangenesse of them, I have begun to keepe a register of them, hoping, if I live, one day to make him ashamed, and blush at himselfe.

His intention in retiring to his library was to enjoy the tranquillity of the contemplative life, but his mind is like an escaped horse (escaped from the restraints of public life) and, whatever it turns to, it produces many 'extravagant Chimeraes, and fantastical monstres' (Florio). To contemplate these, to view the folly, means writing them down. The paradoxical movement of looking inwards rather than forwards, of watching the minute changes of mind, within an intellectual framework, and of controlling, if he can, the behaviour of the mind, has an excitement which is vigorous and vehement and calls to mind the heady discovery of Proust:

Et je compris que tous ces matériaux de l'œuvre littéraire, c'était ma vie passée; je compris qu'ils étaient venus à moi, dans les plaisirs frivoles, dans la paresse, dans la tendresse, dans la douleur, emmagasinés par moi, sans que je devinasse plus leur destination, leur survivance même, que la graine mettant en réserve tous les aliments qui nourriront la plante.[9]

The role of introspection in both authors is vital, and the Montaigne passage lays stress on this from the beginning to the end. A reader has to give of his intellect and sensibility when trying to rediscover all the semantic, literal and symbolical senses of words in their historical and aesthetic perspective. All writers are addressing readers who, they hope, will find something of value in their artistic work. In this seńe Montaigne is a 'committed' author destined to be read on all the different levels he gives to his words. Literary criticism has as its main aim the exploration and the defining of the particular experience of a particular poem or passage of literary prose. To understand a written piece profoundly we are obliged to engrain ourselves in the text and to read it scrupulously over and over again. We are concerned with what certain words are *doing*.

The first quality of this *moi* is ambiguous: 'qui ne manie que terre à

terre' captured finely by Florio 'who but grovells on the ground'. The
phrase makes us think of a labourer working in the fields or of
someone on the bottom rung of society. And this picture is hurled
against the following words 'hay cette inhumaine sapience': a strong
personal hatred barks through the 'hay' and the 'inhumaine'. There is
a paradox here, and it opens the reader's perception-box: the self is
seen in three different lights; it is ordinary, extraordinary and simple.
It plays with philosophy (perhaps with Stoicism enlarding it?); drops
it; picks up the inhumanity of it and dismisses it; accepts 'la culture du
corps', thus introducing a vast and important theme running through
the *Essais* – the indivisibility of mind and body. We note that for the
sense of *culture* Cotgrave simply gives its first meaning: 'culture',
'tillage', 'husbandrie'. But the text of Montaigne is giving it a
metaphorical sense: the physical culture which develops the body
through a loving gradual series of exercises. In this sense the body
becomes as vital as the soul: it is through intellectual exercises that the
body is cultivated. The emphasis has changed from the pleasurable
things to the higher and loftier aim in 'la culture'. And it is
immediately followed by 'J'estime' (substituted for 'Ie trouve'),
thereby confirming its importance. The 'voluptez naturelles' are to be
accepted; neither excessive hatred nor excessive desire is wanted. The
short sentence that follows is made stronger by the deletion of the 1588
'mais' and by a heavier use of punctuation – introducing the
semicolon after 'fuir' so as to read in 1592: 'Il les faut ny suyvre ny
fuir; il les faut receuoir.' The personal example is then introduced so
as to make the seemingly authoritarian statements closer to what in
fact Montaigne practises. 'Je les reçois un peu plus grassement et
gratieusement, et me laisse plus volontiers aller vers la pante
naturelle.' The two adverbs are used in an interesting manner:
'grassement' has the pejorative associations (e.g., 'les paroles grasses')
completely cut out and is edging its way towards generosity, flanked
by the debonair, benign and courteous 'gratieusement'.

We are made to be aware of Montaigne's language in the first
few lines: for instance, the semi-alike phrases 'prendre à contre
cœur' and 'prendre trop à cœur', the very ordinary words like 'terre à
terre', the double-strength of two adjectives 'desdaigneux et ennemis',
the quasi-repetition of *recevoir* in 'Je les reçois', the alliteration in
'culture du corps', the repetition of *prendre*, and so on. Throughout
the *Essais* his delight in manipulating language is evident; puns,
paradoxes, innuendoes, innovation in making up words, in using quite
coarse terms like 'le catze', irony, comic sarcasm, the imagery which is

often 'poetic' in that it sheds light on obscure parts of our activities or brain-movements. He peppers the *Essais* with anecdotes, and our (C) passage is such a one. The anecdote about Xerxes fits the general argument; for Xerxes was a 'ninny-hammer' (Florio), and Montaigne condemns his sottishness while adding a general statement: 'Mais non guere moins fat est celuy qui retranche celles que nature luy a trouvées.'

Words like 'voluptez naturelles', 'nature' and 'la pante naturelle' are keynotes in this first musical development. Montaigne is pulverizing the effects of philosophy by pitting it against nature and humanity; from twice saying 'il faut', thereby suggesting that this is a piece of authoritarian advice, we move immediately to the register of *je* and then to a class of *nous*. This introduces us to the infinitely rich mixtures of voices that Montaigne uses throughout the *Essais*: here we have 'nostre esprit'/'nostre'/'nos'/'il'/'on'/'faut'/'moi'/'je' voices in the background of talking about self. This is no neurotic speaking but a creative author who knows how to play different instruments in his fictional orchestra. The introspection is not solipsistic mainly because Montaigne knows that his mind copes with a secondhand form of knowledge as well – from the books he reads, from the anecdotes of current life in France in the sixteenth century, from the philosophies he has studied and the men and women whom he knows.

'Mercy à nostre esprit' is a fresh statement with intensely personal and quite comic concretization: the qualifying adjectives he puts around 'esprit' are funny – 'maladif' and 'rabat-joye'; Florio translates this passage well: 'Godamercy our weake, crazed, and joy-diminishing spirit, which makes us distaste both them and himselfe.' The sicklie 'maladif' personifies 'nostre esprit': it transforms it into a queasy, distempered, diseased body – again showing the indivisibility of mind and body. A twentieth-century reader translates 'rabat-joye' as spoilsport or killjoy, 'personne chagrine, renfrognée et triste, qui vient troubler la joie, le plaisir des autres' (Robert, *Dictionnaire*), whilst in the sixteenth century it meant 'a bringer of ill tidings, a teller of ill newes' (Cotgrave). The modern meaning is an extension of the sixteenth-century one. And I think both exist in the sense that no one today can claim that he is a sixteenth-century reader of Montaigne. Words are not metallic counters which communicate. They serve to suggest, and if that personification implies a mind who is a spoilsport, then that may be, perhaps, in our reaction to it. 'Meaning' always transcends direct abstract statement; it is always linked through absorption into the oblique suggestiveness of concrete language with

the sensuous properties of rhythm and imagery which are inherent to
it.

The second half of the sentence shows us the extraordinary features
of our minds; they are self-reflexive; all the external circumstances
make them behave differently – 'tantost avant tantost arriere'; our
minds are exercising themselves; they adopt various angles; they focus
in varying ways – they are with-drawn, fore-drawn, out-drawn and
around-drawn in space and in time; their being is 'insatiable,
vagabond et versatile'. Concretely they are wandering, strolling
around; they are things that turn or move around, and they cannot be
satisfied; they never have enough. Nothing is stable. There is
continual movement and flux everywhere. The outside world as
captured by the mind is fragmentary and motionful. This is a key
theme in the *Essais*. We need only one example to show this
point – 'De l'inconstance de nos actions' (II.1) where the movement is
very similar: 'Nostre façon ordinaire, c'est d'aller apres les inclinations
de nostre apetit, à gauche, à dextre, contre-mont, contre-bas, selon
que le vent des occasions nous emporte. Nous ne pensons ce que nous
voulons qu'à l'instant que nous le voulons . . . ' (Villey-Saulnier,
p. 333: 'Our ordinary manner is to follow the inclination of our
appetite this way and that way, on the left and on the right hand;
upward and downeward, according as the winde of occasions doth
transport us: we never thinke on what we would have, but at the
instant we would have it'). The wind image in both passages I shall
deal with in a minute.

We have before that the line from Horace's *Epistles*, 1.2.54, which
reads in English thus; 'If the vessel is not pure, everything you pour in
will sour.' This quotation initiates us to the fact that the *Essais* is
littered with quotations: from Virgil and Horace, from Cicero and
Quintilian, from Plutarch and Caesar, from Catullus, Propertius and
Martial, and so on. They are put there for a purpose, to thicken the
strata of meaning: to ask the reader to consider two contexts instead of
one. Montaigne assumes that we are not naïve or stupid; he assumes
also that we shall have no difficulty in checking the second
context – even though he does not even give the writer! Fortunately,
modern editions of the *Essais* have detected almost all the authors and
translated them into French. But Horace is a case in point. For
Montaigne alters tenses, changes punctuation and puts in or crosses
out link-words like *Et* or *Sed*. One example is enough here: in 'De
l'amitié' (I.28) – which at times reads like a prose poem – he uses
Horace a great deal and it is worth our noticing this quotation: '(B) et

ipse/Notus in fratres animi paterni' (*Odes*, 2.2.6; Villey-Saulnier, p. 185). The quotation is made up. There is no mention of the phrase 'et ipse' in the ode at all. By putting in this phrase Montaigne is able to show how generous he has been towards his own brothers after the death of his father Pierre Eyquem. Thus by 'remaking' his Horace text, and by 'shifting' the emotional tone, he is able to create the 'resonance' appropriate to the circumstance. The phrase 'et ipse' puts his position less blatantly than 'ego', and in any case 'et ego' would not scan. The French editions (e.g., Villey-Saulnier) do not make it clear as they all translate 'et ipse' as 'moi-même'.[10]

The Horatian line in our passage is suggestive only if we know the context. The epistle is written to a young man, Lollius Maximus, who is reading Homer's *Iliad* and *Odyssey*. It is a grave and serious epistle in which Horace is giving advice to the young, according to his own *art de vivre* – we must conquer our passions with as much ardour as we usually apply to satisfy them. The next line (55) – 'Sperne voluptates: nocet empta dolore voluptas' – makes two plays on the word *voluptas*. The whole nature of the passage in Montaigne centres around 'voluptez naturelles'. Themes of this epistle are interwoven with the text of Montaigne: *mediocritas* (meaning 'moderation', not 'mediocrity') as the main aim of man during his life; the leitmotif of 'quod satis est cui contingit, nihil amplius optet'; we must be the masters of our inner, genuine and authentic life –

> animum rege, qui nisi paret,
> Imperat: hunc frenis, hunc tu compesce catena.

The overwhelming aim is to be healthy. These concurrent interwoven meanings give a sense of pattern: it is Montaigne first rehearsing in his own mind and then speaking Horace's words in order to 'try' at the thought that they contain. After this quotation Montaigne dives into his own life and writing.

> Moi qui me uante d'enbrasser si curieusement les commoditez de la uie, et si particulieremant n'y trouue [a crossed-out word, which is illegible] quand i'y regarde einsi finemant, a peu pres que du uent. Mais quoi, [first written 'nostre esprit c'est de mesmes', then crossed out].
>
> (I quote from EP, pl. 1012)

The *moi* takes control of the argument again. The Horace quotation has pulled the demonstration over to a particular focus: and with the thick double texture this has allowed Montaigne to make generaliz-ations on a number of key themes in the *Essais – voluptez, santé, mediocritas*, and so on. Now we have the minute psychological investigation. So the shape of the passage reveals itself already to us: not a clear logical linear shape but a series of perceptive observations ranging from very general ones – as we found around the Horace quotation – to finely concrete particularizations of the *moi*. Montaigne, in studying the self's consciousness, finds it impossible to grasp the states of mind except through a metaphor: an accurate and sensitive language is needed to convey man's innermost reactions, and that language is concrete. The wind metaphor Montaigne had used before – in 'De l'inconstance de nos actions' as we saw – but this time the tone of voice is different. 'Mais quoy, nous sommes par tout vent' is wryly ironic, a shrug of the shoulders; an awareness of human absurdity and an acceptance of that absurdity. He goes one step further in this debunking of the pride of mankind to suggest that the wind is 'plus sagement que nous' in that it accepts precisely that its own qualities are 'to bluster and to be in agitation, and is pleased with his owne offices, without desiring stability or solidity, qualities that be not his owne' (Florio).

The next paragraph is governed by a statement which is ironic: the clue is 'disent aucuns'. 'Some say' is tossing it away – maybe that it is true but I am such a clumsy man that I cannot take it with my imagination. 'Tant pis pour moi' – I cannot make my imagination work like that. The second part of the sentence is 'les desplesirs . . . sont les plus grans comme l'exprimoit la balance de Critolaüs'. This casual throw-off of an allusion is typical of Montaigne: we have now to turn to the Ciceronian context:

> quo loco quaero quam vim habeat libra illa Critolai, qui cum in alteram lancem animi bona inponat, in alteram corporis et externa, tantum propendere illam lancem putet ut terram et maria deprimat. (*Ciceronis Tusculanae disputationes*, 5.17.51)

At which point I ask what force that balance of Critolaus has: in one pan he puts the mental values whilst he puts the values of the body and external things in the other; he reckons that the first pan is so weighty that it outweighs the earth and seas.

Critolaus was leader of the Peripatetic School of Philosophy in

Athens; it followed the tradition of Aristotle, and in the second century BC Critolaus illustrates the relative merits of the *bona animi* and the *bona corporis et externa*. However, Montaigne has given the balance a new and different significance; for here it is the pleasures 'purs de l'imagination' that are being weighed against displeasure, and so the *bona animi* – pointing very definitely to an ethical scale – are no longer relevant. Montaigne follows this by a picturesque image of imagination doing her work: 'Ce n'est pas merueille: Elle les compose à sa poste, et se les taille en plein drap', which is translated by Florio as 'It is no wonder she composeth them at her pleasure, and cuts them out of the whole cloath'. The tailor-like image is set upon the *composer*, 'To compound, make, frame; dispose, order, digest; to write verses, compose, or poetize it' (Cotgrave), and we are thinking of a *composeur*, 'A composer, poet, writer, maker; a setter in Musicke' (Cotgrave).[11] 'J'en uoi tous les iours des examples insignes, et à lauanture desirable.' But he cannot do such things: it is almost a *recusatio*, but a refusal that is both full and mature, both dense and of a sure wit:

> [a new sentence] Mais moi, d'une condition mixte [an illegible crossed-out adjective] grossier, [written on top] ne puis mordre [another two words crossed and they are illegible] si a faict a ce seul obiect, si simple [three words crossed out] que ie ne me laisse [a crossed-out plus and above written] tout lourdement [two words crossed out and therefore written first of all above the 'lourdement'; on second thoughts they are erased] aux [word erased] ~~plai~~ presente ainsi de la ~~proscription naturelle~~ loi humaine [written above] generalle:
>
> (EP, pl. 1012)

And now, after all this playing with language, which is in fact a sort of serious processing of his thought, there comes the famous phrase, with no alteration at all: Montaigne's pleasures are 'intellectuellement sensibles, sensiblement intellectuels'. We shall come back to these in a later chapter.

The statement 'Quand ie dance, ie dance' gives us the 'texture' of Montaigne's 'try-outs'. Dancing and sleeping are activities to which Montaigne gives his whole being; the concentration, the lucidity and the penetration are an example of the balance of mind and body. The move away from abstraction, the dealing with concrete description and the adhesion to immediate experience – all are new and prefigure writers like Proust, Valéry and Sartre. 'Le nettoyage de la situation

verbale' (Valéry) is crucial in all these writers; take the following
passage:

> Quand ie dance, ie dance, quand ie dors, ie dors: voyre, & quand ie
> me promeine solitairement en vn beau vergier, si mes pensées se
> sont entre-tenues des occurrences estrangieres quelque partie du
> temps, quelque autre partie, ie les rameine à la promenade, au
> vergier, à la douceur de cette solitude, & à moy.
>
> (EP, pl. 1012)

The need for self-absorption in a particular event, the importance of
clearing away contingent events which might prevent self-absorption,
solitude and introspection are attached to and are adherent in beautiful
things – 'vn *beau* vergier' – and are seen as 'la douceur de cette
solitude'. This is someone who views solitude as something natural,
who sees it as serving the mind and body, who sees it as non-
Pascalian: 'Qui se considérera de la sorte s'effrayera de soi-même, et,
se considérant soutenu dans la masse que la nature lui a donnée, entre
ces deux abïmes de l'infini et du néant, il tremblera dans la vue de ces
merveilles.'[12] Self-absorption entails consciousness. What is it that is
conscious of itself? It is the self thinking of itself; Montaigne is dealing
with his thoughts, with inspiration, with the power the self has of
concentrating entirely on itself, and with the processes of thought. Is it
not what Valéry did each morning? Since the appearance of the
Cahiers[13] we know that he got up at four each morning for forty years
and thought and wrote: a sort of autodissection. It is here that we
read:

> Nous attribuons à la légère à certains résultats obtenus inconsciem-
> ment une valeur propre – tandis que cette valeur elle-même résulte
> du jugement par lequel nous acceptons ces idées.
>   Une inspiration qui me vient, n'entre en valeur que si je ne
> l'écarte pas – mais avant cette décision du moi, elle n'est plus ni
> moins gratuite que telle herbe/algue/folle continuelle du cerveau.
>
> (Vol. 3, p. 834)

It is as if the *Cahiers* were the *Essais* of Valéry; like Montaigne, Valéry
was infinitely aware of the imprecision of his ideas, of the ambiguity of
language and the artificial nature of most philosophical problems.
Montaigne prefigured Valéry in his analysis of the *moi*, the pluralities
of the *moi*, pluralities made of contradictory, strange and distinctive

elements so that the effort of consciousness never encapsulates them all. But there is a *douceur* in Montaigne that one never quite sees in Valéry. In the last sentence Montaigne states the other side of life, and it is seen as under the maternal power of Nature:

> Nature a maternellement obserué cela, que les actions qu'elle nous a enioinctes pour nostre besoing, nous fussent aussi voluptueuses: & nous y conuie non seulement par la raison, mais aussi par l'appetit: c'est iniustice de corrompre ses regles.
>
> (EP, pl. 1012)

Note the words 'maternellement', 'besoing' and 'voluptueuses'; it is as if Montaigne has arrived at an ethical code within his concept of nature. It is not only a rational quality that nature wants of man; rather, it is at once rational but also 'voluptueuses'.

We have seen how the imagination and the sensibility of Montaigne were in full harmony the one with the other. The emotional resonance, the poetic lyricism and the spirit of criticism are all there: and this must mean that the slowness of reading Montaigne is crucial. The heavy concentration of additions means that these are themes and problems close to his heart. We can see the qualities of a mature Montaigne: self-mastery, control and discipline, moderation in everything, inner peace; the cultivation of insensibility to external things; the need to be honest with oneself and with others; the aesthetic intellectual pattern in his *art de vivre* and the emotional value of his realization that the universe had a doubleness in everything. We find here a basic curiosity about the human condition in so far as it concerns directly each individual.

Having discovered through the close reading of one page the 'ondoyants et divers' aspects of Montaigne's world, the powerful originality of his thoughts, the savoury, juicy and nourishing concrete style and the rich vein of his anecdotes, we can now consider some of the general orientations of his *Essais*.

CHAPTER 3
Intellectual and Philosophical Background

In this chapter I shall discuss briefly three inter-related topics –
Renaissance humanism, Stoicism and Epicureanism.

(i) RENAISSANCE HUMANISM

Montaigne is not Rabelais. He comes at the end of the Renaissance
and is severely critical of certain aspects of it. Where Rabelais can say,
'Grecque, sans laquelle c'est honte que une personne se die sçavant,
Hebraïcque, Caldaïcque, Latine . . . ,'[1] Montaigne reflects rather
sorrowfully: 'C'est un bel et grand agencement sans doubte que le
Grec et Latin, *mais on l'achepte trop cher*' ('De l'institution des enfants',
I.26; Villey-Saulnier, p. 173: my italics). The first half of the sixteenth
century saw an upsurge of writers who, through their rediscovery of
ancient Rome and Greece, through their experimentation with forms
like mock-praises and dialogues (Erasmus comes to mind immediately
but others, such as the author of the *Epistolae obscurorum virorum*,
could be cited), through their translation of Greek and Latin books
and through their attempt to synthesize antiquity and Christianity,
were the most influential men of their time. Since Petrarch, *studia
humanitatis* (classical studies) had been recognized pre-eminently as
studies befitting a human being; they were humaneness, civilization,
erudition and culture. Montaigne says of his father:

> mon pere . . . eschauffé de cette ardeur nouvelle dequoy le Roy
> François premier embrassa les lettres et les mit en credit, recharcha
> avec grand soing et despence l'accointance des hommes doctes . . .
> car il n'avoit aucune connoissance des lettres, non plus que ses
> predecesseurs.
> ('Apologie de Raimond Sebond', II.12; Villey-Saulnier, p. 438)

my father . . . set on fire by that new kinde of earnestness
wherewith King Francis the first imbraced Letters, and raised them
unto credit, did with great diligence and much cost endevour to
purchase the acquaintance of learned men . . . for hee had no
knowledge of Letters no more than his predecessors before him.

And then adds; 'Moy, je les ayme bien, mais, je ne les adore pas.'
Why does Montaigne not adore classical authors? The answer is
twofold: first, the decline of classicism in France generally in the late
sixteenth century; and, second, and more profoundly, Montaigne's
attitude, which was unique.

The world of the Renaissance was eager to possess classical texts.
Edition after edition of all authors multiplied; authors not really
known in the Middle Ages such as Catullus, Lucretius and Longinus
were edited; printing and classical scholarship interacted with creative
writing in the vernacular. Take the text of Horace as an example.
Horace is a fully 'impure' author from the beginning: no manuscript
is older than the ninth century, and even today Professor Brink can
say that 'a sound text has yet to be established on the foundation
of a sound selection of manuscripts'.[2] Scholiasts of Horace – such
as 'Acro', Porphyrio, Josse Bade, Aldus, Benedictus Philologus
(Benedetto Riccardini) and Bonfinus (Matteo Bonfini) – are laborious
and long, so that the text itself is like a tiny island surrounded by an
ocean of annotations (or *adversaria, variae lectiones, recensatio* or even
annotatunculi – all these being the terms given to a scholar's
interpretation), or rather like an exquisite flower blooming in a desert,
waiting to be discovered by a true critical scholar. Montaigne had one
of these editions of Horace in his possession – now in the Municipal
Library in Libourne: it is *Horatii Flacci opera*, an edition published by
Josse Bade, whose house was up until his death in 1535 a centre for all
Parisian humanists. It is dated 1543; it is a folio edition, and the
commentaries are prolix and diffuse. That Montaigne had read them
as well as the text is very possible: we have a 1539 edition of Vergil
(now in the Bibliothèque Nationale in Paris) with the proof that
Montaigne knew of the commentator. Written in his own handwriting
is found the following note: 'Micael Montanus me possidet, anno D.
1549, aetatis prope 16. Cal. Januarii, venundatur 44 ss. *cum indice
Erythraei*' (my italics).

Now, during the 1550s and until the outbreak of civil war in 1562,
Paris experienced the heyday of such Latin scholars as Turnebus,
Muret, Dorat, Scaliger, Denys Lambin (Lambinus), and others. And

it was in 1561 that Lambin produced his edition of Horace. We have
no actual proof that Montaigne possessed a copy of it, but it is likely.
The edition is the best one until Bentley (Cambridge, 1711) and is the
first to collate several manuscripts. A rich suggestion in this edition
sums up the position of Horace in the 1560s in Europe:

> Sic igitur Horatius in hac ad Pisones epistola, cum de omni poëseos
> genere disputat, tum maxime de comoedia, & tragoedia utilissima
> praecepta dat, *non ut philosophus, sed, ut poëta.* (My italics)[3]

This is a break away from medieval moralizing comments on poetry
and, in particular, on Horace, who often has to fight (even in the
twentieth century) against critics who see didacticism in his poetry. As
a poet Horace is deeply ingrained in Montaigne, and Lambin's edition
in 1561 is significant: from this time onwards, it will be only classical
scholars who will go on collating the texts, emending the words and
reviewing past texts.

Let us take another example of the 'decline' in classical studies in the
second half of the century. Adrianus Turnebus is also a person of first-rate
eminence in the world of classical scholarship, and furthermore he is a
friend of Montaigne. Turnebus was a philologist, and his main works
are commentaries on classical (in particular Greek) authors: for instance,
his *Adversaria* (1564) is full of explanations and emendations of numerous passages in these authors.[4] He is in the second generation of French
scholars and, as Jean Jehasse has pointed out,[5] they are the starting-
point of textual criticism. They are the fathers of Bentley, Lachmann
and Housman. They abandon certain critics or scholiasts like 'Acro' and
Porphyrio with regard to Horace's works or they jettison Servius in
Virgilian criticism.[6] They also see the danger of over-emending the text.
We must also remember the devastation of literature teaching during
the civil wars; there is a magnificent speech at the beginning of an edition
by Denys Lambin which describes the chaos of war everywhere.[7]

If we assume that Montaigne read the *Adversaria* of the man whom
he describes as almost perfect –

> Car au dedans c'estoit l'ame la plus polie du monde. Je l'ay souvent
> à mon esciant jetté en propos eslongnez de son usage; il y voyoit si
> cler, d'une apprehension si prompte, d'un jugement si sain, qu'il
> sembloit qu'il n'eut jamais faict autre mestier que la guerre et
> affaires d'Estat. Ce sont natures belles et fortes.
>
> (Villey-Saulnier, p. 139)

For his inward parts, I deeme him to have been one of the most unspotted and truly honest minds that ever was. I have sundry times of purpose urged him to speak of matters furthest from his study, wherein he was so cleare-sighted, and could with so quicke an apprehension conceive, and with so sound a judgment distinguish them, that he seemed never to have professed or studied other facultie than warre, and matters of state. Such spirits, such natures may be termed worthy, goodly, and solid.

– what are the characteristics of his writing? This book is dominated by close and careful scholarship, and the general taste and liveliness of its author make it delightful to read. And, in particular, the concretè language and the literary criticism are very thick and dense. In the first place Montaigne would have come across evaluative terms on classical literature: for instance, 'Elegantissimi sunt versus doctissimi, & politissimi poëtae Catulli . . . ' (p. 5r), or 'Dulcissimus omnium poëtarum & politissimus . . . Catullus . . . ' (p. 225v), or the adjective *suauissimus* attached to Catullan poetry. Montaigne calls him 'Nostre bon Catulle' (II.33) or 'ce bon compaignon' (I.38) – equally approving. Turnebus describes another poet 'lepidissimus & nitidissimus poëta Propertius', while Virgil was a 'doctissimus poëta' to him and to Montaigne he is 'le maistre du chœur' (I.37). Not only does Montaigne agree with him, but also at times his evaluation is almost a translation of Turnebus: for instance, when he is talking about books ('Des livres', II.10; Villey-Saulnier, p. 412) he uses the same terms – 'l'egale polissure et cette perpetuelle douceur et beauté fleurissante des Epigrammes de Catulle . . . '.

However, Montaigne was not really a 'classical scholar', that is, he was not a humanist in the Renaissance sense of the term. He was not a professional scholar of Greek or Latin; he edited no text nor did he write commentaries on ancient authors. Rabelais is, on the contrary, truly a Renaissance humanist. In 1524 he translates the first book of Herodotus and some works of Lucian from Greek into Latin, and in 1532 dedicates Manardi's *Epistolae medicinales* to Tiraqueau and *Hippocratis ac Galeni libri aliquot* to Bishop Geoffrey d'Estissac. He was an enthusiastic student of Greek, and it is a source of great regret that his translation of Lucian is lost. Whereas in fact, at times in his *Essais*, Montaigne is deliberately anti-humanist. We can think of shaggy-elephant stories in the 'Apologie de Raimond Sebond' or anecdotes of bees, swallows and the spider who 'spins her artificial web thicke in one place and thin in another' (Florio). The glory of man's reason is brought down to animals' behaviour as in 'Quand je me jouë à ma chatte, qui sçait si elle passe son temps de moy plus que je ne fay d'elle . . . ' (Villey-Saulnier, p. 452), and we shall see this in the next chapter.

Nevertheless, there is one area where the interaction of the humanists and Montaigne is positive – the language they use in 'close reading' ancient authors. Turnebus in the *Adversaria* gives us an example of this: after quoting two lines from an epistle of Horace (*Epistulae*, I.4) –

> An tacitum sylvas inter reptare salubres
> Curantem quicquid dignum sapiente bonoque est?

– the language he uses is very concrete; 'sub ipso verborum *tectorio* . . . Et ut *sub putamine nucleus* latet, ita quoque sub ipsa *velut nuce*, quae frangenda est, quiddam tanquam salubre, *eduleque* reconditur' (p. 12: my italics). Phrases like *sub tectorio*, *sub putamine nucleus* and *edule* are metaphors calling up *tego* and *sermo verbis tectus* (Cicero, *Ad familiares*, 9.22.1); the shell-and-kernel phrase seems rare in classical writers, who used the words only in a literal sense, and the *edule* calls to the metaphor of food. Turnebus uses the weaving, the interweaving, the interlacing and intertwining metaphor many times (e.g. p. 128v, *retexebat omnia*; or p. 203, *annotationibus intexere*). Both he and Montaigne may have had in mind the famous phrase of Seneca (*Epistulae morales*, 33) 'Contextus totus virilis est; non sunt circa flosculos occupati' (Villey-Saulnier, p. 873), which Montaigne uses in his most dense piece of literary criticism. He makes the important statement a little further on; 'Le maniement et emploite des beaux espris donne prix à la langue, non pas l'innovant tant comme la remplissant de plus vigoreux et divers services, l'estirant et ployant.' Are not the dislike of innovation in language and the spirit of criticism here the same as Turnebus' attitude to emendation? Hear him on page 100r:

> Ut moribus antiquis stabat res Romana, sic Romana lingua stat antiquis exemplaribus, à quibus cum recedunt editiones, merito doctis suspectae sunt, & prope falsi condemnantur. Etsi enim aliquid plerunque non incommode fingunt, novitium tamen id est & nuperum, non cana illa vetustate venerandum. Itaque etiam cum minus fidem facit antiquitas, tamen eam quoquo pacto possumus, interpretari & retinere malumus, quam quicquam innovare . . .

Just as the fortunes of Rome were based on the ancient code of behaviour, so the Roman tongue is based on the ancient models, and when editions depart from these, they are deservedly suspect in the eyes of scholars and very nearly condemned as false. For even if on the whole they manufacture something that is not infelicitously done, it is innovatory and fresh nevertheless and not to be revered for that white-headed old age. Hence even when antiquity does not carry conviction, we nevertheless prefer to translate that and keep to it in any way we can rather than make any innovation . . . (DGC)

Words like *tissure* (used only twice by Montaigne)[8] and *nerveux* (a neologism of Montaigne in Robert's dictionary; the example he gives is 'un parler succulent et nerveux, court et serré, non tant delicat et peigné comme vehement et brusque . . . ': (Villey-Saulnier, p. 171) and *succulent* are grooved into French by Montaigne.[9] They may be compared to a passage such as this one in Turnebus:

Est ut longa iam maturitate victorum fructuum, ac conditaneorum ipsa temporis diuturnitate rugosorum iucundissimus succus: ita vetustissimorum scriptorum suavissimus gustus, habetque, ut vinum vetus gratam palato salivam, sic antiquitas saporem quendam intelligentibus suavem. (p. 195r)[10]

Just as fruit juice is most enjoyable when the fruits have been ripe for a long time and that of pickles when they have grown wrinkled by the sheer passage of time, so tasting the oldest authors is most delightful, and just as old wine has a flavour that is pleasing to the palate, so antiquity tastes delightful, as it were, to those who are discerning. (DGC)

His delight in savouring, digesting, relishing classical texts may be compared to Montaigne, who chews over words from Virgil and Lucretius in his essay 'Sur des vers de Virgile': *la gaillardise de l'imagination* dominates both writers. The words of the classical texts for both of them 'signifient plus qu'elles [paroles] ne disent'.

Turnebus and other scholars gave the world good texts of classical writers, but the heyday of the scholarly printing world is over when he dies in 1565. Vernacular literature has won the day. Montaigne (as Eliot saw) made French prose mature, expressive and sophisticated, and it was French prose heavily underpinned by Latin.

The second reason for Montaigne not adulating the classics is

original, too. We may consider the differences between him and
Rabelais in the sphere of education. In *Pantagruel* there is the famous
letter from Gargantua to Pantagruel on education (ch. 8): it is a hymn
of praise to the progress of knowledge in the French Renaissance, with
images of spring, rebirth and reflowering conveying the fresh
enthusiasm of letters and humanism of the time (the book was
published in 1532). The tone in the letter is that of a humanist giving
an orthodox view about immortality before he begins to talk of
education. Etienne Gilson in 1932 said, 'Apprenons la langue de
Rabelais avant de le lire . . . Pas une d'elles [expressions] qui ne porte
et qui ne prouve la survivance d'un théologien fort compétent chez
l'auteur de *Pantagruel*', and showed how most of the ideas in this letter
were a mixture of patristic thought, with a large dose of ancient
thought, and of the everyday religious practice of a Franciscan.[11] The
picture of the ideal educated man described by Rabelais corresponds
closely to the views expounded by writers such as Leonardo da Vinci
and Du Bellay: man should be a polymath, a walking encyclopaedia –
'que je voy un abysme de science', said Rabelais. And at the top of the
hierarchy of values comes God, 'parce que . . . s012ence sans conscience
n'est que ruine de l'ame – il te convient servir, aymer et craindre
Dieu, et en luy mettre toutes tes pensées et tout ton espoir'.[12]

It is easy to see how Montaigne hated pedants in that a whole essay
turns on them: 'Du pedantisme' (I.25). And there is a passage on
pedants in 'L'Art de conferer' (III.8) where he states that he would
prefer his (hypothetical) son to learn 'aux tavernes à parler, qu'aux
escholes de la parlerie' (Villey-Saulnier, p. 927). But he goes much
further than mere hatred. In 'Du pedantisme' and in the following
essay, 'De l'institution des enfans', he contrasts constantly the 'habile
homme' and the 'homme sçavant', 'sagesse' and 'science' and
'boni'/'docti'. Good men have judgement within them in so far as they
are 'natures belles et fortes' (he says this of Turnebus, as we have just
seen), whilst men relying on pedantic knowledge have nothing within
them. The Stoic terminology will be analysed in a minute. God is not
mentioned in Montaigne's scheme of secular education. His reflections
on the education of children are explicitly concerned with the training
of a gentleman (the essay is addressed to the pregnant Diane de Foix,
comtesse de Gurson, with whom Montaigne had close contacts), but
implicitly they are based on his own personal experience and are to be
'copied' by Locke, Rousseau, the Swiss educationalist Pestalozzi, who
founded a school that became a European model, Froebel, Maria
Montessori and all modern pedagogists.

The interdependence of moral and intellectual traits in education is basic to the sixteenth century: I need only mention Erasmus, Thomas More or Vives. Montaigne says ('Du pedantisme'; Villey-Saulnier, p. 136); 'Nous ne travaillons qu'à remplir la memoire, et laissons l'entendement et la conscience vuide.' This straightforward line of demarcation between mere voluntary memory or repetitiveness, and understanding the 'sens et la substance' ('De l'institution des enfans'; Villey-Saulnier, p. 151), enables Montaigne to state that memory is nothing compared with judgement. The meditation takes an inward turn when he asks himself questions like 'Mais nous, que disons nous nous mesmes? que jugeons nous? que faisons nous?' (Villey-Saulnier, p. 137) and answers finely and ironically: 'Autant en diroit bien un perroquet.' When he makes this statement, 'Nous prenons en garde les opinions et le sçavoir d'autruy, et puis c'est tout. Il les faut faire nostres . . .'(ibid.), he is very close to the observation of Proust; 'On ne recoit pas la sagesse, il faut la découvrir soi-même après un trajet que personne ne peut faire pour nous, ne peut nous épargner, car elle est un point de vue sur les choses.'[13] And, indeed, Montaigne comes soon to a conclusion that 'Quand bien nous pourrions estre sçavans du sçavoir d'autruy, au moins sages ne pouvons nous estre que de nostre propre sagesse' (Villey-Saulnier, p. 138).

The whole concept of teaching children through pleasure, of making them 'gouster les choses' and 'les choisir et discerner d'elle mesme [ame]' (ibid., p. 150), and of aiming at forming 'la teste bien faicte que bien pleine' is basically Erasmian. But Montaigne goes further than Erasmus in seeing that 'Ce n'est pas une ame, ce n'est pas un corps qu'on dresse, c'est un homme' (ibid., p. 165). The indivisibility of body and mind runs through the *Essais* in many interesting ways, but to make it a basis for education is quite original in western Europe. Of course, the *mens sana in corpore sano* (Juvenal, *Satires*, 10.356) was well known, but harnessing it to education was not. Thus Montaigne argues that 'Les jeux mesmes et les exercices seront une bonne partie de l'estude: la course, la luite, (C) la musique, (A) la danse, la chasse, le maniement des chevaux et des armes' (Villey-Saulnier, p. 165: 'All sports and exercises shall be a part of his study; running, wrestling, musicke, dancing, and managing of armes and horses'). Or in a (C) passage of 'De la coustume' (I.23; Villey-Saulnier, p. 110) this pre-Freudian remark, 'Je trouve que nos plus grands vices prennent leur ply de nostre plus tendre enfance, et que nostre principal gouvernement est entre les mains des nourrices' ('I finde that our greatest vices make their first habit in us from our infancie, and that our chiefe

government and education lieth in our nurses hands'), is followed by
'il faut noter que les jeux des enfans ne sont pas jeux'. Physical
exercises favour the harmonious blossoming of the child, whose mind
is kept alert by the tiniest event and whose body 'stretches' at each
exercise; it is very important that every faculty, every sense of man
whose 'condition est merveilleusement corporelle' (I.1), should work
together. The extreme concreteness of Montaigne's language means
that the reader sees put into practice the theoretical considerations of
twentieth-century pedagogists. The basic curiosity of every human
being, the 'grand monde' being 'le livre de l'escolier' (society rather
than books) (Villey-Saulnier, p. 157), the atmosphere of joy in
learning ('J'y ferai pourtraire la joye': ibid., p. 166), judgement and
understanding being incomparably better than memory ('Tout passer
par l'estamine' – the strainer being judgement), never accepting a
thing 'par simple autorité et à credit' (ibid., p. 151) – these are some
of the qualities in Montaigne's educational programme.

Furthermore he recommends the absorption and full digestion of
knowledge, making it an integral part of yourself: 'Les abeilles
pillotent deçà, delà les fleurs, mais elles en font apres le miel, qui est
tout leur; ce n'est plus thin ny marjolaine' (ibid., p. 152). The lesson
of adaptability and relativity is learned through travelling, which rids
one of provincialism – 'frotter et limer nostre cervelle contre celle
d'autruy' (ibid., p. 153). The whole purpose of education is to
'allécher l'appétit et l'affection' (ibid., p. 177) so that self-education
will continue throughout one's life. Montaigne can say in a marginal
note in 'De la phisionomie' (III.10; Villey-Saulnier, p. 1039), 'Les
livres m'ont servi non tant d'instruction que d'exercitation'; the act of
reading is not to gain information but to exercise the intellect and to
shape a human being.

The very humaneness of Montaigne, which we find here and which
we shall see in later chapters, is something that scholars or historians
would vaguely call Montaigne's humanism, but he is not a
Renaissance humanist. He is a humanist in the word's wide sense of
being concerned with the dignity of man, and he has inscribed on his
library ceiling that saying from Terence on the human condition
'Homo sum, humani a me nihil alienum puto' – 'I am a man, I
consider nothing human to be alien to me'. And the intimate joy of
reading comforts him in his old age:

Il me console en la vieillesse et en la solitude. Il me descharge du
pois d'une oisiveté ennuyeuse; et me deffaict à toute heure des

compaignies qui me faschent. Il emousse les pointures de la douleur, si elle n'est du tout extreme et maistresse.

('De trois commerces', III.3; Villey-Saulnier, p. 827)

Reading comforts me in age and solaceth me in solitarinesse; it easeth mee of the burthen of a wearysome sloth: and at all times rids me of tedious companies: it abateth the edge of fretting sorrow, on condition it be not extreme and over-insolent.

Montaigne is humane and cultured in the sense that ancient classics and poetry have refined him; he may best be understood, then, under the term *umanità* or *litterae humaniores*. We move on now to the philosophical background.

(ii) STOICISM AND EPICUREANISM

Categories like Stoic, Sceptic, Neoplatonic, Epicurean, and so on, are almost meaningless in the sixteenth century, which was so syncretic in philosophy. The terminology and the vocabulary of both French and Latin writers were so non-static that we must be careful in feeling our way to the norm. Villey divided Montaigne's intellectual life into three: a Stoic period, followed by a Pyrrhonic one and finally a mature one where Epicureanism reigned.[14] The three stages of development corresponded to the three books of the *Essais*. This is not the moment to attack Villey's famous thesis, and it has been done anyway by other scholars.[15] I merely want to say here that a more intimate knowledge of the *Essais* does not support the thesis and, in particular, that the (A), (B) and (C) passages completely deny it.[16]

Nature and reason, in the sixteenth century, were the two aspects of man: the Neoplatonists in Italy and Erasmus in northern Europe both focus attention on the rational quality of man in a generic sense – as contrasted with animals, who live according to *their* nature. That there was a particle of the divine in man was an idea in antiquity, reshaped by the Christian fathers and coupled in the sixteenth century with the maxim *suivre la nature* which carried implications about value judgements. Living a life which was in agreement with nature has a strong Stoic flavour: indeed, in the very terminology of 'living consistently with one's nature' we are pushed back to Cicero's *De natura deorum* or *De finibus*. *Naturae convenienter vivere* is the pass-phrase amongst ancient Stoics like Seneca or Renaissance ones like Budé.

The individual can only have peace of mind when his will is directed in harmony with Divine Will. (The technical phrase was 'in agreement with Nature' – meaning the ruling principle in the universe, which was Reason and God.) But tranquillity and independence depended on a selection principle – a resort again to nature; in a strict sense only one thing is natural – to have one's reason in perfect activity. But there was a sense in which certain other conditions were natural to it, for instance, the instinct of self-preservation to man in an animal state. When Reason supervened upon animal life, the old law of instinct was superseded by a higher law of Reason, and what had been natural for animals was no longer natural, in the true sense of the word, for man. In a civilized society many things are 'appropriate' which are not natural in a purely animal life and 'natural' according to the norm which man ought to be realizing. Altruistic action was required – a wise man should not concern himself with men *but* serve them; benevolence was needed and not love; we engage in action without desire; we sacrifice anything but not our own internal calm.[17]

The Stoic theory of indifference is argued by Cicero and Seneca with certain things of a high degree (*commoda*) and certain things of a low degree (*incommoda*). It is the attitude of mind that endows them with value. Erasmus spread the doctrine of indifference in a Christian framework, and Rabelais used the episode of the fancy dress ('a long, plain-seamed and single-stitch'd Gown': Urquhart) donned by Panurge to talk about the theory: 'Chascun abonde en son sens: mesmement en choses foraines, externes et indifferentes, lesquelles de soy ne sont bonnes ne maulvaises, pource qu'elles ne sortent de nos cœurs et pensées' (*Tiers Livre*, ch. 7). The wise man will look on clothes, riches, food, drink, and so on, as essentially neutral or indifferent but promotable by the reason of man. Compare Pantagruel's words at the end of chapter 35 of the *Tiers Livre* –

Je interprete . . . avoir et n'avoir femme en ceste façon; que femme avoir est l'avoir à usaige tel que Nature la créa, qui est pour l'ayde, esbatement et societé de l'homme; n'avoir femme est ne soy apoiltronner au tour d'elle, pour elle ne contaminer celle unicque et supreme affection que doibt l'homme à Dieu; ne laisser les offices qu'il doibt naturellement à sa patrie, à la Republicque, à ses amys; ne mettre en non chaloir ses estudes et negoces, pour continuellement à sa femme complaire.

I thus interpret (quoth Pantagruel) the having and not having of a

Wife. To have a Wife, is to have the use of her in such a way as Nature hath ordained, which is for the Aid, Society and Solace of Man, and propagating of his Race: To have no Wife is not to be uxorious, play the Coward, and be lazy about her, and not for her sake to distain the Lustre of that Affection which Man owes to God; or yet for her to leave those Offices and Duties which he owes unto his Country, unto his Friends and Kindred; or for her to abandon and forsake his precious Studies, and other business of Account, to wait still on her Will, her Beck and her Buttocks. (Urquhart)

– with these words of Montaigne; 'Il faut avoir femmes, enfans, biens, et sur tout de la santé, qui peut; mais non pas s'y attacher en maniere que nostre heur en despende' (Villey-Saulnier, p. 241). It is quite clear that both writers take seriously the indifference theory as seen in Seneca's *De beneficiis*, 5.15, or Cicero's *Tusculan Disputations*, 4.5.10, where the Stoic obedience of the passions and desires to reason (*tranquillitas*) is contrasted with *perturbatio*, which was a disordered state:

Vacandum autem omni est animi perturbatione, cum cupiditate et metu, tum etiam aegritudine et voluptate nimia et iracundia, ut tranquillitas animi et securitas adsit, quae affert cum constantiam tum etiam dignitatem.

But one must be free of all mental disturbance – not only desire and fear but also illness, excessive pleasure and anger – to ensure the presence of peace of mind and freedom from anxiety, which brings both stability and the right to be respected. (DGC)

But Montaigne also owned the *editio princeps* of Diogenes Laertius (1533) in Greek and there, in the life of Zeno, he could have read this well-known passage:

Thus the end (according to Zeno) is to live in conformity with Nature (whereby is meant both our own nature and the nature of the universe), and to do nothing that is forbidden by the universal law, which is right reason pervading all things and is identical with Zeus the guide and governor of the whole universe. And the virtue and even flow of life of the happy man consist in this, that his actions conform to his individual genius, working in harmony with the will of the governor of the universe. (7.88–9)[18]

Our individual nature must be known in order to realize that we are in a given action or mood departing from it: as Cicero says, 'That is most fitting to every man which is most in conformity with himself. Let everyone then know his own nature and constitute himself a clear-sighted judge of his own virtues and vices' (*De officiis*, I.31.113–14).

These Stoic ideas form part of the background culture in France (and, indeed, in Europe as a whole), and Montaigne, like Rabelais or Erasmus, was not unaware of them. But he has the clairvoyance to see that the whole Stoic doctrine is a harsh and rigid system; he rejects the Stoic conception of a man endowed with virtue since it is 'd'une vertu excessive' and makes his own comment; 'Il y a pour moy assez affaire sans aller si avant' (Villey-Saulnier, p. 243). He condemns it because by actual experience he finds that he is not the man to go by the Stoic rules of living. When he discusses suicide in the essay 'Coustume de l'isle de Cea' (II.3) he finds that '(B) La douleur (C) insupportable (B) et une pire mort me semblent les plus excusables incitations' (Villey-Saulnier, p. 362). Willpower or reasoning do nothing to help excruciating pain, and we notice that the adjective *insupportable* is added in a (C) passage. He debunks the false values of Stoicism: for example, the separation of body and soul (this falseness was important for his suggestions on education as we have seen and important, too, in ethical questions discussed in 'Du repentir' and 'De la vanité') or the *chasse à la perfection* which man pursues for ever – about which we read in the last and most perfect essay, 'De l'experience' (III.13). We can see him exploring where his emotional and intellectual position lies through an orchestration of Stoic themes. I shall take one example to show this.

On the philosophical front *apprentissage* is a Stoic theme which Montaigne uses time and time again. Vernon Arnold gives us a brief yet penetrating résumé of what *apprentissage* means –

> Virtue comes by training, not by birth; by art, not by nature. In the period that precedes the attainment of virtue, there exist states of the soul which are the semblances and the fore-runners of virtue; and he who is on his way towards wisdom, and whom we call 'the probationer' (*proficiens*), by learning and practice comes daily nearer his goal . . . (*Roman Stoicism*, p. 294)

– and refers to Diogenes Laertius, 7.127, where the author talks of the state of moral improvement. Now, Diogenes Laertius is one writer that Montaigne comes back to again and again – especially in the marginalia of the 1588 edition – and given that he could have used the *editio princeps* it is not surprising that the whole conception of progress towards wisdom was a seductive theory for him. But Montaigne did not accept the Stoic view that in the end a man acquired wisdom. Instead he explored suggestively the probationer's task. For example, in 'De l'institution des enfants' (I.26) Montaigne makes use of the semi-metaphors of 'apprenticeship' and 'school' many times: 'Or, à cet apprentissage, tout ce qui se presente à nos yeux sert de livre suffisant . . . ',[19] or 'En cette eschole du commerce des hommes . . . '.[20] Another example may be taken from 'Coustume de l'isle de Cea' (II.3) where he is talking of his *fantaisies*:

> Si philosopher c'est douter, comme ils disent, à plus forte raison niaiser et fantastiquer, comme je fais, doit estre doubter. Car c'est aux apprentifs à enquerir et à debatre, et au cathedrant de resoudre.[21] (Villey-Saulnier, p. 350)

> If, as some say, to philosophate be to doubt; with much more reason to rave and fantastiquize, as I doe, must necessarily be to doubt: For, to enquire and debate belongeth to a schollor, and to resolve appertains to a cathedrall master.

Note that Montaigne includes himself as an *apprenti*, an *apprenti* on the road to wisdom and an *apprenti* in writing down his *fantaisies*. There are two other examples worth noticing. The first is in a crucial essay, 'De l'exercitation' (II.6), where his own loss of consciousness is recorded and analysed with regard to our feelings about death:

> On se peut, par usage et par experience, fortifier contre les douleurs, la honte, l'indigence et tels autres accidents; mais, quant à la mort, nous ne la pouvons essayer qu'une fois; nous y sommes tous apprentifs quand nous y venons.
> (Villey-Saulnier, p. 371: an (A) passage)

> A man may, by custome and experience, fortifie himself against griefe, sorrow, shame, want, and such like accidents; but concerning death, we can but once feele and trie the same. We are all novices and new to learne when we come unto it.

The use of his own experience as an example makes his thoughts about death particularly interesting. He recounts how he went for a ride in the neighbourhood, astride an easygoing nag; on the return home one of his men mounted upon a strong-headed horse came right on his path, 'and as a Colossus with his weight riding over me and my nag, that were both very little, he overthrew us both, and made us fall with our heeles upward' (Florio, p. 186). This 'swowning', this loss of consciousness – the only time Montaigne experienced unconsciousness – is the raw material for his analysis of the moments before death. Some writers, he says, have tried to *gouster* and *savourer* death – 'Il me semble toutefois qu'il y a quelque façon de nous *apprivoiser* à elle et de l'essayer aucunement' (my italics). Words like *essayer* (repeated a few pages later) and *experimenter* often surround this *apprentissage* in his analysis of the fall. He describes moments when 'I closed mine eyes to help (as me seemed) to send it [his life] forth, and tooke a kinde of pleasyre to linger and languishingly to let my self goe from my selfe'. Many psychological and physiological 'facts' stand out in the analysis: for instance, the memory of the body, the unconscious movements of a leg or an arm, the voicing of instructions 'contre l'advis de nostre volonté' and the sweetness of death in life. Montaigne can, in 1588, end his essay in this penetrating and emotional tone: 'Ce n'est pas ci ma doctrine, c'est mon estude, et n'est pas la leçon d'autruy, c'est la mienne' (Villey-Saulnier, p. 377). When Montaigne subsequently reread this essay he felt it necessary to make a long addition after this phrase. In the 1588 version he had made his basic point; now he adds further remarks like 'Et ne me doit on sçavoir mauvais gré pour tant si je la communique. Ce qui me sert, peut aussi par accident servir à un autre' (ibid., p. 377: 'Yet ought no man to blame me if I impart the same. What serves my turne may haply serve another mans').

The 'playing' with a philosophical formula is also important in my last example: this time through 're-creation' of a Virgil passage. It comes in 'Couardise mere de la cruauté' (II.27): 'Si faudroit-il, suyvant l'ordre de la discipline, mettre la theorique avant la practique: nous trahissons nostre apprentissage' (Villey-Saulnier, p. 697; a (B) passage: 'It were requisite, according to the order of true discipline, we should preferre the theorike before the practike. We betray our apprentisage'). He quotes then from Virgil (*Aeneid*, 11.156 ff.):

Primitiae juvenus miserae, bellique futuri
Dura rudimenta.[22]

Bitter the first fruits of your youth, harsh your apprenticeship in this war so near home.

This is from the speech of Evander as his son's body is brought before him; the question of duelling, earlier mentioned by Aeneas, the chill putting into words of the deep grief felt by the citizens of Pallanteum and by Evander himself, the stock points about death and the father's asking Aeneas to take vengeance on Turnus are dominant in the context. Montaigne takes over the associations in this essay where he discusses duels, fighting, cowardice and bravery. I am struck by the word *rudimenta*: in a military context it means finishing one's initiation or apprenticeship. In later centuries it appeared in the singular, meaning a first attempt, trial or essay in military idiom and in more general terms simply a beginning or commencement. Montaigne gives a hint of translating the phrase when he says 'nous trahissons nostre apprentissage'; then he quotes the phrase, and the noun *rudimenta* is translated by the word *apprentissage* in Villey-Saulnier. Hence Montaigne's mind is always going to 'try out', to make a first attempt, to essay, because 'Si mon ame pouvoit prendre pied, je ne m'essaierois pas, je me resoudrois: elle est toujours en apprentissage et en espreuve' (Villey-Saulnier, p. 805; (B) passage).

We can see now that *apprentissage* was an aesthetic and moral notion, that it was present in the *Essais* in both French and Latin passages, and that the Virgilian *rudimenta* underlies Montaigne *apprentissage*.

Of Epicurus (341–270 BC) only a very small corpus is extant: three letters, a book of maxims and some fragments. The first four are preserved for us in the tenth book of Diogenes Laertius, whose *editio princeps* in Greek was owned by Montaigne. Modern understanding and appreciation of Epicurus are due, largely, to his transmission in Lucretius' epic *De rerum natura*. Lucretius, whom Montaigne reckons to be the best poet after Virgil and yet 'mais j'ay bien à faire à me r'asseurer en cette creance, quand je me treuve attaché à quelque beau lieu de ceux de Lucrece' (Villey-Saulnier, p. 411). Epicurean epistemology and psychology do not attract Montaigne, but he is taken by the theory of pleasure as expounded by Diogenes Laertius:

It is not the succession of banquets and revels nor enjoyment of boys and women nor of fish and all the things that may load an expensive table, that produces the life of pleasure, but sober calculation which examines the grounds for every choice and refuses and banishes those beliefs through which so much confusion occupies our minds. (10.132) (Robert Coleman)

Pleasure is really a state in which some desire is completely satisfied or fulfilled, and mental pleasures are superior to physical ones. Far from offering a hedonistic state the Epicureans recommend plain fare, bread and water which confer the highest possible pleasure when they are brought to thirsty lips. Their real aim was to lead man to a quiet life untroubled by fears of the external world, to that state of *ataraxia*, tranquillity of mind or *securitas*. Pains of the mind are worse than pains of the body.

Throughout the Middle Ages, Lucretius was neglected, and it was only in the Renaissance that he was discovered both as a poet and as a philosopher. Lambin made a valuable contribution to the text when he published his edition in 1563 (he dedicated the second book to Ronsard). It is possible that Montaigne possessed a Lambin text, but anyway he owned a text of Lucretius. Therein he might have noticed that the Stoics are never mentioned by name but always called *stulti*, *stolidi* or, even worse, *quidam* and often they are set aside with a contemptuous *delirium* or *desipere est*. Now, Montaigne was far more intelligent than scholars and critics allow; he could read, understand and appreciate the writings of Cicero and Seneca, Diogenes Laertius and Lucretius. Thus it is not surprising that he wove meditations out of their works without being a toy soldier marching to the Stoics' camp and without being like swine wallowing in the 'hedonistic' mire of Epicurus.

To show that this is so I am going to analyse briefly 'Que philosopher, c'est apprendre à mourir' (I.20), as it is often known as a self-contradictory, paradoxical and, at times, absurd essay. It is a meditation around death and life from a non-religious, non-philosophical and non-intellectual point of view. And it asks the reader to use his imagination in trying to understand one man's experience. The whole meditation on death is like a broken series of improvisations upon themes in a variety of keys. The essay is full of clichés, Stoic ideas, themes that Montaigne had read in ancient literature, in Christian works, in improvised schema, and commonplace stock-in-trade thoughts about death. We might say that the whole web of the discourse was secondhand. But, if the thoughts are not original, the writer's personality sets the scene, analyses a cluster of ideas around life and death and, by so doing, manages to convince the reader of the truth and profundity of the intellectual clichés. Thus, for example, his quotations of Horace and Lucretius are there to expand the theme in another kind of poetic language, one that should elicit from the reader collaboration because he will know the contexts of each quotation. Or, again, Montaigne creates bits of quasi-dialogues – for example, the one with nature doing the talking – which animate the discourse, for with a potential interlocutor present the argument comes alive.

It is a kind of internal composition, worked out with moving, touching details, and it follows the rhythm of Montaigne's thought. He reads and rereads this essay as a means of self-interpretation; therefore, there is coherence in it, but not on the logical and rational level where many scholars believe it should be. Villey's thesis that this essay is Stoic can be confuted. For example, the typical Montaigne thought about death is written in 1580; he wants it to be his own kind of death, 'que la mort me treuve plantant mes chous, mais nonchalant d'elle, et encore plus de mon jardin imparfait' (Villey-Saulnier, p. 89: an (A) passage). We can think of or, rather, imagine a man, living life as well as he can, being caught in his garden planting cabbages and totally *nonchalant* (Cotgrave gives 'carelesse, negligent' as translations) of death.[23] This beautiful particularization of the self and death is the same as what he says in 1588 in the last essay, 'De l'experience': 'Je me compose pourtant à la [vie] perdre sans regret, mais comme perdable de sa condition, non comme moleste et importune' (Villey-Saulnier, p. 1111).

The interlinking of nature with life and death is there in the 1580 edition. We may look at the whole argument which starts with 'On me dira que . . . '. The harsh voices of the Stoics are there and, indeed, of all philosophy, which is abstract and against the 'lived in' shape of the Montaigne argument: 'Laissez les dire' – let them say as they will, it is not *my* experience; 'il y a plus: Nature mesme nous preste la main et nous donne courage' (cf. III.13, where the voice of nature is in a (C) passage – that is to say, the marginalia of the *exemplaire* – 'Le plus simplement se commettre à nature, c'est s'y commettre le plus sagement': Villey-Saulnier, p. 1073). In this argument Montaigne introduces a key idea: that of the paradoxical relationship between pleasure and pain, which has its origin in Epicurean philosophy:

> j'ay trouvé que sain j'avois eu les maladies beaucoup plus en horreur, que lors que je les ay senties; l'alegresse où je suis, le plaisir et la force me font paroistre l'autre estat si disproportionné à celuy-là, que par imagination je grossis ces incommoditez de moitié, et les conçoy plus poisantes, que je ne les trouve, quand je les ay sur les espaules. J'espere qu'il m'en adviendra ainsi de la mort.
>
> (ibid., p. 90: an (A) passage)

I have found that being in perfect health, I have much more beene frighted with sickness, than when I have felt it. The jollitie wherein I live, the pleasure and the strength make the other seeme so disproportionable from that, that by imagination I amplifie these commodities by one moitie, and apprehended them much more heavie and burthensome, than I feele them when I have them upon my shoulders. The same I hope will happen to me of death.

The Epicurean fusion of pleasure with pain found an echo in his own suffering from gallstones. He had been struck by an attack of biliary colic in 1577–8 – that is to say, before the first edition of the *Essais* – and he suffered for the rest of his life from gallstones as well as from rheumatism and gout. The pain he endured was acute; we hear him say in 'De la ressemblance des enfans aux peres' (II.8): '(C) Je suis aus prises avec la pire de toutes les maladies, la plus soudaine, la plus douloureuse, la plus mortelle et la plus irremediable' (Villey-Saulnier, p. 760). The sentence is profoundly moving and yet encased in a fine stylistic pattern. This is typical Montaigne – realizing that he must 'put across' the intense feeling to the reader he uses all the procedures of rhetoric. With the passage of a stone through the bile-duct, a person often breaks out in profuse sweat and may vomit. As Montaigne describes it:

> (A) En accidents si extremes c'est cruauté de requerir de nous une démarche si composée. Si nous avons beau jeu, c'est peu que nous avons mauvaise mine. Si le corps se soulage en se plaignant, qu'il le face; si l'agitation luy plaist, qu'il se tourneboule et tracasse à sa fantaisie; s'il luy semble que le mal s'évapore aucunement . . . pour pousser hors la voix avec plus grande violence, ou, s'il en amuse son tourment, qu'il crie tout à faict.
>
> (ibid., p. 761)

In so extreme accidents it is cruelty to require so composed a warde at our hands. If we have a good game it skills not, though we have an ill countenance. If the body be any whit eased by complaining, let him doe it; if stirring or agitation please him, let him turne, rowle, and tosse himself as long as he list: if with raising his voyce, or sending it forth with more violence, he think his griefe any thing alayed or vented . . . feare he not to do it; or if he may but entertaine his torment, let him mainly cry out.

The sharp violence of pain may indeed make him wish to die in order to escape it. A few pages later, and still in the 1580 version, Montaigne comes face to face with one of the great leitmotifs of the *Essais*, namely, the precious gift of health in a man's life;

> (A) C'est une pretieuse chose que la santé, et la seule qui merite à la verité— qu'on y employe, non le temps seulement, la sueur, la peine, les biens, mais encore la vie à sa poursuite; d'autant que sans elle la vie nous vient à estre penible et injurieuse. La volupté, la sagesse, la science et la vertu, sans elle, se ternissent et esvanouissent.

(ibid., p. 765)

> health is a very precious jewel, and the onely thing that in pursuite of it deserveth a man should not onely employ time, labour, sweate and goods, but also life to get it; forasmuch as without it life becommeth injurious unto us. Voluptuousnes, science and vertue, without it, tarnish and varnish away.

On 25 February 1578 he started reading Caesar's *Civil War* and finished it on 21 July.[24]

And in this paragraph of the essay I.20, a paragraph which unites pain, pleasure, experience, death and life, there is a reminiscence of Caesar and of his own suffering in that he says; 'Tout ainsi que j'ay essayé en plusieurs autres occurrences ce que dit Cesar . . . ' Reading that things appear much larger when seen from a distance than they really are is coupled to the experience that Montaigne has had: the power of the imagination is detrimental, from many points of view, to his thoughts of illness and pain.

Therefore, in the (A) passages, there is quite clearly a Montaigne argument composed partly of his own experience and partly of reading what philosophers say about life and death, pain and pleasure.

Furthermore, there are innumerable threads of Stoic philosophy in the (C) passages. For instance, this statement, 'La vie n'est de soy ny bien ny mal: c'est la place du bien et du mal selon que vous la leur faictes' (Villey-Saulnier, p. 93), is vigorously making a reference to the indifference theory which we saw earlier in this chapter, or again to the fashion of nature advising Thales (and Justus Lipsius called Montaigne the 'French Thales'), 'le premier de vos sages, que le vivre et le mourir estoit indifferent; par où, à celuy qui luy demanda pourquoy donc 'il ne mouroit, il respondit très sagement: "Par ce qu'il est indifferent" ' (ibid., p. 96). Thus it is clear that Montaigne makes traits of Stoic philosophy overlap with Epicureanism in the three books and there is not, as Villey had stated, a distinct separation of Stoic, Pyrrhonic and Epicurean ideas.

However, there is the violent attack on Stoicism in a long addition coming in the (C) version where Montaigne wages war on the 'sectes Philosophiques' (by which he means the Stoics) and dismisses the debates and dissensions as *verbales*: 'Quoy qu'ils dient, en la vertu mesme, le dernier but de nostre visée, c'est la volupté.' And the sheer joy Montaigne has in making this war is found in the following sentence: 'Il me plaist de battre leurs oreilles de ce mot qui leur est si fort à contrecoeur' (ibid., p. 82: a (C) passage. Florio translates it thus: 'It pleaseth me to importune their cares still with this word, which so much offends their hearing'). Here is a fusion of virtue with voluptuousness, a theme which will run through the *Essais* and particularly the third book, where *voluptez* (as we saw in our critical commentary in the last chapter) are of crucial value in Montaigne's *art de vivre*.

In this essay he allies virtue, pleasure, voluptuousness in a totally new way, saying that virtue should actually be called pleasure, and it should not be confused with a merely fleshly pleasure; 'Cette volupté, pour estre plus gaillarde, nerveuse, robuste, virile, n'en est que plus serieusement voluptueuse. Et luy devions donner le nom du plaisir, plus favorable, plus doux et naturel: non celuy de la vigueur, duquel nous l'avons denommée' (ibid.). The adjectives in these two sentences are favourites of Montaigne:[25] *gaillarde* – lusty frolicksomeness; *nerveuse* – sinewy strength; *robuste* – tough sinew; and *virile* – virile manliness. We shall see them again. Suffice it to say here that they concretize voluptuousness very well. The lower voluptuousness is sexual, and Montaigne would give it a place in the hierarchy of values but not a privileged one; rather, one *en concurrence*. If we were to compare virtue with voluptuousness, 'Outre que son goust est plus momentanée, fluide et caduque, elle a ses veillées, ses jeusnes et ses travaux et la sueur et le sang'. As opposed to the adjectives qualifying virtue the adjectives he ascribes to the lower sensuality are amorphous and noisome; *fluide* – thin waterishness; and *caduque* – frail, feeble ruinousness.

Throughout this (C) addition Montaigne is pitting himself against philosophers: for instance, he starts with 'Quoy qu'ils dient', follows this by 'Celuy-là est certes bien indigne'; then we hear him say 'Ceux qui nous vont instruisant' before reaching his stunning climax in 'Mais ils se trompent'. It is as if philosophers were merely theorizing, never having known virtue in its true form; they are for making it difficult; they tell us how hard and laborious is the path to virtue and how even the most perfect seekers after her never possess her. But they are deceived: for the human truth is that the pursuit of a worthwhile pleasure is in itself pleasurable: 'L'enterprise se sent de la qualité de la chose qu'elle regarde, car c'est une bonne portion de l'effect et consubstancielle.' If the purpose of life lies in a preparation for not fearing death, then this quest for and gain of voluptuousness in virtue are worthwhile and this in turn is beneficial in our *mépris de la mort*. When he compares the death of Cato to that of Socrates, the former makes Montaigne see or read into this action 'je ne sçay quelle esjouissance de son ame, et une émotion de plaisir extraordinaire et d'une volupté virile' ('De la cruauté', II.11; Villey-Saulnier, p. 424) whilst Socrates

> A ce tressaillir, du plaisir qu'il sent à gratter sa jambe apres que les fers en furent hors, accuse il pas une pareille douceur et joye en son ame, pour estre desenforgée des incommodités passées, et à mesme d'entrer en cognoissance des choses advenir? (A) Caton me pardonnera, s'il luy plaist; sa mort est plus tragique et plus tendue, mais cette-cy est encore, je ne sçay comment, plus belle. (ibid., p. 425)

> By the startling at the pleasure, which he feeleth in clawing of his legges after his fetters were taken-off; doth he not manifestly declare an equal glee and joy in his soule for being rid of his former incommodities, and entering into the knowledge of things to come? Cato shall pardon me (if he please) his death is more tragical, and further extended, whereas this in a certaine manner is more faire and glorious.

Here again voluptuousness, virtue and pleasure are linked in the same way, and Montaigne reflects that '(C) Toute mort doit estre de mesmes sa vie. Nous ne devenons pas autres pour mourir'.

Montaigne channels his thought inward: 'Que philosopher, c'est apprendre à mourir' is a meditation on death/life considered not humanistically, but psychologically and artistically. Death is lucidly probed with 'poetic' movements, with lyrical passages and finely observed details. It is up to the reader to weigh and measure

Montaigne's way of thinking, and it is certainly a fine challenge. He is
moving backwards and forwards through the skein of his memories.
His *Essais* demands from the reader a high degree of participation and
a slowness in reading. It seems as if Montaigne were putting minims
between the sentences. His thought is always turning back and
growing out of itself and yet reaching out to the universal plane.
Words which do not allow themselves to be pinned down to one
simple sense are richly allusive; they evoke associations, sensations,
complex images and interwoven themes.

This single example of Montaigne's transformation of Stoic and
Epicurean philosophical ideas may be backed up by the preceding
essay, 'Qu'il ne faut juger de nostre heur, qu'apres la mort'. Here he
sees death almost like a tableau, something that every person
composes as he wills; or like the last act of a drama, 'Mais à ce dernier
rolle de la mort et de nous, il n'y a plus que faindre, il faut parler
François, il faut montrer ce qu'il y a de bon et de net dans le fond du
pot . . . ' (Villey-Saulnier, p. 80). Life is regarded as a work of art.
Meeting death is not an idea or a piece of knowledge: he does not say
how many ways of dying there are, nor the concepts underlying each
one nor what the ancients say about it. But, rather, death is something
which every individual *composes* for himself; 'Je remets à la mort
l'essay du fruict de mes estudes. Nous verrons là si mes discours me
partent de la bouche, ou du cœur' (ibid.). Both passages are there in
the 1580 edition. The meditation on death is something we can call
aesthetic.

Thus we can conclude that Montaigne put up a scaffolding of ideas
from Stoic and Epicurean writings, but it was erected so as to make it
possible for him to get inside the building, so to speak, and
structuralize ideas coming from his own experience and his own life.
The result is a full-blooded textural pattern which is uniquely that of
Montaigne.

CHAPTER 4

The 'Apologie de Raimond Sebond': Religion and Scepticism

'Que sais-je?'

The 'Apologie' is the most lengthy and, in many ways, the most difficult of the essays – although, perhaps, not the most exciting. It is crucial for understanding Montaigne's meditations on religion, on the concept of reason and the way man decides, reaches or does not reach knowledge of anything.

Montaigne was not a systematic thinker; this essay was written for, it is thought, Marguerite de Valois (first wife of Henri de Navarre), a Catholic with a Protestant husband and a circle of Protestants in Nérac around her. Nérac is a small town which is today in the *département* of Lot-et-Garonne, but in the sixteenth century was the capital of the kingdom of Navarre. It proved a safe refuge for Protestants: for example, Calvin, Lefèvre d'Etaples, Marot, Nostradamus and Du Bartas stayed there at different times. The queen of Navarre was very distinguished in letters, wrote her *Mémoires* (published in 1628), founded an academy which was run by Pibrac. The court of Nérac is the setting of *Love's Labour's Lost*. The atmosphere of gallantry, pageantry and continual entertainment meant that Catholics and Protestants met on an equal footing in this court, finely associated with the tradition of academies in France: 'Navarre shall be the wonder of the world;/Our court shall be a little academe,/Still and contemplative in living art.'[1] It seems as if the 'Apologie' was written in several parts before 1580, and there are numerous passages inserted in 1588 and in the *exemplaire*. We start by drawing a rather schematic plan on the content of the essay:

(1) Montaigne explains how he came to translate Raimond Sebond's work. In the 1560s his father had been given by Pierre Bunel, a humanist and a personal friend of his, the *Theologia naturalis* of Sebond. Sebond was a fifteenth-century Catalan scholar, who taught in the University of Toulouse and who produced this hefty work, trying to prove the existence of God by using human reason alone (not coupled with revelation). Pierre Montaigne asked his son to translate it for him. Which he did.

(2) Montaigne states that there were two objections to Sebond's work: the first one, that no Christian could argue from purely rational or human reasons the proof of Christianity, which is the work of faith or revelation. The second one, that Sebond's arguments are weak and inapt for proving the rightness of Christianity. Montaigne comments on the first one by saying that our faculties must aid in a necessarily human endeavour and prepares for the counter-attack against the second objection.

(3) Montaigne affirms, first, that Sebond's arguments are not weak seeing that there is the interaction of faith and reason – 'la foy venant à teindre et illustrer les argumens de Sebond, elle les rend fermes et solides' (Villey-Saulnier, p. 447). Are there better arguments? Is there a better method? This takes Montaigne into a résumé of human reason. He shows that man and animals are on an equal footing in nature; if man has reason, this makes him neither happy nor good. Furthermore, Montaigne goes on to demonstrate that man knows nothing: his ignorance of God or the gods, of himself in general, of the nature of the soul and reason, and lastly of his own body.

(4) A two-page warning to Queen Margot that what will follow is a dangerous fencer's trick, to be used only as a last resort, by which you abandon your own weapon – that of reason – to make your adversary lose his:

> C'est un coup desesperé, auquel il faut abandonner vos armes pour faire perdre à vostre adversaire les siennes, et un tour secret, duquel il se faut servir rarement et reservéement. C'est grande temerité de vous perdre vous mesmes pour perdre un autre. (ibid., p. 558)

> It is a desperate thrust, gainst which you must forsake your weapons, to force your adversary to renounce his, and a secret slight, which must seldome and very sparingly be put in

practice. It is a great fond hardnesse to lose our selfe for the losse of another.

This is the most exciting part of the 'Apologie', to which I shall return. It concerns the argument that man is a creature of flux and all the instruments of knowledge, notably the senses, are demonstrably deficient and deceptive.

(5) The conclusion praises Seneca's feeling that man must raise himself above humanity, but Montaigne pronounces it absurd from Seneca's point of view, for it is God alone, by His grace, can work such a miracle.

In the introduction Montaigne refers to an important principle: 'Ce seroit mieux la charge d'un homme versé en la Theologie, que de moy qui n'y sçay rien . . . ' (ibid., p. 440). Since the Council of Trent (1545–63), theology was left to the professionals; it was right for them to pursue and declare doctrinal, ecclesiastical and metaphysical points; Montaigne confesses that he is a layman, yet 'Toutefois je juge ainsi'. In other words, his whole argument on faith and reason is that of a non-specialist but, he seems to hint, it is worth hearing.

There are a few things that need to be investigated before we tackle in more detail the contents of the 'Apologie'. The first is atheism. Busson has demonstrated that between 1540 and 1560 many words like *athée*, *déiste*, *achriste* and *libertin* were born in the French language.[2] He has shown the effect in France of the rationalist treatise *Tractatus de immortalitate animae* published in Italy in 1516 by Pomponazzi. Etienne Dolet, a scholar and printer (he printed Rabelais' books in 1542 without the author's consent), was imprisoned three times for atheism and then was tortured and burned in Paris on 3 August 1546. Vicomercato, a pupil of Pomponazzi, held the royal chair of philosophy in Paris from 1542 and proclaimed that the soul was mortal and that God was the true Aristotelian one, not a creative power but merely the unmoved mover of the eternal heavens. The Elder Pliny, in whose works Montaigne delighted, was regarded as blasphemous, atheistic and impious; Lucretius, who so often comes into the 'Apologie', was similarly an atheist, and Cicero's *De natura deorum* and *De divinatione* (which Montaigne had read) were arsenals for atheistic ideas. But Montaigne, in a very adamant tone of voice, dismisses atheism as 'execrable' (Villey-Saulnier, p. 439), and a little further on states: 'L'Atheisme estant une proposition come desnaturée et monstrueuse, difficile aussi et malaisée d'establir en l'esprit humain, pour insolent et desreglé qu'il puisse estre' (ibid., p. 446). Thus, in no sense can we see him as an atheist nor as an existentialist, a person who rejects the essentialist world and believes that our existence is all. We must not be a Sainte-Beuve nor a Gide in this matter.

Many critics accept that he was a Catholic in the sense that people can be today: they accept that God exists, that Christ was sent to earth and that there are ceremonies laid down by the church such as the last confession which they will receive. They can cite the passage in 'Des prieres' (I.56):

> (C) tenant pour *execrable*, s'il se trouve chose ditte par moy ignorament ou inadvertament contre les sainctes prescriptions de l'Eglise catholique, apostolique et Romaine, en laquelle je meurs et en laquelle je suis nay. (Villey-Saulnier, p. 318: my italics)

> deeming it absurd and impious if anything be either ignorantly or unadvisedly set downe in this rapsody, contrarie unto the sacred resolutions and repugnant to the holy prescriptions of the Catholike, Apostolike, and Romane Church, wherein I was borne, and out of which I purpose not to die.

They can take external evidence of the fact that Montaigne was a Catholic from the *Journal de voyage*.[3] On first coming to a village or town Montaigne at once makes for a theologian – be he a Lutheran, Zwinglian, Benedictine, Jesuit – and it comes as a surprise that he likes particularly the Jesuits. For instance, being in Rome during Lent, Montaigne can indulge himself with a good supply of sermons – both from Jews and from Christians; especially Padre Toledo:

> (en profondeur de sçavoir, en pertinance et disposition, c'est home très rare); un autre très éloquent et populere, qui prechoit aux jesuites, non sans beaucoup de suffisance parmi son excellence de langage; les deux derniers sont jesuites. (p. 1230)

> he was an outstanding man through the depths of his knowledge, and in the aptness and disposition of his natural humor; another one, very eloquent and popular, used to preach to the Jesuits very ably and with an excellent tongue; the last two are Jesuits. (DGC)

Immediately following this comes a paragraph of enthusiastic

admiration for the Jesuit order, complimenting them on their efficient
services and ending up by saying: 'C'est celui de nos mambres qui
menasse le plus les hérétiques de nostre tamps.' The military precision
of the Society, the high average of intelligence in a large body of men
and the firmness of their institution would be approved of in a time of
religious wars.

But we can dismiss all the *préchi-précha* scholars who have tried to
prove that he was a fully devout and orthodox Catholic[4] and move to a
position that was an acceptable one in the sixteenth century, that of
fideism. What is meant by this term? The *Oxford Dictionary of the
Christian Church* states: 'A term applied to a variety of doctrines which
hold in common belief the incapacity of the intellect to attain to
knowledge of divine matters and correspondingly put an excessive
emphasis on faith.' Admittedly, the term was only invented in 1838,
but that does not mean that we cannot use it in connection with
Montaigne. Ideas exist without the terminology that later ages give
them, and we are not being ahistorical when we superimpose a
structure of language on previously blurred outlines. To quote Busson
here: 'Parce que le mot *fidéisme* date de 1838, quel historien de la
théologie refusera de voir du fidéisme jusque dans le moyen âge?' (*Le
Rationalisme* (Paris: Vrin, 1957), p. 12: author's italics).

The ideology connected with fideism is present throughout the
'Apologie'. Montaigne does not disparage reason, but man's mind –
its capacity for seeing and knowing truth: 'J'appelle tousjours raison
cette apparence de discours que chacun forge en soy' (Villey-Saulnier,
p. 565). Because it is human reason it is in reality *apparence*, and in
one of the key sentences in the 'Apologie' Montaigne makes the
distinction between divine and human reason quite clear, and indeed
makes them move in separate ways: 'C'est aux Chrestiens une occasion
de croire que de rencontrer une chose incroiable. Elle est d'autant plus
selon raison qu'elle est *contre l'humaine raison*' (ibid., p. 499: my
italics). In other words, divine reason is totally outside our reach; God
moves in a mysterious way and is not, in any way, hedged by our
human reason. All we can do is to recognize this fact and live with it.
The *humaine raison* is incapable of a knowledge of God and of all
supernatural things. There is a suspension of judgement in Montaigne
and a lack of concern over faith in general, over grace, over sin and
over Jesus Christ but, nevertheless, throughout the *Essais* there are
theological overtones when he speaks about the 'faiblesse', the vanity
and misery of the human condition and the 'imbecillité de nostre
jugement'.

The disproportion between man and God is vast: 'C'est à Dieu seul de se cognoistre et d'interpreter ses ouvrages. Et le faict en nostre langue, improprement, pour s'avaller et descendre à nous, qui sommes à terre, couchez' (ibid., p. 499). Montaigne enthrones God on high, and nothing that human reason, language or experience can do can ever make us know His behaviour. Even the most important dogmas of the church like the immortality of the soul cannot be proved by reason but must be believed. He recognized God as an incomprehensible power beside whom our 'raisons' are 'humaines et naturelles': 'nos raisons et discours humains, c'est comme la matiere lourde et sterile: la grace de Dieu en est la forme; c'est elle qui y donne la façon et le pris' (ibid., p. 447). This is a scholastic argument or, rather, an Aristotelian concept, clothed in Christian form, with *forme* being the essence given by God to matter which is shapeless and clumsy. The marks of truth in this universe are man's incomprehension:

> Ce n'est pas par discours ou par nostre entendement que nous avons receu nostre religion, c'est par authorité et par commandement estranger. La faiblesse de nostre jugement nous y ayde plus que la force, et nostre aveuglement plus que nostre cler-voyance. (ibid., p. 500)

> It is not by our discourse or understanding that we have received our religion, it is by a forreine authority and commandement. The weaknesse of our judgement helps us more than our strength to compasse the same, and our blindnesse more than our clear-sighted eies.

And in this he follows what St Paul and St Augustine said, that anything human added to the concept of divinity would mark it with imperfection:

> rien du nostre ne se peut assortir ou raporter, en quelque façon que ce soit, à la nature divine, qui ne la tache et marque d'autant d'imperfection. Cette infinie beauté, puissance et bonté, comment peut elle souffrir quelque correspondance et similitude à chose si abjecte que nous sommes, sans un extreme interest et dechet de sa divine grandeur. (ibid., p. 523: cf. St Paul, I Corinthians, 1.25)

> Now can nothing of ours, in what manner soever, be either compared or referred unto divine nature, that doth not blemish and

defile the same with as much imperfection. How can this infinite beauty, power, and goodness admit any correspondencie or similitude with a thing so base and abject as we are, without extreme interest and manifest derogation from his divine greatnesse?

Montaigne states very strongly that the first law of God is obedience:

ce fust un commandement nud et simple où l'homme n'eut rien à connoistre et à causer, d'autant que l'obeyr est le principal office d'une ame raisonnable, recognoissant un celeste superieur et bienfacteur. De l'obeyr et ceder naist toute autre vertu, comme du cuider tout péché. (Villey-Saulnier, p. 488)

It was a bare and simple commandement whereof man should enquire and know no further: forasmuch as to obey is the proper dutie of a reasonable soul, acknowledging a heavenly and superior benefactor. From obeying and yeelding unto him proceed all other vertues, even as all sinnes derive from selfe-overweening.

And the sentence which is famous in that Pascal copied it ('cela vous fera croire et vous abêtira') – 'Il nous faut abestir pour nous assagir et nous esblouir pour nous guider . . . ' (Villey-Saulnier, p. 492: a (C) passage) – is a call for the humility of man *vis-à-vis* the dazzling greatness of God.[5] In fact it is pure presumption on the part of man to think himself in any way related to God. The sixteenth century had brought forth many heresies (Luther, Calvin and the whole Reformation) which try to bring God's behaviour and actions nearer to man; Montaigne denies categorically that this is ever possible, for God is unknowable. This view of the *condition humaine* is something on which Montaigne never goes back, and his influence on the next century's pessimism is primordial.[6] Nevertheless, in Montaigne's case there is something inherently beautiful in what some would call the external trappings of religion. For instance, the incensing of the altar, church and people he finds pleasant: 'l'invention des encens et parfums aux Eglises, si ancienne et espandue en toutes nations et religions, regarde à cela de nous resjouir, esveiller et purifier le sens pour nous rendre plus propres à la contemplation' (ibid., p. 315). Montaigne is very sensitive to perfume, and he chooses frankincense as the most common religious incense in Egyptian, Jewish, Buddhist, Roman, and so on, worship of the gods.

The account of the 'Apologie' so far is clear, but we have omitted to include the enigmatic, ambiguous, paradoxical and fascinating parts. There are innumerable insinuations behind this defence of Sebond's natural theology. For a start, it achieves the opposite of what it was trying to do, in that it is a sceptic's demolition of the pretensions of human reason.[7] Montaigne is not only a sceptic but also an ironical, wry, humorous, oblique sceptic who is triggered off by Pliny's or Herodotus' anecdotes to play on the reader, constantly. The humour of these paradoxes is keen. How is it that man, who lives in the mire of this world, 'fast tied and nailed to the worst, most senselesse, and drooping part of the world, in the vilest corner of the house, the farthest from heavens coape' (Florio), can imagine that he is nobler than beasts, birds and fish? How does he know the inward movements of beasts? The fact that my cat does not communicate with me may well be my fault, not hers: 'Nous avons quelque moyenne intelligence de leur sens; aussi ont les bestes du nostre, environ à mesme mesure. Elles nous flatent, nous menassent et nous requierent; et nous, elles' (Villey-Saulnier, p. 453). At which point Montaigne's rhetoric sweeps along like Rabelais' oratory, in the prologue to the *Tiers Livre*, where he lists all the motions of Diogenes: Montaigne asks what we do with our hands and answers with a list of verbs – 'Doe we not sue and entreat, promise and performe, call men unto us and discharge them, bid them farewell and be gone, threaten, pray, beseech, deny, refuse, demand, admire, number, confesse, repent, feare, bee ashamed' (Florio), and so on. Verbs are a dominant feature in Montaigne's writing: the rhythm of the phrases and the words themselves are responsible for the ebullience, vitality and dynamics which give us something of the author's great delight in manipulating language, in developing paradoxes and puns and in his creativeness in linguistic formulation. This part of the 'Apologie' is not meant to be taken seriously but is intended to be enjoyed enormously. It is part of Montaigne's anti-philosophy, his anti-humanism. We are amused by weird stories like the blind men with dogs, the spider teaching man to weave, the oxen with the buckets, the swallow showing us her house-building technique, the innumerable stories about elephants, the caged birds not having been to school under their parents and thus being unable to sing, the tunny fish in battle array, the elephant who 'tastoit les tetins' of the girl he is in love with, and so on. Montaigne's joy of showing us the strange behaviour of animals comes through very strongly.

The tone of joy and irony in undermining man's presumption makes his thoughts relatively easy to read, to understand and to interpret. But other sides are also present – a fact which makes us read his basic ambiguity tentatively and suggestively. We can look at his famous statement, 'Nous sommes Chrestiens à mesme titre que nous sommes ou Perigordins ou Alemans' (Villey-Saulnier, p. 445), which seems to deny any absolute truth whatsoever to the Christian religion. Everything is relative, and there is nothing absolute in any philosophical system or any religion. It is an addition in the 1588 edition, but when we look at the context we see that it is an illustration of something that was already in the 1580 edition, namely, 'nous ne recevons nostre religion qu'à nostre façon et par nos mains, et non autrement que comme les autres religions se reçoyvent. Nous nous sommes rencontrez au païs où elle estoit en usage' (ibid.). He argues that a pure faith is idealistic and impossible.[8] It is custom, usage and milieu which determine our religious conduct. It is precisely this concept of relativity, which was new in western European thought, that tinges all the arguments of the 'Apologie'. Montaigne explored relativity most fully in the 'Apologie', but scattered around the *Essais* there are numerous instances of it: for example, in 'Des cannibales' (I.31) he tells us of how he had met (in Rouen 1562) three Brazilians and had talked to them through an interpreter; he states that other nations are not barbarous, only different from us; we are blind to our faults and yet we like to judge the faults of others. French culture is seen by an almost eighteenth-century critical stranger: the Amerindians are surprised that 'un enfan [Charles IX] commande à des vieillards' and find the French as odd as the French found them. Montaigne admires the superiority of unspoiled natural man in Latin America; they are not corrupted by our laws nor by a government such as ours; they are simple in dress, words and activities; he admires their sex habits:

> Les hommes y ont plusieurs femmes, et en ont d'autant plus grand nombre qu'ils sont en meilleure reputation de vaillance: c'est une beauté remerquable en leurs mariages, que la mesme jalousie que nos femmes ont pour nous empescher de l'amitié et bien-veuillance d'autres femmes, les leurs l'ont toute pareille pour la leur acquerir.
>
> (Villey-Saulnier, p. 212)

> Their men have many wives, and by how much more they are reputed valiant so much the greater is their number. The manner and beautie of their marriages is wondrous strange and remarkable: For, the same jealousie our wives have to keepe us from the love and affection of other women, the same have theirs to procure it.

The primitive happy tribes deny the basic institutions of European society, and Montaigne concludes with seeing the equality of mankind wherever he goes and then throws out a wry ironic remark: 'Tout cela ne va pas trop mal: mais quoy, ils ne portent point de haut de chausses.'[9] We are witness to the fact that he distrusts everything that man thinks is supernatural. European witch-trials were rampant at the end of the sixteenth century; authors like Jean Bodin, who published his *De la demonomanie des sorciers* in 1580, believed in the reality of witchcraft. Montaigne, however, talked to a supposed witch possibly in Lorraine where witch-hunting was acute, and said 'A tuer les gens, il faut une clarté lumineuse et nette' and he would have given her 'de l'ellebore que de la cicue' ('Des Boyteux', III.11; Villey-Saulnier, p. 1031). The sane, humane and enlightened attitude exposed here will, in the eighteenth century, be regarded as the 'true' Montaigne by people such as Diderot or Voltaire. Relativity is an absolute bedrock of Montaigne on questions like suicide, superstition, immortality, witches, and so on, and his views look beyond the horizon of his western European culture as he comments on the invention of artillery, 'd'autres hommes, un autre bout du monde à la Chine, en jouyssoit mille ans auparavant' ('Des coches', III.6; Villey-Saulnier, p. 908); or when he describes a king of Peru 'bruslé tout vif' (ibid., p. 912); or when he affirms that the people of Mexico are more civilized than other Amerindians (ibid., p. 913).

The oratorical phrase which almost concludes the 'Apologie', 'O la vile chose . . . et abjecte que l'homme, s'il ne s'esleve au dessus de l'humanité', is destroyed if we remember phrases like 'Quoy qu'on nous presche, quoy que nous aprenons, il faudroit tousjours se souvenir que c'est l'homme qui donne et l'homme qui reçoit; c'est une mortelle main qui nous le presente, c'est une mortelle main qui l'accepte' (ibid., p. 563). The force of Christianity comes through God's grace and only if we are born in certain countries; otherwise we would be a Buddhist or a Muslim. Even more devastating is 'comparez nos mœurs à un Mohometan, à un Payen; vous demeurez tousjours au dessoubs' (ibid., p. 442), where he uses *tousjours*, and a (C) passage from the *exemplaire* makes a harsh remark:

Toutes autres apparances sont communes à toutes religions; esperance, confiance, evenemens, ceremonies, penitence, martyres. La marque peculiere de nostre verité devroit estre nostre vertu . . . (ibid., p. 442)

All other outward shewes and exterior apparences are common to
all religions: As hope, affiance, events, ceremonies, penitence and
martyrdom. The peculiar badge of our truth should be vertue . . .

The denial of truth to Christianity on the metaphysical level is
countered by the denial of ethical value in Christians. In addition his
interest in comparative religion is strong, and there is a veiled attack
on Christianity and on values that man takes for granted. For instance,
ideas about the afterlife that the Mohammedan religion propounds,
'quand Mahumet promet aux siens un paradis tapissé, paré d'or et de
pierrerie, peuplé de garses d'excellente beauté, de vins et de vivres
singuliers . . . ' (ibid., p. 518: 'when Mahomet promiseth unto his
followers a paradise all tapestried, adorned with gold and precious
stones, peopled with exceeding beauteous damsels, stored with wines
and singular cates . . . '), are close to the view of the Garden of Eden;
he adds in the *exemplaire* the statement, 'Si, sont aucuns des nostres
tombez en pareille erreur, se promettant apres la resurrection une vie
terrestre et temporelle accompaignée de toutes sortes de plaisirs et
commoditez mondaines' ('Even so are some of our men falne into like
errours by promising unto themselves after their resurrection a
terrastriall and temporal life accompanied with all sorts of pleasures
and worldly commodities'), which is a frontal attack on man's
idealistic concept of 'heaven'. And when he is talking about
metempsychosis as developed by Pythagoras he states that 'Ce qui a
cessé une fois d'estre, n'est plus' and follows it with a long quotation
from Lucretius (3.847) which 'proves' the point.

He examines the contradictory philosophies of the Stoics, Epicureans
and Peripatetics, who are all dogmatists and who think they have
found Truth whereas they 'n'ont pas tant pensé nous establir quelque
certitude, que nous montrer jusques où ils estoyent allés en cette
chasse de la verité . . . ' (Villey-Saulnier, p. 507). They have merely
moved to 'amuser la curiosité de nostre Esprit, lui donnant où se
paistre, à ronger cet os creux et descharné . . . ' (ibid., p. 508): 'They
have not so much gone about to establish any certainty in us, as to
show how farre they had waded in seeking out the truth'). Other
philosophers like the Academicians or Pyrrhonists remain faithful to
the doubt that Truth can ever be known. All of them show the
'vacillation de l'esprit humain autour de toute matiere' (ibid., p. 510).

His attack on anthropomorphism, the ascribing of a human form to
the Deity, is vehement –

Mais d'avoir faict des dieux de nostre condition, de laquelle nous devons connoistre l'imperfection, leur avoir attribué le desir, la cholere, les vengeances, les mariages, les generations et les parentelles, l'amour et la jalousie, nos membres et nos os, nos fievres et nos plaisirs, (C) nos morts, nos sepultures, (A) il faut que cela soit party d'une marveilleuse yvresse de l'entendement humain . . .

(ibid., p. 516)

But to have made Gods of our conditions, whose imperfections we should know, and to have attributed desire, choler, revenge, marriages, generation, alliances, love, and jealousie, our limbs and our bones, our infirmities, our pleasures, our deaths, and our sepulchres unto them, hath of necessity proceeded from a meere and egregious sottishnesse or drunkennesse of man's wit.

– and is 'proven' by two lines from Lucretius, followed by a long (C) addition of the words of Cicero in his *De natura deorum*.

Montaigne makes a delightfully fresh announcement of the way he would have chosen a God, if he had been forced to make a decision: that God would be the sun, 'parmy cette cecité universelle, je me fusse, ce me semble, plus volontiers attaché à ceux qui adoroient le Soleil' (Villey-Saulnier, p. 514). And he quotes a long passage from Ronsard's *hymne au soleil* which is a very moving digression in the *Remonstrance au peuple de France*. Montaigne was a very fine literary critic (as we shall see later), and he chose from a contemporary poet a superb piece of artistic creation in the newly fashioned (by Ronsard himself) alexandrine line.

Montaigne's way of arguing is not on a straight line of logic; he throws in pell-mell all examples – be they philosophical, anthropological, personal experience, current themes from the civil war raging in France, anecdotal comments from Plutarch or Pliny – to create the dense texture of this essay. His demonstration that man knows nothing, has known nothing from time immemorial and will never know anything lacks the urgent metaphysical push towards faith that we find in certain authors.[10] He is much more interested in epistemology, the problem of knowledge or 'The philosophical discipline which examines the nature and validity of human cognition' (*Oxford Dictionary of the Christian Church*).

Take the famous analogy of the cat that I have quoted before: 'Quand je me joüe à ma chatte, qui sçait si elle passe son temps de moy plus que je ne fay d'elle?' (Villey-Saulnier, p. 452). Man and cat understand nothing of each other; they are simply living. Language is a mode of communication between men in the same way as miaowing is the cat's terminology, 'se plaindre, de se resjouyir, de s'entr'appeler au secours, se convier à l'amour'. Man is no better and no worse than animals: 'Nostre parler a ses foiblesses et ses defauts, comme tout le reste. La plus part des occasions des troubles du monde sont Grammairiennes' (ibid., p. 527). One man can discourse, quarrel, put forward propositions, and the other man can interpret it in a way that suits his ideas; the syntax, the vocabulary and the tone of voice do not make a proposition true or valid; it depends entirely on a pact built up by speaker and listener, and we have to enter that pact if we wish to be understood. Thus, 'On couche volontieres le sens des escris d'autruy à la faveur des opinions qu'on a prejugées en soi . . . ' (ibid., p. 448).

Montaigne enters that pact in the last part of his argument and if he were to find no way out he would be imprisoned in a solipsistic tower where he was completely alone and where both the imperfection of language and the emptiness of knowledge would make a terrific impact on the reader's mind. Montaigne affirms the difficulty of knowing oneself and that it is precisely because of his actual experience that he can see that it is impossible for man to know anything. Montaigne places his experience in a religious framework, but everything human beneath it is analysable: 'la difficulté ne me doit pas desesperer, ny aussi peu mon impuissance, car ce n'est que la mienne' (ibid., p. 561). He affirms that what he is doing, testing out every opinion, can be of value. He was aware that he was breaking through modern European thinking when he stated: 'en retastant et pétrissant cette nouvelle matiere, la remuant et l'eschaufant, j'ouvre à celuy qui me suit quelque facilité pour en jouir plus à son ayse, et la luy rends plus souple et plus maniable . . . ' (ibid., p. 560: 'and in handling and kneading this new matter, and with removing and chasing it, I open some faculty for him that shall follow me, that with mere ease he may enjoy the same, and make it more facile, more supple and more pliable').

The degree of introspection entailed in this study of man looks forward (of course to Proust, but he is so much later) to a person like La Rochefoucauld who, in the next century, explores man's feelings and emotions with just such a subjective approach. There is man's perpetual curiosity, the *chasse à la vérité*, the impossibility of knowing anything and yet, as Montaigne hints, human beings will always try to gain a lucid comprehension of the universe within and outwith themselves. Others may go much further than Montaigne, but he is pushing back certain frontiers when he states: 'Que les choses ne logent pas chez nous en leur forme et en leur essence . . . ' (ibid., p. 562).

We are unable to know or to reach the essence of things because we are at the mercy of our senses; they falsify things; we misinterpret things as a result, but it is only through our senses that we can reach the outside world. It is a subjective judgement we make on everything. Taste differs in every man so that what one finds sweet, another will find sour; a healthy man will have a totally different impression of wine from a sick man. And so 'Les subjets estrangers se rendent donc à nostre mercy; ils logent chez nous comme il nous plaist' (ibid., p. 562). He is pushing a new point on western European minds. Proust will make exactly the same point more than three centuries later; 'seule la perception grossière et erronée place tout dans l'objet, quand tout est dans l'esprit'.[11]

Furthermore, not only the object but also the subject changes every minute of the day; the relationship between the observed and the observer is complex and shifting; the subjective value is in itself variable; 'Ce que je tiens aujourdhuy et ce que je croy, je le tiens et le croy de toute ma croyance . . . Je ne sçaurois ambrasser aucune verité ny conserver avec plus de force que je fay cette cy. J'y suis tout entier, j'y suis voyrement . . . ' (Villey-Saulnier, p. 563). So fully am I committed to this or that view that I cannot even think of changing my adherence to an opposite viewpoint. But 'ne m'est il pas advenu, non une fois, mais cent, mais mille, et tous les jours, d'avoir ambrassé quelqu'autre chose à tout ces mesmes instrumens, en cette mesme condition, que depuis j'aye jugée fauce?' (ibid., p. 563). The diversity of Montaigne (and of all of us) is such that one moment he thinks this and another moment quite the opposite; he thinks them with the same reason, the same judgement, the same senses as he thought exactly opposite things a moment ago. Our judgement and all the faculties of our mind move together with the movement of the body. Montaigne makes absolute man's inability to reach contact with the outside world when he says:

Finalement, il n'y a aucune constante existence, ny de nostre estre, ny de celuy des objects. Et nous, et nostre jugement, et toutes choses mortelles, vont coulant et roulant sans cesse. Ainsi il ne se peut establir rien de certain de l'un à l'autre, et le jugeant et le jugé estans en continuelle mutation et bransle. (ibid., p. 601)

In few, there is no constant existence, neither of our being, nor of the objects. And we and our judgement and all mortall things else do uncessantly rowle, turne and passe away. Thus can nothing be certainely established, nor of the one nor of the other; both the judgeing and the judged being in continuall alteration and motion.

The opinion that we make is subject to changes of the body, to climate, to humours and to physical health. This fact is central to Montesquieu in the eighteenth century, for in *De l'esprit des lois* we have whole chapters on the relationship between a hot country producing servitude and an island giving Englanders 'une fierté naturelle'. Montesquieu's doctrine of determinism is touched on by Montaigne: 'elles ont leur revolution, leur saison, leur naissance, leur mort, comme les chous . . . ' (Villey-Saulnier, p. 575). That is, there are human as well as physical cycles. Not only opinions are relative but moral laws, too: 'la forme de nostre estre depend de l'air du climat et du terroir où nous naissons . . . ' (ibid., p. 575). In a way religious beliefs bring a certain feeling of comfort – 'me tien en l'assiette où Dieu m'a mis' (ibid., p. 569) – but everything is conditioned by environment. The only form of knowledge is through the senses, but 'des sens, ausquels gist le plus grand fondement et preuve de nostre ignorance . . . ' (ibid., p. 587) because there is, perhaps, an insufficient number of them. Montaigne suggests that animals are, perhaps, better off: for instance, cocks always crow at the right time, magnets attract iron always and snakes know which herb in the fields will cure them of a disease. Perhaps we should have eight or ten senses to reach truth? It is their falsitude and uncertainty that strike Montaigne. He affirms that there are really no criteria in this world of shifting appearances: we are asleep or awake; awake or asleep; we do not know: 'Nous veillons dormans, et veillans dormons. Je ne vois pas si clair dans le sommeil; mais, quand au veiller, je ne le trouve jamais assez pur et sans nuage . . . ' (ibid., p. 596). We recognize the words which are the opening lines in Proust's novel: 'Longtemps, je me suis couché de bonne heure. Parfois, à peine ma bougie éteinte, mes yeux se fermaient si vite que je n'avais pas le temps de me dire: Je m'endors.'

Since we cannot know anything but ourselves, and in particular our own sense impressions, our starting-point in the quest of knowledge must be ourselves. Our mind is 'curieux et avide' and thus cannot bear to have itself tied:

On le bride et garrote de religions, de loix, de coustumes, de
science, de preceptes, de peines et recompanses mortelles et
immortelles; encores voit-on que, par sa volubilité et dissolution, il
eschappe à toutes ces liaisons.

(Villey-Saulnier, p. 559)

He is bridled and fettered with and by religions, lawes, customes,
knowledge, precepts, paines, and recompences, both mortall and
immortall; yet we see him, by meanes of his volubility and
dissolution, escape all these bonds.

Once Montaigne has recognized this about the human mind he is
ready to take the next step: knowledge can only be got by looking
deeply into his own mind and, in particular, watching the behaviour
of his own body 'avant toute autre chose'. It is precisely through his
own body that he can have some relationship between himself and the
outside world.

Thus the 'Apologie' may be seen as the centre of the *Essais*. It gives
epistemology a sort of metaphysical basis. The quest for knowledge
through *scientia* or through religion is negative. But the quest for self-
knowledge is resoundingly positive: 'Moy qui m'espie de plus prez,
qui ay les yeux incessamment tendus sur moy . . . ' (ibid., p. 565). I,
the observer, the critic, the spectator have my eyes always on *moi*, the
thing doing the actions. Montaigne gives us tiny examples in this self-
analysis like 'à jun je me sens autre qu'après', like feeling healthy
makes me happy, like the same step of my horse now seems rough
now easy, like feeling able to do all things, like feeling unable to do
anything at all, like experiencing now pain now pleasure out of the
same external cause. Montaigne's own personality is different
depending on which angle he has chosen to view it. And so writing on
everything became a means for 'trying out', for 'essaying' and
'assaying' everything with the *je* and the *moi* of himself.

Therefore, in the 'Apologie' Montaigne has separated the study of
self from the study of philosophy and he is totally fascinated by the
solitude, the difficulty and the challenge of his quest. His *arriere-
boutique* ('back-shop') is an imaginary space more real than reality, a
layered protection of the self. As Proust withdrew into his cork-lined
room, so Montaigne secluded himself in his library alone. The
independence he sought was that of being far from 'occupations
domestiques' ('De la solitude', I.39; Villey-Saulnier, p. 238); the
arriere-boutique was where he established 'nostre vraye liberté et

principale retraicte et solitude' and where he could unburden the mind of ambition, avarice, fear and concupiscence. The tête-à-tête with himself ('faisons que nostre contentement despende de nous'; ibid., p. 240), the happy relations with himself ('La plus grande chose du monde, c'est de sçavoir estre à soy'; ibid., p. 242), the forsaking of books if they do nothing to keep gaiety and health within us ('Les livres sont plaisans; mais, si de leur frequentation nous en perdons en fin la gayeté et la santé, nos meilleures pieces, quittons les'; ibid., p. 245), the rejection of glory and ambition, the refusal of self-abnegation, of asceticism, of spiritual life, of excessive study and research ('il y a pour moy assez affaire sans aller si avant': ibid., p. 243) – all make a first sketch of his subsequent *art de vivre*. But, unlike Proust who became gradually more isolated from people, Montaigne knew that 'Il n'est rien si dissociable et sociable que l'homme: l'un par son vice, l'autre par sa nature' (ibid., p. 238).

CHAPTER 5
Political and Ethical Ideas

'War, and the pity of War' filled the whole of Montaigne's adult life. When the Chancellor of France, Michel de l'Hospital (a friend of Montaigne), spokesman of Catherine de Medici, gave the Huguenots a restricted right to worship, the Massacre of Vassy took place on 1 March 1562, and that was effectively the outbreak of eight fratricidal wars. Montaigne was 29. When he died in September 1592, Henri de Navarre had come to the throne, but he was still a Protestant, had not yet been crowned or received an absolution from the Pope, and the Edict of Nantes would not be issued until 1598. From 1581 to 1585, Montaigne served two terms as mayor of Bordeaux. He had to ensure that the city remained loyal to their king (Henri III), to unite its warring factions and finally to face the disaster of the plague in the first half of 1585. When Catherine de Medici died on 5 January 1589, Henri III cried out, 'Now I alone am king', but his kingdom was minute: the only French towns who recognized him as king were Blois, Tours and, significantly, Bordeaux.[1] It is fundamental that the Bordeaux *parlement* remained loyal to the king: Montaigne was not a schizophrenic talker, reader and writer to himself with no concern for France and French people. And Bordeaux was really the centre of resistance to the Protestants, who were a majority of the population in nearby Languedoc.

A glance at 'De la vanité' (III.9), which describes, among other themes, the rampant yet anarchic civil war which raged around Castillon, Libourne, Bergerac and other places in the Dordogne valley in the summer of 1585 (when Montaigne and his family had to leave their home and become a sort of caravanserai on the move), will prove how much personal and communal suffering underlies this leitmotif of war: in a 'siecle desbordé' (Villey-Saulnier, p. 946) every man (Montaigne included, for he uses the word *nous*) contributes to the 'corruption du siecle'; the people in power are guilty of treason, injustice, irreligion, avarice and cruelty; others are weaker (like Montaigne) and impart foolishness, vanity and idleness to war. The

French people is 'perdu de toute sorte de vices execrables', and 'la desolation de cet estat' (i.e. France) is manifest (ibid., p. 947). Montaigne in particular is 'over-pressed' (Florio) by it: 'Car en mon voisinage, nous sommes tantost par la longue licence de ces guerres civiles envieillis en une forme d'estat si desbordée . . . qu'à la verité c'est merveille qu'elle se puisse maintenir' (Villey-Saulnier, p. 956: 'For round about where I dwell we are, by the over-long licentiousness of our intestine civill warres, almost grown old, in so licentious and riotous a forme of state . . . that in good truth it were a wonder if it should continue and maintaine it selfe'). He talks of the devastation this corner of France has suffered; of the extremes of danger, of the terror and intimidation the people have felt, and of how civil war is the worst type of war: 'Les guerres civiles ont cela de pire que les autres guerres, de nous mettre-chacun en eschauguette en sa propre maison' (ibid., p. 971: 'Civill warres have this one thing worse then other warres, to cause every one of us to make a watch-tower of his owne house'). He speaks of his own experiences at night, when his imagination plays on him at the edge of sleep and makes him visualize being murdered in his bed 'mille fois' (ibid., p. 970). We may note how concrete his vocabulary is here: 'je me plonge la teste baissée stupidement dans la mort'; his reactions are not intelligent at all; the fear, the threat of being killed, the nervous response, fearing the worst, all are brought out in his imagination, and it is as if he sensed death through the working of his body – 'Je m'enveloppe et me tapis en cet orage, qui me doibt aveugler et ravir de furie, d'une charge prompte et insensible'. This man is in the heat of civil wars, 'en ces desmambremens de la France', and is living his life 'en un temps malade comme cettuy-cy' (ibid., p. 993).

Here is a clear-sighted indignation at wars. He is suffering personally, there are sieges around his home, 'tout crolle autour de nous' (ibid., p. 961). The state of the world occasions in him, if not actual despair, a deep depression of mind so that when one looks at his attitude to politics, to power, to the government of France it is tinged emotionally by this depression. For example, Montaigne is for preserving the form of government which already exists, however bad that may be, rather than innovating a new form of government. He compares it to repairing a building rather than uprooting and changing its foundations: 'Les vieux batiments ausquels l'aage a desrobé le pied, sans croute et sans ciment, qui pourtant vivent.' The state of France, however shakily based, 'tien à plus d'un clou' (ibid., p. 960). The search for ideal forms of government is good for intellectual gymnastics but is no use for practical purposes. He condemns the pleasure people experience in witnessing torture; savages may 'rotir et manger les corps des trepassés' but we are ten times worse, for we torment them and persecute them while they are alive. The moral insensibility, the hatred between man and man ('extreme de tous les vices'), the invention of new tortures, and so on – Montaigne thinks that these are streaks of inhumanity inherent in our make-up *qua* human beings: 'Nature, à ce creins-je, elle mesme attache à l'homme quelque instinct à l'inhumanité' (ibid., p. 433).

'Monstrueuse guerre' is also one of the themes in 'De la phisionomie' (III.12), when 'en un siecle si foible' 'les hommes ne s'enflent que de vent, et se manient à bonds, comme les balons'. Montaigne's irony and mocking attitude make the world suspicious of him, and each side curses him: 'Je fus pelaudé à toutes mains: au Gibelin j'estois Guelphe, au Guelphe Gibelin' (Villey-Saulnier, p. 1044). Beneath this statement we 'feel' that the tolerance, the honesty and the non-commitment of Montaigne are being harshly treated. The skirmishes of war around his property and the disaster of the plague meant that most of his buildings (except the château itself) were ravaged and most of his servants died. He used to keep a good house and invite friends to dinner or to stay the night, but now 'Moy qui suis si hospitalier, fus en tres penible queste de retraicte pour ma famille; une famille esgarée, faisant peur à ses amis et à soy-mesme, et horreur où qu'elle cerchast à se placer' (p. 1048). Not only his personal suffering is brought out but also his compassion and sympathy for 'le peuple'. He gives us a realistic description of his own servants:

> Or lors, quel exemple de resolution ne vismes nous en la simplicité de tout ce peuple? Generalement chacun renonçoit au soing de la vie. Les raisins demeurerent suspendus aux vignes, le bien principal du pays, tous indifferemment se preparans et attendans la mort à ce soir, ou au lendemain, d'un visage et d'une voix si peu effroyée qu'il sembloit qu'ils eussent compromis à cette necessité et que ce fut une condemnation universelle et inevitable.
>
> (ibid.)

What examples of resolution saw we not then in all this peoples simplicity? Each one generally renounced all care of life. The grapes (which are the countries chiefe commoditie) hung still and rotted upon the vines untoucht; all indifferently preparing themselves, and expecting death either that night or the next morrow; with countenance and voice so little daunted that they seemed to have compromitted to this necessitie, and that it was an universall and inevitable condemnation.

We may contrast this humane human being with this description by La Bruyère –

L'on voit certains animaux farouches, des mâles et des femelles, répandus par la campagne, noirs, livides et tout brûlés du soleil, attachés à la terre qu'ils fouillent et qu'ils remuent avec une opiniâtreté invincible: ils ont comme une voix articulée, et quand ils se levent sur leurs pieds, ils montrent une face humaine, et en effet ils sont des hommes.

(*Les Caractères* (Paris: Hachette, n.d.), *De l'homme*, p. 229)

Certain wild animals can be seen, male and female, scattered in the fields; they are black, pallid and sunburned; they are attached to the soil they are digging and turning over with unrelenting stubbornness; they have an articulate voice, and when they stand up they show a human face, and indeed they are men. (DGC)

– where, in spite of the fact that he is indignant at man's lot, he is an outsider, whereas one 'feels' that Montaigne is an insider, not only experiencing the same fate as his servants but also gaining from these terrible events an understanding of what life and death can mean to man.

Linked to this hatred of war is the harsh attitude to the Spanish cruelty while colonizing Latin America:

Tant de villes rasées, tant de nations exterminées, tant de millions de peuples passez au fil de l'espée, et la plus riche et belle partie du monde bouleversée pour la negotiation des perles et du poivre: mechaniques victoires. Jamais l'ambition, jamais les inimitiez publiques ne pousserent les hommes les uns contre les autres à si horribles hostilitez et calamitez si miserables.

(Des coches', III.6; Villey-Saulnier, p. 910)

So many goodly citties ransacked and razed; so many nations destroyed and made desolate; so infinite millions of harmelesse people of all sexes, states and ages, massacred, ravaged and put to

the sword; and the richest, the fairest and the best part of the world
topsiturvied, ruined and defaced for the traffick of pearls and
pepper. Oh mechanicall victories! oh base conquest! Never did
greedy revenge, publik wrongs or general enmities, so moodily
enrage and so passionately incense men against men, unto so
horrible hostilities, bloody dissipation, and miserable calamities.

The attitude is extremely liberal; the indignation is passionate, the
violence is held up against humanity; it is far more than merely
displaying anti-Spanish feelings; it is the freedom, the disinterestedness
and the benevolence towards other men. It is almost an eighteenth-
century feeling.

In the second half of his mayoralty Montaigne played an active and
personal role against the Ligue. Vaillac was the governor of the
Château Trompette in Bordeaux and was hoping to deliver the town to
the Leaguers. Through the extant correspondence between Montaigne
and Matignon we know that Montaigne acted as the intermediary
between Matignon, lieutenant of the king in Guyenne, and Du Plessis-
Mornay, who acted for Henri de Navarre. Thus, Montaigne and
Matignon were in charge. There are two letters dated 22 and 27 May
1585 in which Montaigne calls back the absent Matignon. If he could
not come, Montaigne promised that he would spare neither his 'soin,
ni, s'il est besoin, sa vie, pour conserver toute chose en l'obéissance du
roi'.

Therefore Montaigne had fulfilled a dangerous political role and
knows what he is talking about when he discusses politics. For
instance, in 'De mesnager sa volonté' (III.10) he puts forward a shrewd
estimation of Henri de Navarre, who 'peut faire promptement par la
vivacité de son esprit'; the quick-wittedness of Henri IV (along with
extreme courage and good-heartedness) is a point on which history
agrees. Furthermore, from the death of the duc d'Anjou in June 1584,
Henri de Navarre was the heir presumptive to the throne. He
remained loyal to the *Politique* party, which included François
de la Noue, who was a Protestant, and Catholics like Pierre de l'Estoile,
Jacques-Auguste de Thou and Etienne Pasquier.

We can see in this essay various aspects of the problem of *les mains
sales* being clearly discussed. The intellectual cannot be an active
political figure: he sees too many of the pros and cons and can never
reach a decision. Montaigne's own political actions or attitude may be
compared with the chairman of any committee: all the members are
partisan, all are committed to the thing they are discussing; the

chairman is uncommitted and leads the argument on from every point of view; then the vote is taken and the chairman does not vote. Montaigne makes a very frank confession here as regards his election as mayor: he is 'sans memoire, sans vigilance, sans experience, et sans vigueur' – all negative terms or qualities; but he is, in compensation, 'sans hayne aussi, sans ambition, sans avarice et sans violence'. He analyses his character further: 'J'ay la veuë clere' – his lucidity in dealing with difficult affairs; by allowing only his judgement and direction to work he could feign, yield, manipulate according to contingent necessities, and thereby be superior and detached from a fanaticism that held in grip the majority of Frenchmen 'Aux presens brouillis de cet estat'; he has 'le sens delicat et mol' – that is, extreme sensitivity to everything – therefore he has to cultivate 'insensibilité par estude et par discours'. His sensitivity is such that he cannot accept anything that costs the blood and life of citizens. He is sensitive to cruelty and inhumanity in 'les invasions, incursions contraires, alternations et vicissitudes de la fortune autour de moi'. He condemns French people for ambition in these civil wars and states that we 'surpassons en toute sorte de barbarie' the newly discovered peoples of Latin America ('Des cannibales', I.31). Montaigne's own attitude towards Amerindians is 'Or, je trouve . . . qu'il n'y a rien de barbare et de sauvage en cette nation, à ce qu'on m'en a rapporté, sinon que chacun appelle barbarie ce qui n'est pas de son usage' (Villey-Saulnier, p. 205).

Montaigne's qualities of lucidity and manoeuvrability underlie his position *vis-à-vis* the civil wars. He sees the Protestants acting with blind zeal, being led and governed by their leaders: 'Leur sens et entandement est entierement estouffé en leur passion. Leur discretion n'a plus d'autre chois que ce qui leur rit et qui conforte leur cause. J'avoy remarqué souverainemant cela au premier de nos parties fiebvrieux' (ibid., p. 1013: 'Their discretion hath no other choise but what pleaseth them and furthereth their cause, which I had especially observed in the beginning of our distempered factions and factious troubles').

The 'nouvelletez de Luther' (ibid., p. 439), which Montaigne saw could lead men to atheism, were intellectually torpid in the 1550s and they gave way to Calvinism in France. From the founding of a college (the academy in 1559 in Geneva) to train ministers and send over his mission to evangelize France, Calvin increased his hold on French people tremendously. On the other hand, the Ligue – the party of extreme Catholics – was set up in 1576 and was no better.

Cet autre qui est nay depuis, en l'imitant le surmonte. Par où je
m'advise que c'est une qualité inseparable des erreurs populaires.
Apres la premiere qui part, les opinions s'entrepoussent suivant le
vent comme les flotz. On n'est pas du corps si on s'en peut desdire,
si on ne vague le train commun. (ibid., p. 1013)

This other which is growne since by imitation surmounteth the
same, whereby I observe that it is an inseparable quality of popular
errours. The first being gone on, opinions entershocke one another,
following the winde as waves doe. They are no members of the
body, if they may renounce it, if they follow not the common
course.

Henri III on his way back to France from Poland met in Milan in
1574 Cardinal Borromeo, 'that supreme representative of Counter-
Reformation spirituality' (Elliott, *Europe Divided*, p. 250) and was
overwhelmed by the fervent religious sensibility and intensely austere
mortification of the flesh in the life of the cardinal.[2] The weakness of
Henri III as head of state was notorious, and yet Montaigne never
accepted any alternative to the legitimate king and he condemns both
the Ligue and the Protestants:

Je me prens fermemant au plus sain des partis, mais je n'affecte pas
qu'on me remarque specialement ennemy des autres, et outre la
raison generalle. J'accuse merveilleusement cette vitieuse forme
d'opiner: Il est de la Ligue, car il admire la grace de Monsieur
de Guise. L'activeté du Roy de Navarre l'estonne: il est Huguenot.
Il treuve cecy à dire aux moeurs du Roy: il est seditieux en son
coeur.

                                              (Villey-Saulnier, p. 1013)

I stand firmely to the sounder parts. But I affect not to be noted a
private enemy to others, and beyond generall reason I greatly
accuse this vicious forme of obstinate contesting. He is of the
League because he admireth the grace of the Duke of Guise; or he
is a Hugenote, forsomuch as the King of Navarres activitie amazeth
him. He finds fault in the Kings behaviours, therefore he is
sedicious in his heart.

He has here an independent and dispassionate judgement. As a
moderate man (of the *Politique* party) Montaigne must be royalist, in

the sense that obedience to the king *qua* king overrides the king's particular defects as a human being. Elsewhere the king's faults are ambiguously – and he is never mentioned by name – picked out: for instance, extravagant dress (I.43; Villey-Saulnier, p. 269), his failure to lead his army (II.21; Villey-Saulnier, p. 676), excessive displays of religiosity (I.30; Villey-Saulnier, p. 197) and debauchery (III.10; Villey-Saulnier, p. 1013).

'In 'De mesnager sa volonté' the problem of commitment is tackled quite vigorously. We hear him say in forceful terms: 'Le Maire et Montaigne ont tousjours esté deux, d'une separation bien claire' (Villey-Saulnier, p. 1012). If that statement came from, say, Nerval or Rousseau, we might instinctively believe that they had a split personality. But Montaigne is advocating that man adopts for living life reasonably two distinct things: a mask or a public self and real essence as a private individual. His self-mastery, his control and his discipline are quite remarkable: for instance, the striking phrase, 'Personne ne distribue son argent à autruy, chacun y distribue son temps et sa vie' (ibid., p. 1004). Or 'il se faut prester à autruy et ne se donner qu'à soy-mesme' (ibid., p. 1003). Or that tiny, seemingly trivial remark which hits at the mark: 'je m'engage difficilement'.

If we look at a different essay – 'De l'utile et l'honeste' (III.1) – we find him questioning deeply and in troubled tones the dilemma between public (the useful and the expedient) and private (the morally just) lives. In the early part we can see the depreciation of what he writes, a nonchalant air of complete disinterestedness and a casual air of 'let no one think that what I say is of any importance whatsoever' – 'Je parle au papier comme je parle au premier que je rencontre' (ibid., p. 790). This self-depreciation is a basic quality of Montaigne and, indeed, of all French people. It is coupled with self-assured qualities which greet the most annoying or the most astonishing occurrences with a shrug of the shoulder, a facial movement and a gesticulation with their hands.

Montaigne makes a distinction between public and private virtue. As private individuals we can adhere to a strict moral code, whereas in public matters there is no such morality. We have to recognize that in dealing with public matters expediency is of prime importance. And this means that as a public man one has to lie. Under this texture there comes a leitmotif of Montaigne; he cannot abide lies and dissimulation; his hatred of lying or cruelty is so extreme that it is almost a moral absolute:

Je hay, entre autres vices, cruellement la cruauté, et par nature et

par jugement, comme l'extreme de tous les vices. Mais c'est jusques
à telle mollesse que je ne voy pas égorger un poulet sans desplaisir,
et ois impatiemment gemir un lievre sous les dens de mes chiens,
quoy que ce soit un plaisir violent que la chasse.

('De la cruauté', II.11; Villey-Saulnier, p. 429)

Amongst all other vices, there is none I hate more than Crueltie,
both by nature and judgement, as the extremest of all vices. But it
is with such an yearning and faint-hartednesse, that if I see but a
chickins necke puld off, or a pigge stickt, I cannot chuce but
grieve, and I cannot well endure a seelie dewbedabled hare to
groane when she is seized upon by the houndes, although hunting
be a violent pleasure.

'Par nature' – Montaigne is by character extremely sensitive and he
discusses cruelty to animals; 'par jugement' – through reading,
meditating and reasoning Montaigne enlarges his moral sensibility to
exceptional depths. To speak of the cruelty of man in the time of civil
war is remarkable simply because it had become trivial and banal;
when these 'ames si monstrueuses' are intent on inventing new forms
of torture simply for the pleasure experienced in witnessing torture,
Montaigne stands firmly to his placing of cruelty uppermost on the
hierarchy of vices. This stand was/is not much discussed by traditional
moral philosophers and certainly not in Christian ethics – witness the
colossal cruelty in the name of religion of the Spaniards in Latin
America as denounced by Montaigne himself in III.6. As a magistrate
one has to be cruel and as a king one is often punishing those whom as
private individuals one would admire and like. Once one is in politics,
vices such as lying become legitimate and, using the Augustinian
metaphor about vices and virtues, Montaigne says 'les vices y trouvent
leur rang et s'employent à la cousture de nostre liaison, comme les
venins à la conservation de nostre santé' (Villey-Saulnier, p. 791),
which is the potential maxim (182) of La Rochefoucauld:

Les vices entrent dans la composition des vertus comme les poisons
entrent dans la composition des remèdes. La prudence les assemble
et les tempère, et elle s'en sert utilement contre les maux de la vie.

Thus it is that the public good must of necessity require one to lie,
to betray and to massacre: 'Le bien public requiert qu'on trahisse et
qu'on mente (C) et qu'on massacre . . .' (Villey-Saulnier, p. 791).

And then comes the position of someone who is a private citizen, '(B) resignons cette commission à gens plus obeissans et plus souples'. There are strains of humaneness in Montaigne's political ideas which he shows when he says: '(B) toutes choses ne sont pas loisibles à un homme de bien pour le service (C) de son Roy ny (B) de la cause generalle et des loix' (ibid., p. 802).

In conducting his public life Montaigne fleshes out the Stoic indifference theory; thus he can have an attitude towards princes: 'Je regarde nos Roys d'une affection simplement legitime et civile, ni emue ni demue par interest privé . . . je ne suis pas subject à ces hypotheques et engagements penetrants et intimes' (ibid., p. 792). Different conduct is appropriate to different circumstances or even to different persons in the same circumstances. Since Montaigne held that morality is relative to place and individual and circumstance he would none the less agree that morality loses its meaning if the same thing can be both right and wrong for the same person in the same circumstances. Every man must establish for himself his own standard. The Stoic ideal was not suitable for Montaigne. He needed a more simple morality, a morality suited to his own temperament. He recognizes that people like Brutus have high political ideals and are willing to sacrifice their lives to their ideals. Others achieve their happiness in a multiplication of love-affairs or in a cult of external beauty like the dandies of this life. We see this in another essay, too ('De la solitude', I.39), where Montaigne compares his *complexion*, which favours retiral into himself –

Celles [complexions] qui ont l'apprehension molle et làche, et un'affection et volonté delicate, et qui ne s'asservit ny s'employe pas aysément, desquels je suis et par naturelle condition et par discours.
(Villey-Saulnier, p. 242)

These which have a tender and demisse apprehension, a squemish affection, a delicate will, and which cannot easily subject or imploy it selfe (of which both by naturall condition and propense discourse I am one)

– to that of other people who are 'les ames actives et occupées qui embrassent tout et s'engagent par tout, qui se passionnent de toutes choses, qui s'offrent, qui se presentent et qui se donnent à toutes occasions' (ibid.: 'active minds and busie spirits; which imbrace all, every where engage, and in all things passionate themselves; that offer, that present and yeeld themselves to all occasions').

Finally, before we turn to the private self and the ethical values embodied in Montaigne's own morality let us look at two additions in the essay 'Que nostre desir s'accroit par la malaisance' (II.15) concerning his final attitude to war and politics.

It is clear that Montaigne came back twice to this essay: first, he added an enormously long addition in French beginning immediately after the last word of the 1588 version – 'hayes'. One can just decipher it; it starts: 'Furem signata sollicitant. Aperta effractarius praeterit.' This is rather severely crossed out perhaps because Montaigne realized that he would need the space at the top of the page to get in everything he wanted to say about the civil wars. Some corrections are immediate: a phrase crossed out with a swift stroke and then hurriedly rewritten. Other corrections are different: rereading made him want to correct, expand or contract his way of saying things. For example, the very last words of the essay read: 'Comment? il y a bien trente ans' (EP, pl. 555). He inserts a word and then deletes it, making it illegible.

We feel the anger and despair of Montaigne living through 'la violence de nos guerres civiles', these 'guerres intestines'. But we perceive that he is not passive: he has not defended his house: the soldiers' conquest of it will be 'lasche et traistresse'; he has an old janitor who will offer it 'plus decemment et gratieusement'. The contrasting adjectives and adverbs make one realize that this passage is carefully worked out. Even though he can say with a certain bitterness that 'Les moyens d'assaillir . . . croissent tous les iours', he can also state: 'Ie n'ay ny garde ny sentinelle que celle que les astres font pour moi.' His attitude is intellectual, and it is also wise, mature and sane.

The second addition comes at the end of the penultimate sentence and is written on the left-hand side of the page, lengthways. It is an example of what he said when he referred to chance events or inspiration coming as 'les saillies poëtiques qui emportent leur autheur et le ravissent hors de soy' (Villey-Saulnier, p. 127).[3] For in the end it is his pride that makes its mark here; and he is 'caught' saying 'Entre tant de maisons armées, moi seul, que ie sache en France, de ma condition, ai fié purement au ciel la protection de la mienne' (EP, pl. 555). It first read, rather brashly and arrogantly, without 'en France' and 'de ma condition'; 'Entre tant de maisons armées, moi seul que ie sache ai fié purement de la mi.' What spur urged him to insert the qualifying phrases? The arrogance of saying he was the only one in the world? A critical sense being there at the instant when he was writing? Maybe. But at least it shows one thing: he *was* proud of his behaviour during the civil wars. And he was proud enough of his conduct to say: 'j'ay tousiours assez duré pour rendre ma durée remerquable et enregistrable'. His behaviour makes it 'worthy the registring' (Florio). And immediately there comes the tongue-in-the-cheek remark: 'What, is not thirtie years a goodly time?' (Florio). He is proud of his decision to leave undefended his ancestral home. Compared with other country houses it is not protected. Is that a reason worth recording? Does it not tie in with other aspects of his ethical behaviour? The hatred of lying, the will to be honest, the 'stoic' resignation as regards death and life, and the patient attempt at keeping 'out of the limelight' – 'J'essaye de soubstraire ce coing à la tempeste publique, comme je fay un autre coing en mon ame' (Villey-Saulnier, p. 617). 'Pour moy, je ne bouge' might well be the answer of Montaigne on political matters and religious warring.

Ethics are not considered by Christians as the most important part of religion since this life is only a small insignificant episode, the prelude to the beyond. If we think back to the 'Apologie', especially to the last part where all knowledge is subjective, we recognize that we are prisoners within ourselves. Once Montaigne had accepted subjectivity and uncertainty in the world he had to act positively, and all actions and discriminations between good and bad became more important and critical as life on earth is an end in itself, and the end. God is not there to come to the rescue.

In 'Du repentir' (III.2), Montaigne distinguishes between what is exterior or acquired through living, through education and through acting, and what is interior or fundamental, found in each of us, that basic nature with which moral philosophy deals – 'une forme sienne, une forme maistresse'. And all moral philosophy can be derived from the study of the *moi* within ourselves. For him, self-knowledge is a source of ethical actions. His concern is to identify philosophical considerations with individual lived experience – hence the concern with writing and style throughout the *Essais*, because this is a very important clue as to his moral philosophy. He prefers a natural style because this will capture the rich fullness of life.

The 'Know yourself' adage in Montaigne is not only a pragmatic and moral precept, but an epistemological one also: the primacy of self-knowledge takes on significance only in regard to the moral study of man. It is the *condition humaine* with all its essential insecurity, doubts and problems that Montaigne is trying to present to his reader. The important adjective *humaine* entails that Montaigne is not thinking of Christian views, but that life on this earth is the only one man has and thus Montaigne wants to savour it to the last drop, 'car enfin c'est nostre estre, c'est nostre tout'. And in another essay (III.9) Montaigne makes it clear that man cannot waste or hinder the enjoyment of life: 'c'est chose tendre que la vie, et aysée à troubler'.

In 'Du repentir' he states that there is something so ugly and so inappropriate about vice that a wise man puts it down to 'betise' and 'ignorance'; very concretely he says, 'Le vice laisse, comme un ulcere en la chair, une repentance en l'ame, qui toujours s'esgratigne et s'ensanglante elle-mesme . . . ' (Villey-Saulnier, p. 806) where one sees the bloody flesh within oneself not at rest. The Stoic term of 'conscience' is awarded to a man by his inner and personal consciousness, even when the whole world disapproves of his actions; it is closely akin to peace of mind. Seneca puts it this way: 'bona conscientia turbam advocat, mala etiam in solitudine anxia atque sollicita est' (*Epistulae morales*, 43.5). It is precisely what Montaigne means by 'un patron au dedans' later on in this essay, which can alone judge 'auquel toucher nos actions et, selon iceluy, nous caresser tantost, tantost nous chatier' (Villey-Saulnier, p. 807). This makes Montaigne a very difficult arbitrator, for nothing that anyone tells about us, whether praise or blame, helps the inner judgement of us *qua* us. The world is seeing everything we have put forward as art; the inner judge is the only one who can see our true nature. 'C'est une vie exquise, celle qui se maintient en ordre jusques en son privé' (ibid., p. 808).

The inner distinctions and criteria are essentially natural rather than supernatural: into this close-textured argument we can see entering leitmotifs like *naiveté, naif, naturel, instinctif* – all of which are evaluated positively by Montaigne. Moral conscience is limited to what can be expected of a man, and when he says 'Je me repens rarement' in this context it means something entirely different from repentance in a Christian context. It takes on another meaning; it is the opposition of our will; it upsets the inward organization; it is 'une desdite de nostre volonté'. Public actions can prove nothing of our basic moral being; to make your morality truly yours you have to know yourself. And in this Montaigne knows more about himself than anyone else: 'je suis le plus savant homme qui vive'. He can say 'jamais aucun ne penetra en sa matiere plus avant ni en eplucha plus particulierement les membres et suite'. Because he finds beneath the chaotic surface of his actions, behaviour, thoughts, and so on, something permanent – 'une forme sienne . . . qui luicte contre l'institution et la tempeste des passions qui luy sont contraires' – he can conclude that 'mes actions sont reglées et conformes à ce que je suis et à ma condition. Je ne puis faire mieux' (ibid., p. 813).[4]

This is a serene non-Christian attitude.[5] Montaigne has no illusions, and has the courage and bravery to debunk false values like the repentence that often comes on with age – 'Au demeurant, je hay cet accidental repentir que l'aage apporte' (ibid., p. 815) – which is a result of physical weakness and debility of mind – 'une vertu lache et catarreuse' (ibid.) or the values of Stoicism. He is a ruthless inner judge of actions and accepts the terrific weight of responsibility on self. In refusing the solemn mask of wisdom he accepts himself and the human condition as they are. His private morality is away from the extreme views of Christians or philosophies like Stoicism but is much more difficult:

> Tancer, rire, vendre, payer, hayr et converser avec les siens et avec soymesme doucement et justement, ne relacher point, ne se desmentir poinct, c'est chose plus rare, plus difficile et moins remerquable. (ibid., p. 809)

> to chide, laugh, sell, pay, love, hate, and mildely and justly to converse both with his owne and with himselfe; not to relent, and not gainesay himselfe, are thinges more rare, more difficult and lesse remarkeable.

We shall see more deeply this private *art de vivre* later, but we can note how lucid and far-seeing he is and how he is at the end of the Renaissance. He can look back on the sixteenth century in France and see that human society, always corrupt and unstable, has not improved much. Since politics is necessary, he would prefer princes to be wholeheartedly and singlemindedly devoted to political efficacy. We may note how near and how far he comes to Machiavelli.[6] His nature is 'trop tendre, et par nature et par usage' (ibid., p. 1003) to give itself up to political negotiation: 'Il faut jouer deuement nostre rolle, mais comme rolle d'un personnage emprunté' (ibid., p. 1011).

CHAPTER 6

The Classical Literary Background: Knowledge and Imagination

> A little learning is a dang'rous thing;
> Drink deep, or taste not the Pierian spring:
> There shallow draughts intoxicate the brain,
> And drinking largely sobers us again.
> Pope, *An Essay on Criticism*, ll.215–18

Montaigne did not have French as his mother tongue: 'Quant à moy, j'avois plus de six ans avant que j'entendisse non plus de François ou de Perigordin que d'Arabesque' (Villey-Saulnier, p. 173). As we saw in Chapter 1, he had Latin. The particular language to which a child is exposed implants in him syntactic structures and also intonation patterns. At the age of 6 Montaigne had the pattern of one language in his mind, and that was Latin. He explains in 1588 ('Du repentir'; Villey-Saulnier, p. 810) how Latin and French operate within his own mind:

> Le langage latin m'est comme naturel, *je l'entens mieux que le François*, mais il y a quarante ans que je ne m'en suis du tout poinct servy à parler, ny à escrire: si est-ce que à *des extremes et soudaines esmotions* où je suis tombé deux ou trois fois en ma vie, et l'une, voyent mon pere tout sain se renverser sur moy, pasmé, j'ay tousjours eslancé du fond des entrailles les premieres paroles Latines. (My italics)

> The Latin tongue is to me in a manner naturall; I understand it better than French: but it is now fortie yeares I have not made use of it to speake, nor much to write; yet in some extreame emotions and suddaine passions, wherein I have twice or thrice falne, since

my yeares of discretion, and namely, when my father being in perfect health, fell all alone upon me in a swoune, I have ever, even from my very hart, uttered my first words in Latine.

This is an extraordinary statement to make: he is writing the creative meditations that are his *Essais* in his second tongue, the tongue which he understood less well than Latin, and yet in moments of extreme emotion Latin (rather than French) rolls out to express his thoughts.

Art is by its very nature a heightening of consciousness. Every writer is striving to convert his private awareness of himself into an expressed multi-dimensional public figure. For this task a special kind of language will be needed, a language which will be more allusive than explicit. Roman and Greek literature are so ingrained in Montaigne that he lives, breathes and eats with living people of ancient Rome and Greece. Paradoxically, he knows the Augustan period in Rome, a period when Virgil, Horace, Propertius, Tibullus and Ovid flourished, the earlier late Republic which embraced Lucretius, Catullus and Cicero, and the later Empire which is represented by Martial, Quintilian, Juvenal, Lucan and Tacitus so well that, in spite of (or because of) his not being a Renaissance Latin scholar, we might call him a classical, sensitive and imaginative intellectual of the sixteenth century. This calls for an explanation.

We define him as an intellectual: meaning that he has that form of mind which is characterized by taking pleasure in applying intelligence to all problems and to anything and then sorting them out, establishing patterns, harmonies and associations between them. The gratuitous element in this intellectuality makes it different from intelligence, which is the faculty of seeing relationships and applying it for practical purposes. Montaigne has a refined sensibility, refined through his early reading of and his love for classical poets. In the essay 'De l'institution des enfans' (I.26) he tells how he started his reading with Ovid; 'je me desrobois de tout autre plaisir pour les lire d'autant que *cette langue estoit la mienne maternelle* . . . ' (Villey-Saulnier, p. 175: my italics). None of the usual books like 'Lancelots du Lac, (B) des Amadis, (A) des Huons de Bordeaus, et tel fatras de livres' was offered to him, their place being taken by Latin poets. He argues in this essay that the sensitivity of children is not yet developed and so the tutor must try to guide them without going against their own *inclination*. His own education is concretely described through culinary terminology: for instance, 'gourmander ces livres' or 'aguisoit ma faim'. Underlying this appetite for books was the lesson of solitude, for '[Mon ame] les digeroit seule, sans aucune communication'.

Montaigne's own concept of imagination has been excellently analysed by McFarlane, and I quote his final statement:

> we may claim that for him the imagination was an incentive to thought and action, an instrument of inner balance and catharsis, a collaborator of experience in our relations with the outside world, and finally an aspect of identity. And what indeed are the *Essais* but the imagination in action?[1]

Everyone knows of Montaigne's love of Latin poets like Catullus, Propertius, Lucretius and, above all, Virgil and Horace: '*j'enfilay tout d'un train* Vergil en l'Æneide et puis Terence, et puis Plaute . . . lurré tousjours par la douceur du subject' (Villey-Saulnier, p. 175: my italics). He confesses that he himself wrote poetry only at an early age, and in Latin (II.17). Why write in prose? Because he would have been a mediocre poet and he has a hatred of that, suggested by the famous lines of Horace:

> mediocribus esse poetis
> non homines, non di, non concessere columnae . . .
> (*Ars poetica*, ll.372–3)

'Neither Gods nor men nor the public approving books have ever allowed poets to be mediocre.' If this failure to write poetry is not a confession of a defect, nothing is. Critics admit that Montaigne is inspired by a creative fictional impulse to select only those events and experiences from his own life which will make up an integrated pattern. They accept, too, the fact that Montaigne's method of composition suggests a cohering of life's complexities rather than a logical and rational *opus*. But this is merely tickling the skin of his writing. Malcolm Bowie in his book on *Mallarmé and the Art of Being Difficult* (Cambridge: Cambridge University Press, 1978) argues finely that the question 'What does this poem mean?' is superficial; what we really ought to ask is 'How can this poem be read fully and with enjoyment?' This must surely be so with every great writer, and Bowie touches on a point that is very close to present Montaigne studies when he says: 'Something is going wrong when criticism conscientiously refuses to take heed of the singular disruptive energies which works of art possess' (p. 154). Montaigne works with two languages:

Latin and French. The result is ambivalent – a dense texture which can be grasped only if we read his prose partly as 'poetry': sensitivity, imagination and the willingness for a phrase to be obscure in itself, knowing that its context will eventually make it clear. And this involves a knowledge of Latin and Greek literature and an understanding of the 'innutrition' theory held by the French Renaissance and by French literature for four centuries afterwards. The word 'innutrition' needs defining: if we look at Blount's dictionary, the 1656 edition,[2] we find that *innutrition* means a 'nourishing or bringing up' of literature. This suggestion of eating, digesting and mentally chewing ancient texts – having them as prime nourishment before giving forth a new text rather than merely imitating or assimilating classical models – is precisely what Montaigne implies in this passage: 'Que nous sert-il d'avoir la panse pleine de viande, si elle ne se digere? si elle ne se trans-forme en nous? si elle ne nous augmente et fortifie?' (I.25).[3] (The digestion metaphor runs through the Renaissance in England, too, so it is not surprising to find Blount commenting on *innutrition*, perhaps a 'hard' new word for the English tongue.) The sensibility of a reader of Montaigne's *Essais* has to react to the deep meaning of all associations with Latin authors given that an emotive symphony rumbles under the surface of the lines. In a revealing passage (I.26) he criticizes authors who try to hide their defects under clothing borrowed from ancient literature; for himself, 'Je ne dis les autres, sinon d'autant plus me dire'.

We shall start by looking closely at a passage in which his fine literary criticism imposes itself on our minds. It is from the essay 'Sur des vers de Virgile' (III.5), and it is a piece of practical criticism based on a comparative analysis of both Virgil and Lucretius passages:

Ce que Virgile dict de Venus & de Vulcan, Lucrece l'auoit dict plus sortablement d'vne iouissance desrobée, d'elle & de Mars:

> belli fera moenera Mauors
> Armipotens regit, in gremium qui saepe tuum se
> Reiicit, aeterno deuinctus vulnere amoris:
> Pascit amore auidos inhians in te, Dea, visus,
> Eque tuo pendet resupini spiritus ore:
> Hunc tu, diua, tuo recubantem corpore sancto
> Circunfusa super, suaueis ex ore loquelas
> Funde.

Quand ie rumine ce, *reiicit, pascit, inhians, molli, fouet, medullas,*
labefacta, pendet, percurrit, & cette noble, *circunfusa,* mere du gentil,
infusus, i'ay desdain de ces menues pointes & allusions verballes,
qui nasquirent depuis. A ces bonnes gens, il ne falloit pas d'aigue &
subtile rencontre: Leur langage est tout plein, & gros d'vne vigueur
naturelle & constante. Ils sont tout epigramme; non la queuë
seulement, mais la teste, l'estomac, & les pieds. Il n'y a rien
d'efforcé, rien de treinant: tout y marche d'vne pareille teneur. '(C)
Contextus totus uirilis est: non sunt circa flosculos occupati.' (B) Ce
n'est pas vne eloquence molle, & seulement sans offence. Elle est
nerueuse & solide, qui ne plaict pas tant, comme elle remplit &
rauit: & rauit, le plus, les plus forts espris. Quand ie voy ces braues
formes de s'expliquer, si vifues, si profondes, ie ne dicts pas que
c'est bien dire, ie dicts que c'est bien penser. C'est la gaillardise de
l'imagination, qui esleue & enfle les parolles. '(C) *Pectus est quod*
disertum facit. ' (B) Nos gens appellent iugement, langage; & beaux
mots les plaines conceptions. Cette peinture est conduitte, non tant
par dexterité de la main, comme pour auoir l'object plus vifuement
empreint en l'ame. Gallus parle simplement, par ce qu'il conçoit
simplement. Horace ne se contente point d'vne superficielle
expression, elle le trahiroit. Il voit plus cler & plus outre dans la
chose: son esprit crochette & furette tout le magasin des mots & des
figures, pour se representer. Et les luy faut outre l'ordinaire,
comme sa conception est outre l'ordinaire. Plutarque dit, qu'il veid
le langage latin par les choses. Icy de mesme; le sens esclaire &
produict les parolles. Non plus de vent, ains de chair & d'os. (C)
Elles signifient plus qu'elles ne disent. (B) Les imbecilles sentent
encores quelque image de cecy. Car en Italie ie disois ce qu'il me
plaisoit en deuis communs, mais aus propos roides ie n'eusse osé
me fier à un Idiome, que ie ne pouuois plier ny contourner, outre
son alleure commune. I'y veux pouuoir quelque chose du mien.

(Basically, this passage is Villey-Saulnier, pp. 872–3; I have
made a few changes in punctuation and orthography)

What Virgill saith of Venus and Vulcan, Lucretius had more
sutably said it of a secretly-stolne enjoying betweene her and Mars:

> Mars, mighty arm'd, rules the fierce feats of armes,
> Yet often casts himselfe into thine armes,
> Oblig'd thereto by endlesse wounds of love,
> Gaping on thee feeds greedy sight with love,

His breath hangs at thy mouth who upward lies;
Goddesse thou circling him, while he so lies,
With thy celestiall body, speeches sweet
Powre from thy mouth (as any nectar sweet).

When I consider this, *reiicit, pascit, inhians, molli, fovet, medullas, labefacta, pendet, percurrit,* and this noble *circumfusa,* mother of gentle *infusus,* I am vexed at these small points and verball allusions, which since have sprung up. To these well-meaning people there need no sharpe encounter or witty equivocation: their speech is altogether full and massie, with a naturall and constant vigor: they are all epigram, not only taile, but head, stomacke and feet. There is nothing forced, nothing wrested, nothing limping; all marcheth with like tenour. *Contextus totus virilis est, non sunt circa flosculos occupati.* The whole composition or text is manly, they are not bebusied about rhetorike flowers. This is not a soft quaint eloquence, and only without offence; it is sinnowie, materiall, and solid; not somuch delighting, as filling and ravishing, and ravisheth most the strongest wits, the wittiest conceits. When I behold these gallant formes of expressing, so lively, so nimble, so deepe, I say not this is to speake well, but to think well. It is the quaintness or livelinesse of the conceit that elevateth and puffes up the words. *Pectus est quod disertum facit:* 'It is a mans owne brest that makes him eloquent.' Our people terme judgement, language; and full conceptions, fine words. This pourtraiture is directed not so much by the hands dexterity as by having the object more lively printed in the minde. Gallus speakes plainly because he conceiveth plainly. Horace is not pleased with a slight or superficiall expressing, it would betray him; he seeth more cleere and further into matters: his spirit pickes and ransacketh the whole store-house of words and figures, to show and present himselfe; and he must have them more then ordinary, as his conceit is beyond ordinary. Plutarch saith that he discerned the Latine tongue by things. Here likewise the sense enlighteneth and produceth the words: no longer windy or spongy, but of flesh and bone. They signifie more then they utter. Even weake ones shew some image of this. For, in Italie, I spake what I listed in ordinary discourses, but in more serious and pithy I durst not have dared to trust to an idiome which I could not winde or turne beyond its common grace or vulgar bias. I will be able to adde and use in it somewhat of mine owne.

In my *Gallo-Roman Muse* I analysed parts of this passage from the point of view of Montaigne's judgement and his re-creation of the Latin passage in French. Now I can go further in my analysis. Throughout the Renaissance and the seventeenth century in France and England the Latin force of masculinity, the muscular imagery, the intellectual character of virility, and the dense vigour dominated in their poetics. In England the cult of 'strong lines' was not a doctrine of obscurity: it was a cult of expressiveness. When 'strong lines' were successful, they were the products of a search for vigorous, pregnant, exciting expression. Muret – one of the many Latin critics who were really expressing the traits of literary criticism in their commentaries on poets like Horace, Catullus, Virgil and so on after 1550 – had been one of Montaigne's teachers at the collège de Guyenne. In Muret's second lecture delivered in Rome in 1580 – a year before Montaigne met him again there – he favours a harsh style, applying the word *asperitas* to it.[4] If we read of the encounter of Muret and Montaigne in the latter's *Journal de voyage en Italie*,[5] we find something quite interesting:

> Disnant un jour à Rome avec nostre ambassadur, où estoit Muret et autres sçavans, je me mis sur le propos de la traduction françoise de Plutarche, et contre ceus qui l'estimoint beaucoup moins que je ne fais, je meintenois au moins cela: 'Que où le traducteur a failli le vrai sans de Plutarque, il y en a substitué un autre vraisemblable et s'entretenant bien aus choses suivantes et précédentes.' Pour me montrer qu'en cela mesme je lui donnois trop, il fut produit deux passages . . .

> Dining in Rome with our ambassador one day in the company of Muret and other learned people I gave my opinion of the French translation of Plutarch saying, against those who reckoned it as inferior, at least this: 'That where the translator failed to get the sense made by Plutarch, he substituted another which was likely and went well with things before and after it.' To demonstrate that I was admiring him too much, two passages were produced . . . (DGC)

The scholars point out the false meaning – due to a misunderstanding of the Greek – given to certain words by Amyot: 'Le latin d'Estiene s'est aproché plus près du vrai.' Montaigne's argument no longer has right on its side:

Au lieu de ce sens cler et aisé, celui que le traducteur y a substitué
est mol et estrange; parquoy recevant leurs presuppositions du
sens propre de la langue, j'avouai de bone foi leur conclusion.

Instead of this clear and easy sense, the one that the translator had
given it was feeble and odd; for that reason accepting their
presuppositions as to the proper meaning of the Greek language, I
granted in good faith their conclusion. (DGC)

Here is a company of scholars discussing seriously the words in a
passage of Greek; it comes as no surprise that Montaigne is one of the
company. Latin philologists/literary critics like Muret, Lambin,
Scaliger, Turnebus and Henri Estienne are active readers from the
1550s onwards and they were known by Montaigne. In the marginalia
of Montaigne's passage in 'Sur des vers de Virgile' he adds the famous
phrase written by Seneca, 'Contextus totus uirilis est: non sunt circa
flosculos occupati' (*Epistulae morales*, 33). This *uirilis* means that it is
the intellectual nature of writing, the fullness, the masculinity and
muscular shape of thought and style that Montaigne enjoys. This was
the style of Montaigne in his last period, and it is the style liked by
Lipsius (who was a great admirer of Montaigne) when he judged style
on the Senecan model:

Est et compositio quaedam et viriles numeri: sed ut structuram
agnoscas, mollitiem abnuas; et pugnae atque arenae omnia, non
delectationi aut scaenae parata.

Style also is apparent, and virile harmony and rhythm, yet in such a
way that, while you recognise artistic construction, you will admit
no effeminate artificiality, and it is for fighting and the arena that
the whole equipment is made, not for pleasure and scenic show.[6]

The virility of this style in a passage centred on sexuality suggests
subconsciously the virility of the mature Montaigne, making love in
his imagination to the young women of the world. He has already said,
when introducing the passage by Virgil earlier in this essay, 'Venus
n'est pas si belle toute nue, et vive, et haletante, comme elle est icy chez
Virgile . . . ,' thereby implying that he prefers 'l'imaginaire' to reality.
Is it not true in life that imagination is often better than reality? In
choosing the scene between Venus and Mars, Montaigne shows fully
his inventiveness: Cicero had rightly called Lucretius' poetry full of

lumina ingenii. The use of the archaic *Mauors*, the coining of a word like *armipotens* (adopted later by Virgil: *Aeneid*, 2.425), the *pascit* . . . *visus* – the Epicurean theory of vision where the eyes do almost literally 'feed upon' the *simulacra* – the alliteration in 'Eque tuo *p*endent resu*p*ini *sp*iritus ore . . . ', the rhyme of the stressed syllable at the third foot with the final sound in the sixth foot, 'hunc tu, diua, tu*o* recubantem corpore sanct*o* . . . ', the diminutive *loquelas* – all make the passage intensely moving, and one can imagine the effect of writing it down, the reading, the rereading of it has on Montaigne, physically. Then he *ruminates*: Cotgrave gives the two senses – literal and figurative – 'To ruminate or chaw the cud; also, to ponder, weigh, examine, consider or thinke of, deliberate or pawse on, revolve in the mind'. He 'chews' the Virgilian and Lucretian words. The word *reiicit* – Mars lets his body sink into Venus' arms – is a powerful concrete downward movement, and the *Oxford Latin Dictionary* actually cites the Lucretian words as examples; similarly *pascit* is cited by the *OLD* from Lucretius; *inhians* would no doubt cause Montaigne to remember the other passage announcing extreme passion;

> verum ubi vementi magis est commota metu mens,
> consentire animam totam per membra videmus,
> sudoresque ita palloremque exsistere toto
> corpore et infringi linguam vocemque aboriri,
> caligare oculos, sonere auris, succidere artus.

Nevertheless, when the understanding is stirred by some stronger fear, we see that the whole soul feels with it throughout the limbs, and then sweat and pallor break out over all the body, and the tongue is crippled and the voice is choked, the eyes grow misty, the ears ring, the limbs give way beneath us.

(De rerum natura, 3.152 ff.)

The next word *molli* comes from the Virgil passage: Montaigne thinks also of 'est mollis flamma medullas' (*Aeneid*, 4.66); when he rolls around his mouth the famous phrase in Latin love-poetry *fouet* – fondling, caressing – he remembers Tibullus, 'Delia furtim nescio quem fouet' (1.6.6), or Ovid's 'sex annis pulchram fouisse Calypso' (*Epistulae ex ponto*, 4.10.13). The Virgilian *labefacta* would remind him of Lucretius, 4.1114, 'membra uoluptatis dum ui labefacta liquescunt'; *pendet* – this time he reverts to the Lucretian passage – is typical of Latin love-poets; they use it for hanging upon a person's neck and embracing, or hanging on the lips of the other partner or gazing intently at the person's face. Thus he might think of 'pendentia bracchia collo' (Tibullus, 3.6.45), or of 'ubi complexu Aeneae colloque pependit' (Virgil, *Aeneid*, 1.715). Then with the mention of *percurrit* he is back to the Virgilian passage. In other words he is using both passages (does he have them in front of him or is it by memory?) to excite his imagination sexually and to recall other love-poetry in Latin. When we come to the next words he is evaluating them, 'et cette noble *circunfusa*, mere du gentil *infusus*'. The first is in the Lucretian passage, the second in Virgil: both are terms used of embraces, but one is rather more suggestive of lovemaking, of drooling over and being encapsulated by each other, of a more intense, excitable fondling, of petting and necking: it is the two prefixes – *circum* and *super* – that make it 'noble'. Whilst the *infusus* is 'gentil' (Cotgrave translates it as 'Gentle, tame, tractable; mild; affable, courteous, gracious; kind, loving; pliant, soft, supple, tender etc') – gentler billing and cooing.

The passage from Lucretius that Montaigne quotes is unlike Botticelli's painting 'Mars and Venus' now in the National Gallery. Botticelli chooses to set his picture after the intercourse. It is the scene of undoubted erotic significance: Mars is in a kind of swooning sleep, but the little satyrs are playing with the god's weapons and armour, one of them putting on his helmet, the second one joining in the fun with a bright grin on his face, the third blowing hard on a trumpet and the fourth looking out of the picture – very fat and smiling. The whole picture seems to be telling one that love is preferable to war. Montaigne, on the other hand, chooses the moments when the animal instinct and its gratification are to the fore. Lucretius brings up the sexual desire or appetite, the excitability, the physical sensitivity and the high tension or pressure that accompanies copulation. And Montaigne uses the passage as a kind of excitant or stimulator to give himself the fever of excitement. We know he is hypersensitive (Villey-Saulnier, p. 1082; 'le moindre bourdonnement de mouche m'assassine'); he tells us in the second page (ibid., p. 841) of this essay, 'Les ans m'entrainent s'ils veulent, mais à reculons'; old age and death are inhabitants of his life. Thus this passage is 'la desbauche par dessein' (ibid., p. 841) – giving himself (and his readers) the tickle of pleasure through the imagination. The virility of Montaigne and of his style.

We have here an evaluation of Latin and French – or, rather, of poetry or poetic prose in both languages. He continues with his sexualogical terms.[7] The Latin used by 'ces bonnes gens' (i.e. Roman writers – note the evaluation here) is 'tout plein et gros d'vne vigueur naturelle & constante'. Cotgrave gives us for *plein*: 'Full; whole, compleat, absolute, large, ample, solide; also gorged, stuft, replenished, well furnished, stored, fraught, with.' For *gros* he gives 'Grosse, great, big, thicke', and for *vigueur* 'Vigor, strength, force, toughness, courage, liuelinesse, efficacie'. Montaigne's language is earthily sensual, grossly concrete and fully vigorous, thereby preparing us for his next metaphor; 'Ils sont tout epigramme, non la queuë seulement, mais la teste, l'estomac & les pieds. Il n'y a rien d'efforcé, rien de treinant: tout y marche d'vne pareille teneur.' An epigram is a 'short poem ending in a witty or ingenious turn of thought, to which the rest of the composition is intended to lead up' (*OED*). The qualities it must have are terseness and 'point' and sometimes 'sting' in the tail; it is sinewy, pithy and forcible, fleshy and brawny, thick and virile. The language of Latin poets is 'all epigram'; their eloquence is 'nerueuse & solide'. This evaluation of Latin as manly calls up many other essays where the same judgement occurs. For example, in 'De l'institution des enfans' (Villey-Saulnier, p. 162) these terms are intermingled with sexuality. Ariosto's *Orlando furioso* has two beautiful heroines – Bradamant and Angelica; Montaigne suggests that the tutor present them to the child:

> Et quand il commencera de se sentir, luy presentant Bradamant ou Angelique pour maistresse à jouir, et d'une beauté naïve, active, genereuse, *non hommasse mais virile*, au prix d'une beauté molle, affettée, delicate, artificielle; l'une travestie en garçon, coiffée d'un morrion luysant, l'autre vestue en garce, coiffée d'un attiffet emperlé: il jugera masle son amour mesme, s'il choisit tout diversement à cet effeminé pasteur de Phrygie. (My italics)

> And when he shall perceive his scholler to have a sensible feeling of himselfe, presenting Bradamant or Angelica before him, as a Mistress to enjoy, embelished with a naturall, active, generous, and unspotted beautie not uglie or Giant-like, but blithe and livelie, in respect of a wanton, soft, affected, and artificial-flaring beautie; the one attired like unto a young man, coyfed with a bright-shining helmet, the other disguised and drest about the head like unto an impudent harlot, with embroyderies, frizelings, and carcanets of pearles: he will no doubt deeme his owne love to be a man and no woman, if in his choice he differ from that effeminate shepherd of Phrygia.

Why does Montaigne analyse in 'Sur des vers de Virgile' first the Virgilian Venus and Vulcan intercourse rather than the chronologically correct one of the Lucretian Venus and Mars? We might guess at the superiority of Virgil, but let us turn to the short but fine essay 'Du jeune Caton' (I.37): here he wants to 'faire luiter ensemble les traits de cinq poëtes Latins sur la louange de Caton' – and they are Martial, Manilius, Lucan, Horace and Virgil. In the 1580 version he quotes from each and then says this on Virgil:

> Et le maistre du chœur, apres avoir étalé les noms des plus grands Romains en sa peinture, finit en cette maniere:

> his dantem jura Catonem
> (p. 232)

The evaluation is crisp and complete. But the post-1588 version brings in a lot of practical criticism: for instance, Martial and Manilius are 'trainans'; Lucan is 'plus verd' but is 'abattu par l'extravagance de sa force'; Horace is excellent and 'il [the reader] joindra ses mains par admiration'. Montaigne evaluates Horace very highly, until he comes to Virgil; 'Au dernier, premier de quelque espace, mais laquelle espace il jurera ne pouvoir estre remplie par nul esprit humain, il s'estonnera, il se transira' (Villey-Saulnier, p. 231). And there follows a magnificent piece of creative and poetic literary criticism. The appreciation of moderately fine poetry can be done rationally, so to speak: one has the rules obtaining when the poem was written, one measures the way the poem comes up to them and one formulates one's criticism by reason and art. But poetry that is 'la bonne, l'excessive, la divine est audessus des regles et de la raison. Quiconque en discerne la beauté d'une veue ferme et rassise, il ne la void pas, non plus que la splendeur d'un esclair. Elle ne pratique point nostre jugement: elle le ravit et ravage.' (ibid., p. 231: 'But the good and loftie, the supreme and divine, is beyond rules and above reason. Whosoever discerneth her beautie, with a constant, quicke-seeing, and setled looke, he can no more see and comprehend the same than the splendour of a lightning flash. It hath no communitie with our judgement; but ransacketh and ravish the same'. Montaigne uses here the terminology of Longinus (which we shall see in a minute) to convey to the readers the kind of startling shock and the ecstasy of sublimity when reading or listening to poetry. And it is in this category of poetry that he places Virgil: he likes him better than

Lucretius. Montaigne shows himself to be literarily refined, a product of a highly cultured sophistication which sees how Virgil pursued expressiveness as a major virtue and realizes that his poetry, in its verbally rich texture, is one of immeasurable richness and complexity.

Montaigne hits on the compression, the allusiveness and the rich texture of all good poetry. When he has spoken of Latin words, the Latin eloquence which is 'nerveuse et solide', the density of Horace's poetry – 'son esprit crochette et furette tout le magasin des mots et des figures' – he finds the right equivalent in a post-1588 version: 'Elles [les paroles] signifient plus qu'elles ne disent.' Words in the best style can never be pinned down to a simple sense or to a simple statement of 'That equals that'. Words are too richly allusive ever to exhaust of significance. The allusions in a poem may or may not be caught; but the right kind of reader is forever inching along with his senses on the alert and his imagination ready to pick an allusion, reference or quotation.

Our analysis of this passage has brought to us more clearly that knowledge, imagination, language and love are interrubbing all the time. His *fantasies* arrive in two ways: if they come in battalions, he records them impressionistically; if they come *à la file*, that is, more logically, he fashions an argument out of them. In other words, Montaigne does not order them in a rhetorical way with divisions and subdivisions; he records them as they strike him and according to the subject he is dealing with: 'Je veux qu'on voye mon pas naturel et ordinaire, ainsin detraqué qu'il est. Je me laisse aller comme je me trouve . . . ' (Villey-Saulnier, p. 409). He shows a creative not a logical intelligence in his *Essais*. Indeed, he can say:

Mais mon ame me desplait de ce qu'elle produict ordinairement ses plus profondes resveries, plus folles et qui me plaisent le mieux, à l'improuveu et lors que je les cerche moins, lesquelles s'esvanouissent soudain, n'ayant sur le champ où les attacher: à cheval, à la table, au lit, mais plus à cheval, où sont mes plus larges entretiens.

(Villey-Saulnier, p. 876)

But my conceit displeaseth me, forsomuch as it commonly produceth most foolish dotages from deepest studies, and such as content me on a suddaine, and when I least looke for them; which as fast fleete away, wanting at that instant some holdefast. On horse-back, at the table, in my bed; but most on horse-back, where my amplest meditations and my farthest reaching conceits are.

Montaigne skips judiciously through ('Je feuillette les livres, je ne les estudie pas') the books of a remarkably vast library which consists of Greek and Roman writers in abundance, some of the best of fifteenth-century books, contemporary works and a sparse amount of Christian books. (In the 'Apologie' almost all the Christian quotations were inscribed on his library ceiling.) We have seen part of his remoulding of classical poets in analysing the passage in 'Sur des vers de Virgile'. (The other way, through intertextuality, will be analysed in the next chapter.)

Most authors on Montaigne have given us the writers he had read,[8] which of them were favourites and which he went back to again and again.[9] The three genres which formed the base of an educational system in the Renaissance – history, poetry and moral philosophy – are his favourites. Classical poets we have seen playing their role in the *Essais*; Cicero and Quintilian and Diogenes Laertius occupy a prominent place, Plutarch and Seneca are often praised and often plagiarized.

I should like to add Longinus to the list of writers, for arguments that I discuss more fully elsewhere.[10] We may recall the possibility that Montaigne owned the 1563 edition of Lucretius produced by Lambin and his fine edition of Horace in 1561. Now, Lambin possessed the *editio princeps* of Longinus, produced by Robortello in Basel in 1554. It is today in the Bibliothèque Nationale (X.3074). If Montaigne frequented the *cénacle* of Federic Morel (a hypothesis discussed in Chapter 1), he would have heard all the eminent Latin and Greek scholars talk about Longinus in the 1560s. Even supposing that his Greek was very rough, he could have read it in Latin – there were at least three translations in the 1560s and 1570s.[11] Longinus is one of the greatest literary critics that antiquity ever produced. (Second to Aristotle, I suppose, but with much more intuitive insight than him.) Nearly a dozen manuscripts of the treatise *De sublimitate* were known in the Renaissance. Lambin, in his copy of the *editio princeps*, annotates, clarifies and corrects according to the tenth-century Paris *Codex regius*, Robortello, whose manuscript was the Bessarion one. He not only checks the version printed in 1554, but he has also the second edition of Longinus produced in 1555 by Paulus Manutius so that, for instance, on page 11 he says 'Sic C. R. autem libri non habent' or 'libri editi, at non C. R.'. The two editions of Longinus caused the Paris scholarly world a good deal of excitement in the 1550s and 1560s: for example, Turnebus and Henri Estienne mention them in their works. Montaigne could have been impressed by Longinus through his association with Paris humanists in the 1560s, and he might have been urged to read him in translation.

Longinus' treatise on 'impressiveness in style' was a *succès de scandale* in France and Italy from roughly 1554 to 1580, partly because it revealed an ode by Sappho which had hitherto not been known except for the Latin version composed by Catullus.[12] Montaigne might well be thinking of this connection when he asks in the 'Apologie de Raimond Sebond', 'Pensez-vous que les vers de Catulle ou de Sapho rient à un vieillart avaritieux et rechigné comme à un jeune homme vigoreux et ardent?' (Villey-Saulnier, p. 564: an (A) passage) – particularly as he had used the Catullan ode as the centre of 'De la tristesse', hinting unambiguously at the strength of lust in himself. But there is more than that in the connection of Longinus to Montaigne. They both see literary criticism as – to use Longinus' words – 'the last and crowning fruit of long experience'.[13] They both believe that the source of greatness in man is his understanding the place of mankind in the universe. Longinus says that 'the effect of elevated language upon an audience is not persuasion but transport. At every time and in every day imposing speech, with the spell it throws over us, prevails over that which aims at persuasion and gratification' (ch. 1). Does this not recall Montaigne's words *ravit* and *ravage* which we saw a moment ago in the discussion on poets in 'Du jeune Caton'? If we look at the Latin translation of Longinus by Paganus we find verbs such as *deturbant* and nouns such as *admirationem* and *stuprem*. Or we can take Portus' commentary where we read that Hermogenes certainly teaches but, 'ut Longinus non solum docet, sed etiam rapit, & quodammodo vim affert lectoribus; incendit quae desiderio istius gloriae, quae proficiscitur ex magnifico & amplo genere dicendi'. Montaigne is deeply preoccupied with the emotive effects of literature as is shown by, for instance, his examination of the effect of ancient writing on himself; 'Les escrits des anciens, je dis les bons escrits, pleins et solides, me *tentent* et *remuent* . . . ' (Villey-Saulnier, p. 569: my italics). Or the remarkable statement, 'Les saillies poëtiques, qui emportent leur autheur et le ravissent hors de soy . . . ' (ibid., p. 127), where he touches on divine inspiration; 'elles surpassent sa suffisance et ses forces, et les reconnoit venir d'ailleurs que de soy, et ne les avoir aucunement en sa puissance' (ibid., p. 127: 'The Poeticall furies, which ravish and transport their Author beyond himselfe, why shall we not ascribe them to his good fortune, since himselfe confesseth that they exceed his strength and sufficencie, and acknowledge to proceed from elsewhere than from himselfe, and that they are not in his power'). The strength of the imagination, the mystery of the creative process, the *je ne sais quoi* of poetry, the interrelation of art and nature in a poetic process – all are hinted at here.

Neither Montaigne nor Longinus accepts a division between prose and poetry. Longinus constantly refers to 'the genius of great poets and prose writers' (ch. 9) or to the 'sublimity in poems and prose writings' (ch. 7), while Montaigne affirms; 'Mille poëtes trainent et languissent à la prosaïque; mais la meilleure prose ancienne (C) (et *je la seme ceans indifferemment pour vers*) (B) reluit par tout de la vigueur et hardiesse poëtique, et represente l'air de sa fureur' (Villey-Saulnier, p. 995 – my italics: 'A thousand poets labour and languish after the prose-manner, but the best antient prose, which I indifferently scatter here and there, shineth everywhere, with a poeticall vigour and boldness, and representeth some air or touch of its fury'). This statement comes in the middle of an intense piece of literary criticism: we look at the EP facsimile (pl. 906) and realize that the margin additions are great and that some of them have been crossed out. (Montaigne's statement, 'J'adjouste mais je ne corrige pas' (Villey-Saulnier, p. 963), is distinctly untrue.) This is proof that he came back to the page between 1588 and 1592. His praise of Plato, who allowed his dialogues 'ainsi rouler au vent' or 'à la sembler' where the qualification underlines precisely the self-conscious art of the poet in prose, is followed by a reference to his own style: 'I'ayme l'alleure poetique, à sauts & à gambades' above which he has inserted in very tiny handwriting 'C'est un' art, comme dict Platon, legere, volage, demoniacle'. After a reference to the skipping structure of Plutarch's style, he remarks that his own manner of thinking and writing 'vont vagabondan de mesmes' and concludes with the sharp admonition: 'C'est l'indiligent lecteur qui pert mon subject, non pas moy: il s'en trouvera tousjours en un coing quelque mot qui ne laisse d'estre bastant, quoy qu'il soit serré' (I am quoting from EP, not from Villey-Saulnier). The kind of reader Montaigne wants is sensitive to allusions in his text, can reconstruct imaginatively hidden metaphors, can see through the multiplicity of strata thoughts from one essay converging with thoughts from another, is unusually keen in scenting out in the text ideas that Montaigne deliberately and ambiguously has put there – in short, an active reader.

Great literature does not evolve or improve or progress. I can say that Sappho's love-poetry is superb but so is the work of that Welsh Ronsard, Dafydd ap Gwilym. The two are radically different, but the evaluation of them does not depend on chronology. We relate the poems and plays and novels we read and see, not to the men who wrote them but directly to ourselves, and then we relate them to each other. The real effort in literature is one of putting words together. Our function, as active readers and as critics, is to interpret every work of literature in the light of all the literature we know and our personal experience of life, to keep struggling to understand what literature is all about. The discipline of 'contextual reading' (Leavis's phrase) can be got only through much intelligent reading of the practical-criticism kind.

Verse and literary prose are different attempts to express things well: Longinus and Montaigne have in mind that the 'meaning' of a literary work is not that of a message, but of an artistic design which is inexhaustible. A writer deals with words: the combination of words, the suggestiveness which they produce, the harmony and patterns of sound, and the delicate balance of sense and sound. Longinus and Montaigne are both subjective enthusiasts. The admiration for Plato is obvious in Longinus' treatise, but the marginalia on EP plate 906 reveal also Montaigne's approval of Plato's way of working. Montaigne has been reading several of his dialogues, in particular the *Phaedrus*. There is one place in the treatise *On the Sublime* where the *Phaedrus* is at the back of Longinus' mind; it is worth our while to read this chapter 36:

Now as regards the manifestations of the sublime in literature, in which grandeur is never, as it sometimes is in nature, found apart from utility and advantage, it is fitting to observe at once that, though writers of this magnitude are far removed from faultlessness, they none the less all rise above what is mortal; that all other qualities prove their possessors to be man, but sublimity raises them near the majesty of God; and that, while immunity from errors relieves from censure, it is grandeur that excites admiration. What need to add thereto that each of these supreme authors often redeems all his failures by a single sublime and happy touch, and (most important of all) that if one were to pick out and mass together the blunders of Homer, Demosthenes, Plato, and all the rest of the greatest writers they would be found to be a very small part, nay an infinitesimal fraction, of the triumphs which those heroes achieve on every hand. This is the reason why the judgement of all posterity – a verdict which envy itself cannot convict of perversity – has brought and offered those needs of victory which up to this day it guards intact and seems likely still to preserve. (pp. 136–7)

In the introduction to his book on Longinus, Rhys Roberts says: 'He breathes the spirit of the *Ion* rather than of the *Poetics*. He is subjective rather than objective. He is an enthusiast rather than an analyst' (p. 30). And the sublimity or heightened expression that Longinus talks of is connected with a sense of uncertainty, obscurity and infinity. It is not surprising to find Plato as one of the most sublime (after Homer, of course) writers in the treatise. Plato's language is often deeply tinged with poetry: for example, he sets out a difficult point by using a metaphor; or we can look at his puns and some affectations of assonance. And, above all, his prose is musical – the rhythm especially strikes me even when I read him in translation. Let us look at one chapter of Longinus – chapter 13 – where important things are said about imitation by way of Plato. Plato is sublime, he states: 'Although Plato thus flows on with noiseless stream, he is none the less elevated. You know this because you have read the *Republic* and are familiar with his manner' (p. 79). Longinus then gives quite a long quotation from the *Republic* before he goes on to say:

This writer shows us, if only we were willing to pay him heed, that another way . . . leads to the sublime . . . It is the imitation and emulation of previous great poets and writers . . . This proceeding is not plagiarism; it is like taking an impression from beautiful form or figures or other works of art.

And Longinus points his finger at Plato:

And it seems to me that there would not have been so fine a bloom of perfection on Plato's philosophical doctrines, and that he would not in many cases have found his way to poetical subject-matter and modes of expression, unless he had with all his heart and mind struggled with Homer for the primacy, entering the lists like a young champion matched against the man whom all will admire, the showing perhaps too much love of contention and breaking a lance with him as it were, but deriving some profit from the contest none the less. For, as Hesiod says, 'This strife is good for mortals.' And in truth that struggle for the crowns of glory is noble and best deserves the victory in which even to be worsted by one's predecessors brings no discredit. (p. 81)

We can see what Longinus and Montaigne shared: the stress on imagination and judgement, and the belief that heightened speech induces ecstasy in the listener or reader. We may recall how Montaigne speaks of Plato in the 'Apologie' with a good deal of irony: 'Platon n'est qu'un poëte descousu' (a (C) passage), 'Platon en ses nuages poetiques; voyez chez luy le jargon des Dieux' (another (C) passage), or 'sous des umbrages fabuleux de la Poesie' (Villey-Saulnier, p. 545). Plato's philosophy is demeaned as part of Montaigne's general attack on human presumption . Did Plato not call nature 'une poësie œnigmatique'? 'Et certes la philosophie n'est qu'une poësie sophistiquée' (ibid., p. 537) – a falsified counterfeit. Montaigne mocks at Plato's philosophy throughout the *Essais*, but he has a certain liking for the way he writes. And this liking gravitates and crystallizes around Montaigne's deep creativity.

CHAPTER 7

The Ambiguous Frontier between Prose and Poetry

C'est l'enfileure de noz aiguilles. (I.37)

If we accept the bilingualism of Montaigne, and if we are convinced of the primary importance of Latin poets in his way of thinking, then we can begin to explore the universe of his consciousness from the hypothesis that the starting-point for his 'poetic' projections was in fact the poetry that he knew best and admired. Thus one way of showing how the 'poetic' passages come about is by taking examples from the Latin poets – Martial, Catullus, Lucretius, Propertius, Horace and Virgil – and seeing how they are the spur which takes Montaigne further and deeper in psychological terms than any writer before him. This chapter will examine this intertextual process in some of the essays.

'De la force de l'imagination' (I.21) (right from the original 1580 version) has this statement from Lucretius:

> Ut quasi transactis saepe omnibus rebus profundant
> Fluminis ingentes fluctus, vestémque cruentent.

Often, as though their function were actually fulfilled, they discharge a flood of liquid and drench their clothes.

(De rerum natura, 4.1035)

This is the spur from literature that governs the essay. Montaigne was attracted to his 'scientific' epic.[1] He was particularly taken by the treatment of physical, physiological and psychological matters. This essay may be linked with 'De la tristesse' (I.2) where the Catullus poem of vehement passion is perhaps underpinned by these words of Lucretius:

audoresque ita palloremque existere toto
corpore et infringi linguam vocemque aboriri,
caligare oculos, sonere auris, succidere artus.

Sweat and pallor break out all over the body. Speech grows
inarticulate; the voice fails; the eyes swim; the ears buzz; the limbs
totter.

(*De rerum natura*, 3.152 ff.)

And it may be coupled with 'Sur des vers de Virgile' (III.5), where the
prayer to the creative force of Nature (personified as Venus), which
begins the epic, is one of the central quotations (alongside those from
Virgil) governing the shape of the essay.

The context of the quotation from Lucretius in 'De la force de
l'imagination' is the pasage on dreams in relation to waking life. It is a
fine vivid piece of description, which Montaigne must surely have
admired. It precedes Lucretius' attack on sex. The context is the
seminal discharge of youths while asleep, without knowledge or
warning and without the consent of the will. Montaigne discusses the
'nouements d'aiguillettes', moments of transient impotence, and it is
clear that he is talking of himself under the guise of relating an episode
which had been experienced by another person.[2]

The essay opens – perhaps surprisingly – with a confession of a
defect, '*Fortis imaginatio generat casum*, disent les clercs. Je suis de
ceux qui sentent tres-grand effort de l'imagination' (Villey-Saulnier,
p. 97),[3] and this, in 1580, leads not to the Lucretian quotation which
Montaigne will use later –

Ut quasi transactis saepe omnibus rebus profundant
Fluminis ingentes fluctus, vestémque cruentent.
(*De rerum natura*, 4.1035)

– but to a splendidly concrete description of what we do not of our
conscious will but through the power of the imagination: 'Nous
tressuons, nous tremblons, nous pallissons et rougissons aux secousses
de nos imaginations et renversez dans la plume sentons nostre corps
agité à leur bransle, quelques-fois jusques à en expirer' (Villey-
Saulnier, p. 98). And then he almost paraphrases Lucretius before
introducing the quotation 'Et la ieunesse bouillante s'eschauffe si avant
en son harnois tout' endormie, qu'elle assouvit en songe ses amoureux
désirs . . . '. We have the impression that he is 'translating' the Latin

of Lucretius into a vivid French prose description. After two short paragraphs (we know that in the *exemplaire* there are no paragraphs, but it is convenient to follow the 'standard edition' here) he talks about the central theme – the potency of man. In 1580 he has 'ces plaisantes liaisons des mariages' (Villey-Saulnier, p. 99), but he then crosses out 'des mariages' in the *exemplaire*. Perhaps he wanted to extend the topic to any kind of transient impotence and turn the reader's attention away from the impotence that can occur on the wedding night. Or maybe he did not want it to be known that *this* experience of impotence was his own. The next sentence is interesting: 'Car ie sçay par *experience*, que tel de qui ie puis respondre, *comme de moy mesme*, en qui il ne pouuoit eschoir soupçon de foiblesse' (EP, pl. 72: my italics). That is how it appears in 1588. There are two possibilities here: either the experience was Montaigne's (the phrase 'par experience' suggests this strongly) or it was La Boëtie's, and the phrase 'comme de moy mesme' seems to hint at his friend. In the *exemplaire*, however, he adds betwen 'soupçon' and 'de foiblesse' an 'aucun'. The 'aucun' makes the point absolute. The reworking of the passage is in fact a warning to readers that it is important.

When we turn to EP plates 73 and 74 the marginalia are colossal. And, what is more, those on plate 74 are all continuations of the notes on plate 73. Here, obviously, is a passage with 'poetic' flavour. For the argument about the penis is extended to other parts of a human being which are also set in motion without the consent of the will. First of all he deals with the wedding night: the 'il' of 1588 is changed into 'le patient'; he is giving advice to the patient:

> Auant la possession prinse, le patient se doit à saillies & diuers tamps legierement essaïer et offrir, sans se piquer & opiniastrer à conveïncre definitiuement soimesmes. Ceux qui sçauent leurs membres de nature dociles, qu'ils se soingnent seulement de contrepiper leur fantasie.
>
> (EP, pl. 73)

> Before possession taken, a patient ought by sallies, and divers times, lightly assay and offer himselfe without vexing or opiniating himselfe, definitely to convince himselfe. Such as know their members docile and tractable by nature, let them only endevour to counterces in their fantasie.

Montaigne's advice is that 'the patient' should try delaying tactics before having sexual intercourse. As he said in 'Sur des vers de Virgile':

'Ie louë la gradation & la longueur en la dispensation de leurs faueurs'
(EP, pl. 803). Then Montaigne is concerned with 'nostre volonte'
when the penis is 'contestant de l'authorité si *imperieusement* auec nostre
uolonté, refusant auec *tant de fierté & d'obstination* noz solicitations
mentales & manuelles' (EP, pl. 73: my italics). We can note the
language here: the penis is behaving *imperieusement* – 'imperiously,
lordly, proudly, loftily, soveraigne-like' (Cotgrave); it is operating with
fierté and *obstination* – wilfulness and stubbornness. Montaigne sees
the penis as having the characteristics that are usualy given to a man's
willpower. We may notice, too, that the marginal comment has grown
so much that Montaigne has to turn to the following page for more
space and his handwriting grows much smaller as he knows now that
he has a lot to say on this topic.

Montaigne extends the argument as if he were speaking like a
barrister in court; half-humorously he states 'il [le membre] m'avoit
payé pour plaider sa cause . . . ', and the legal language is echoed
later on by 'a l'adventure mettroy-je en souspeçon noz autres
membres' and 'le chargeant malignement seul de leur faute commune'.
Florio has caught the flavour of the language here: 'drawes a triall' and
'would pay me for to plead his cause'. But unfortunately he translates
il as a 'man'. We readers are like the jury in court being addressed by
Montaigne: 'Car je vous donne à penser.' What we are being told is:
's'il y a une sule des parties de nostre corps qui ne refuse a nostre
uolanté souuant son operation et qui souuent ne lexerce contre nostre
uolanté'. Montaigne extends the argument from the penis to all
involuntary actions: 'Elles [les parties] ont chacune des passions
propres, qui les esueillent et endorment sans nostre congé.' The
physiological comes from the psychological so that muscles, veins,
lungs, heart are brought into play, without our consent.

This whole area of man's being is important to Montaigne, and it is
fascinating to see the way he starts to map it. For instance, EP plate 73
has about eight lines crossed off, and one can 'hear' the tone in the
1588 text: authoritatively counselling as a wise monitor with terms like
'mon conseil est' and 'Mais il faut aussi'; a warning guide to the
behaviour of women in France at this time: 'Mais il faut aussi que
celles, à qui legitimement on le peut demander, ostent ces façons
ceremonieuses & affectuées de rigueur & de refus, & qu'elles se
contraignent un peu pour s'accomoder à la necessité de ce siecle.' This
last sentence is transformed in the *exemplaire*. Gone are the
imperatives, gone the air of authority; instead there is a humorous
anecdote with a warm-hearted and down-to-earth touch:

Or elles ont tort de nous recueiller de ces contenances mineuses quereleuses et fuiardes, qui nous esteignent en nous allumant. La bru de Pythagoras disoit que la femme qui se couche avec un home doit avec la cotte laisser aussi la honte: et la reprendre avec le cotillon.

Now they wrong us, to receive and admit us with their wanton, squeamish, quarellous countenances, which setting us afire, extinguish us. Pythagoras his neece was wont to say, That a woman which lies with a man ought, together with her petie-coate, leave off all bashfulness, and with her petie-coate, take the same again.

The final marginalia, from 'Si je come bien, qu'un autre come pour moy', vouch for the authenticity of what he writes in this psychological study of man: 'Aussi en l'estude que ie traitte de noz mœurs et mouuements; les tesmoinages fabuleux pouruue qu'ils soient possibles, y seruent come les vrais.' The *vraisemblants* and the *vrais*. A pretty authoritarian position.

It was the quotation from Lucretius that was the catalyst for this essay. Montaigne, however, has gone much further than his inspirer: he is, perhaps, the first European to explore this independence of our bodies from our will. We find in the final version a depth of assimilation and a very creative 'try-out' of personal ideas. And the 'poetic' passage provoked by the Latin quotation comes into the French text in a lively and rich manner.

The essay 'Des senteurs' (I.55) works in a different way. Here the poet is, first, Martial, who is present from the 1580 edition onwards.[4] Two quotations from him are introduced this way: 'D'où naissent ces rencontres des Poëtes anciens: c'est puïr que de santir bon' (Villey-Saulnier, p. 314). Cotgrave gives several meanings to *rencontres*: 'an accidental getting, obtaining or lighting on; also, an occurance; also, an apt or unpremeditated iest, conceit, wittie saying'. The witty conceits of ancient poets. The two quotations are from two epigrams, both of which are concerned with homosexuality. The tone is light and frivolous.
Epigram 6.55:

> Quod semper cassiaque cinnamoque
> et nido niger alitis superbae
> fragras plumbea Nicerotiana,
> rides nos, Coracine, nil olentis,
> malo quam bene olere nil olere.

Because, constantly smeared darkly with cassia and cinnamon and
the perfumes from the nest of the phoenix, you reek of the leaden
jars of Niceros, you laugh at us, Coracinus, who smell of nothing.
To smelling of scent I prefer smelling of nothing.

Epigram 2.12:

> Esse quid hoc dicam quod olent tua basia murram
>   quodque tibi est numquam non alienus odor?
> hoc mihi suspectum est, quod oles bene, Postume, semper:
>   Postume, non bene olet qui bene semper olet.

How shall I explain this, that your kisses smell of myrrh, and that
there is about you invariably some foreign odour? This is suspect to
me your being well-scented, Postumus, always. Postumus, he is not
well scented who is always well-scented.

Montaigne uses the last two lines of epigram 6.55 and the last line of
2.12, both of which suggest that the best way to smell is to smell of
nothing. He is thinking of the contexts of the two poems. For
example, the sentence 'Et les bonnes senteurs *estrangieres*, on a raison
de les tenir pour *suspectes* . . . ' (my italics) corresponds to the two
phrases in 2.12 – 'alienus odor' and 'hoc mihi suspectum est'. The
shortness of the essay makes me think that it was an early one: it is a
witty type of discourse. And the additions from Latin poetry are apt.
Reading the essay between 1580 and 1588, Montaigne adds a good
deal. There appear now three lines from a Horatian epode.

> Namque sagacius unus odoror,
> Polypus, an gravis hirsutis cubet hircus in alis,
> Quam canis acer ubi lateat sus.

For I have a nose finely and uniquely sensitive to smell a polypus or
the putrid goaty smell in hairy armpits; keener even than a dog
finds the boar's lair by its smell. (DGC)

(Epodes, 13.4–6)

The original Horatian poem is full of coarse sexuality. It is an attack
on an ageing woman: gross physical details are mentioned; sexual
intercourse, the impotent penis and the orgasmic power of women.
The scholiasts 'Acro' and Porphyrio comment on it quite fully: they

give it a title – 'In mulierem libidinosam'. They mention the sweat in intercourse: when it is a *coitu finito* the *sudor* is *humida* and *humefacta*. 'Acro' explains the word *sagacius* thus: 'Sagacitam suam inueniendo muliebrium membrorum putor cani comparauit feras quaerenti . . . ' In Lambin's edition the note to the previous line is even more sexually charged:

> nigris dignissima barria/valentissimi ac mentulatissimis amatoribus dignissima: vel propria & litterata, elephantis digna, non viris, nonnulli existimant significaria nefarium concubitum, id, est, aversam, in cod. Faer, neque usquam alibi, si bene memini, scriptum est *longis dign. barr.*

(Lambin's italics)

It seems certain that Montaigne knew the poem, and probable that he was aware of the commentators' views. He has read the essay once again, and immediately following the quotation there is a passage on women: 'Les senteurs plus simples et naturelles me semblent plus agreables. Et touche ce soing principalement les dames.' Then there is a statement: 'Quelque odeur que ce soit, c'est merueille combien elle s'attache à moy, et combien j'ay la peau propre à s'en abreuver' (Villey-Saulnier, p. 315). The sentence introducing the Horace lines is very personal and highly emotional: 'j'ayme pourtant *bien fort* à estre entretenu de bonnes senteurs, et hay *outre mesure* les mauvaises, que je tire *de plus loing que tout autre*' (my italics).

Then personal comments and his sensuality come in: 'Les estroits baisers de la ieunesse, savoureux & gourmans, s'y colloyent autresfois, & s'y tenoient plusieurs heures apres.' He reads it again between 1588 and his death and poetically 'invents' two different adjectives to qualify *baisers*, savouring the *gl* in both: 'Les estroits baisers de la ieunesse, savoureux, gloutons et gluans . . . ' Thus in this essay a witty conceit ends up as a sensual and poetic elaboration on his moustache and on the nature of passionate kissing. Aesthetic and pleasing.

Finally, we might analyse the essay 'Que nostre desir s'accroit par la malaisance' (II.15) as an example of *la difficulté vaincue*. This phrase means two things. In 'Sur des vers de Virgile' (III.5) he spells out the conditions. The first lies in the exercise of love; difficulty before reaching the intercourse stage is primarily what Montaigne desires – 'L'amour se fonde au seul plaisir, et l'a de vray plus chatouillant, plus vif et plus aigu; un plaisir attizé par la difficulté. Il y faut de la piqueure et de la cuison' (Villey-Saulnier, p. 854: 'Love melts in onely pleasure; and truly it hath it more ticklish, more lively, more quaint, and more sharpe, a pleasure inflamed by difficulty; there must be a kinde of stinging, tingling and smarting'). Aware of his own temperament, his hypersensitive nervous system, his impetuous excitability – 'Ce souhait est mieux à propos en cette volupté viste et precipiteuse, mesmes à telles natures comme est la mienne, qui suis vitieux en soudaineté . . . ' (ibid., p. 880) – he wants infinitely to extend the pre-coition period.[5] And, second, *la difficulté vaincue* is the difficulty of expressing things about sex in any language. There is an intimate connection between Montaigne's way of making sense of experience and his verbal language. All words are ambiguous, especially the words governing sex, and the difficulty lies in what is publicly producible. The kind of language Montaigne uses is concrete, manly and malleable: for instance, beauty is 'non hommasse mais virile' (I.26); his ideal youth must not be 'un beau garçon et dameret' but 'un garçon vert et vigoureux' (ibid.), and he adds the comment in the marginal notes of 1588–92 that 'Enfant, homme, vieil, j'ay tousjours creu et jugé de mesme'. The nouns which indicate libido/concupiscence/carnal desire/unslaked and unquenchable lust are exceedingly numerous in Montaigne – 'lasciveté'/'concupiscence'/ 'atouchement'/'accointance'/'desbordements'/'extreme volupté' – and, furthermore, the 1588–92 marginalia show very clearly, by crossing out the redistribution, that Montaigne was concerned with the different variations in style, level and tone around the essential *volupté* up to his death in 1592.

This essay (II.15) is an example in which the Latin quotations are from love-poets – inserted before 1588 – and the French passage is found in the marginalia of the *exemplaire*. The first main theme is again sex: the *volupté* is ten times stronger if it is made more difficult; *aisance* is opposed to *rareté et difficulté*. Before looking at this more closely it is worth noting what the marginalia/corrections reveal. First, his stylistic rereading cuts out both the exaggeration and the symmetry: for example, 'Ie remachois tantost ce tresbeau mot & tres veritable' becomes 'Ie remachois tantost ce beau mot' (EP, pl. 551). Second, he alters adjectives to make them more precise. For example, 'd'autant plus ferme' becomes 'd'autant plus estroit' (ibid.). Third, he removes the difficulty of getting at women because of their custom of wearing bastions ('Ouvrage de fortification faisant saillie sur l'enceinte d'une place forte' – Robert): 'Et à quoy seruent ces gros bastions, dequoy les nostres viennent d'armer leurs flancs, qu'à lurrer nostre appetit *par la difficulté* . . . ' (EP, pl. 553).

And, last, his admiration for Italian women gets closely cropped when he cancels his earlier praise – 'Voyez en Italie, où il y a plus de beauté à vendre, & de la plus ~~parfaite qu'en aucune autre nation . . .~~ ' (ibid.) – and substitutes merely one adjective: *fine*.

In the 1580 version five poets are quoted: Martial, Horace, Lucretius, Virgil and Ovid. Let us see what the Roman context brings to the French. The Martial line

> Galla, nega: satiatur amor nisi gaudia torquent
> (*Epigrams*, 4.38)

is not in fact followed by the second line of the epigram – 'sed noli nimium, Galla, negare diu' – but one feels sure that Montaigne meant us to have in mind this witty expression of the woman's short-lived refusal and rapid capitulation. Montaigne goes on immediately with the statement 'Pour tenir l'amour en haleine': this shows what he was using the Martial for. And he has not altered the quotation. With the quotation from Horace, Montaigne has juggled with the lines; a modern critical edition gives them thus:

> In quis amantem languor et silentium
> Arguit et latere petitus imo spiritus.
> (*Epodes*, 11.9–10)

With Montaigne they appear as

> & languor, & silentium,
> Et latere petitus imo spiritus,
> (EP, pl. 551)

Montaigne here has rejected the context he found in Horace – where the author regrets the way he behaved when in love with Inachia – and has created a new one, in the present tense instead of the past; and surrounded it with French conveying the pleasure he has known himself. The sentence begins: 'La difficulté des assignations, le dangier des surprises, le honte du lendemain . . . ' Then come the Horatian-inspired lines, and then . . . what is really Montaigne's own re-enjoyment of the pleasure and ironic expression of it – 'c'est ce qui donne pointe à la sauce' (EP, pl. 552). In the marginalia he adds this very ambiguous sentence: 'Combien de jeux tres lascivement plaisants naissent de l'honeste et vergongneuse maniere de parler des ouvrages de l'amour' (ibid.). Is he leaving it to the imagination of the reader to

wander at will across the ambivalence and ambiguity of these lines? I
expect that Montaigne would have smiled at doing that. This
quotation gets us almost to the point of intercourse, but it is in fact the
Lucretian lines that push us further in that direction. They are not
accurately quoted. Lucretius has, in the modern edition of Bailey
(Oxford: Clarendon Press, 1947):

> quod petiere, premunt arte faciuntque dolorem
> corporis et dentis inlidunt saepe labellis
> osculaque adfligunt, quia non est pura voluptas
> et stimuli subsunt qui instigant laedere id ipsum
> quodcumque est, rabies unde illaec germina surgunt.
>
> (4.1079–83)

What they have grasped, they closely press and cause pain to the
body, and often fasten their teeth in the lips, and dash mouth
against mouth in kissing, because their pleasure is not unalloyed,
and there are secret stings which spur them to hurt even the very
thing, be it what it may, whence arise those germs of madness.

Montaigne leaves out the line 'osculaque adfligunt, quia non est pura
voluptas'. Why? Now, Lucretius at this point is attacking the passion
of love, on the grounds that it is a cause of mental disturbance. The
singleminded pursuit of sex is a kind of disease for Lucretius, and so
he inserts 'quia non est pura voluptas'. Montaigne is different: he
relishes the words themselves, he delights in the alliterative 'petiere,
premunt', and lingers over 'dentes inlidunt saepe labellis' – the very
visualization and the 'hearing' of two lovers grasping and fondling. He
follows the question with 'Il en va ainsi par tout, la difficulté donne
pris aux choses' (EP, pl. 552). His point is perfectly clear: the
enjoyment of a sexual encounter.

Later on in this essay there is a line from Virgil's *Eclogues*, 3.65:

> et fugit ad salices et se cupit ante uideri

The previous line in Virgil reads:

> Malo me Galatea petit, *lasciua puella*
> (My italics)

Montaigne would surely expect his readers to know this context. The
bisexual tradition in Greek and Roman poetry would be known by

Montaigne, and the choice of one line from a homosexual context –
clearly with the Galatea as the main focus and boys as the subsidiary
one – is suggestive. Finally, he quotes a line from Ovid's *Amores*,
2.19.3, to finish off his example of Roman views on marriage:

> Quod licet, ingratum est: quod non licet, acrius urit.

This means that he already knew that the *Amores* can help in this
question of lust/love and marriage. He will remember Ovid in the
1588 additions – and even use quotations from the same poem.

The 1588 version has further quotations from Roman poets: Ovid,
Amores (three times) and Propertius (twice). The first Ovid quotation is

> Si numquam Danaen habuisset aenea turris
> Non esset Danae de Iove facta parens
> (ll.27–8: EP, pl. 551)

The second comes a little later:

> nisi tu seruare puellam
> Incipis, incipiet desinere esse mea
> (ll.47–8: EP, pl. 552)

The third comes from a few lines earlier in the *Amores*:

> Si qua volet regnare diu contemnat amantem

But this is a 'made-up' line and it is not in fact accurate. The Ovid line
should be

> si qua volet regnare diu, deludat amantem
> (l.33)

There is no evidence of a manuscript variant here. (See Ovid, *Amores*,
ed. E. J. Kenney, Oxford Classical Texts, 1961, p. 65.) So we have to
ask whether Montaigne deliberately chose to say *contemnat* or (and this
is perfectly possible) half-forgot the Ovid and was influenced by the
next two lines, which are themselves a quotation from Propertius:

> contemnite amantes,
> Sic hodie veniet si qua negauit heri.
> (2.14.19–20)

The second possibility is my guess. What kind of a poem is this one of Ovid? Is it in any way fitting to what Montaigne wishes to convey to his reader? The poem is witty and naughty; Ovid as the lover asks the husband to make his task more difficult: 'Guard your girl, stupid – if only to please *me*./I want to want her more' (I quote Guy Lee's very fresh rendering of the *Amores*). The difficulty of the task is precisely what Montaigne is arguing throughout his essay. Before the first quotation one reads: 'que nostre volonté s'esguise aussi par le contraste'; note that he uses *s'esguise* – 'even so our will is *whetted* on by that which doth resist it' (Florio). Before the second one reads: 'Nous defendre quelque chose, c'est nous en donner envie'. Before the third one we find a fully developed sentence: 'mais la satieté engendre le dégoust: c'est vne passion mousse, hebetée, lasse & endormie' (EP, pl. 553). 'Whereas satiety begets distaste: it is a dull, blunt, weary, and drouzy passion' (Florio). Montaigne sees the pre-coition period in love/lust as crucial to the lovemaking and hints that it can never be long enough.

The Ovidian context is precisely on the length of the pre-coition period:

> quo mihi formosam quae numquam fallere curet?
> (*Amores*, 2.19.7)

> I write off beautiful women who won't bother to deceive me.
> (Guy Lee's translation)

Or, later in the poem, Ovid says: 'Love on a plate soon palls.' The power of deception is something about which Montaigne agrees with Ovid, who states that 'if you want your power to last deceive your lover'. I think the last four lines of the poem are suggestive:

> quid nihi cum facili, quid cum lenone marito?
>   corrumpit vitio gaudia nostra suo.
>
> quin alium quem tanta iuvet patientia quaeris?
>   me tibi rivalem si iuvat esse, veta.
>
> I don't approve of uncomplaining, pimping husbands –
>   their immorality ruins my pleasure.
>
> Find someone who can appreciate your perversion,
>   or, if you value *me* as a rival, use your veto.
>   (Guy Lee's translation)

The poem was well-known to Montaigne, and Ovid's offer of a pose of frank sensuality expressed in verbal wit was, as it were, 'taken up' by him in this essay.

But was it really 'taken up' by Montaigne? We saw earlier that he read Ovid for fun at an age when other children were reading romances of chivalry, and we saw, too, how his taste changed with the years. Nowhere was Montaigne's purpose in using two registers – poetry and prose – and two languages – Latin and French – clearer than in this essay. For his ideas on sex, on the pre-coition period in intercourse – 'rien qui l'éguise tant que la rareté et difficulté' – and on the whole adoption of a Roman view on love, with the quotations from Propertius sealing this register, are all important. But Montaigne's attitude is far more sophisticated than Roman views on love, lust and sex. Montaigne's experience was a long one: there was his childhood, adolescence and premature puberty in the Collège de Guyenne; there was the hypothetical period in Paris where Trinquet speaks of his 'fougue intempérante, des élans irraisonnés';[6] a period of extreme friendship with La Boëtie, followed by a stage when *la difficulté vaincue* was his motto towards women of a certain rank; then there was the period of his marriage and, as an old man, of his composition and revision of the *Essais*. Throughout, his experience of lust/love/sex was particularly rich. Qualities like discretion, moderation he rates quite highly, and time is important – he declares that one must delay. 'Qui me demanderoit la premiere partie en l'amour, je responderois que c'est sçavoir prendre le temps; la seconde de mesme, et encore la tierce: c'est un poinct qui peut tout' (Villey-Saulnier, p. 866). We shall return to his attitude towards women, towards old age and towards sex in the next chapter. Meanwhile, let us look finally at the essay 'Des prognostications' (I.11) where we find again an experiment of creative imitation. It is inherent in Stoic philosophy to regard the concepts of time past and time future with indifference, as having no value in themselves, as something outside man's control. Present time alone may be considered as being under one's control. So a statement like 'Notable exemple de la forcenée curiosité de nostre nature, s'amusant à preoccuper les choses futures, comme si elle n'auoit pas assez affaire à digerer les presentes . . . ' (EP, pl. 29) should cause us no surprise. After the anecdote of Francis Marquis of Saluzzo, however, Montaigne quotes parts of Horatian odes (3.29, 29–32 and 41–4 and two lines from another ode, 2.16,25–6).

Prudens futuri temporis exitus
Caliginose nocte premit Deus,
Ridétque si mortalis ultra
Fas trepidat.
  Ille potens sui
Laet usque deget, cui licet in diem
Dixisse, vixi, cras vel atra
Nube polum pater occupato
Vel sole puro.
Laetus in praesens animus, quod vltra est,
Oderit curare.

(EP, pl. 30)

A god hides the future in the darkness of night and mocks man whose fears go beyond the limits fixed by him. He will be master of himself and will live happily; every day he will say 'I have lived'. Let Jupiter cover the sky with black clouds or fill it with pure sunshine. Content for the moment, the mind must not preoccupy itself with the future. (DGC)

This is at the heart of the 1580 version of the essay. Why should he have quoted so many lines from Horace? Much as the Catullus quotation formed the centre of 'De la tristesse' (I.2), so this Horatian quotation seems to be of crucial importance. Why should he have quoted from two odes, without letting us know that they are two? It is another example by which we see that two structures are superimposed in the *Essais*: Montaigne's bilingualism is so significant that we hardly dare guess which was the language he was thinking in. We have to retexture the quotations by looking at their exact contexts in Horace. The importance of context has been well stated by J. Petter:

Around the writer, and at the very center of the inspiration that makes him a writer, we must re-establish the presence of a literary universe . . . to have the idea of expressing oneself in writing, one must know that this is possible and be concerned with what others have written . . . In a non-literary civilisation, *je* would not have written; living in another literary atmosphere, the same man would have written something else; brought up among the mute he would never have spoken.[7]

In Montaigne we have two contexts: that of Horace and that of Montaigne. The first ode is a dramatization of Horace's inner tranquillity of mind; the two important words are *Dixisse* and *vixi*. They have fired Montaigne's imagination and become a leitmotif in the *Essais*. For example, his whole *art de vivre* is an intellectualization of the present – how to suck all the enjoyments of the moment and at the same time to enjoy them over again as memory. 'De l'experience' (III.13) is a fully mature criss-cross pattern woven around these two Horatian words *Dixisse* and *vixi*. The second ode is on the same theme, but the context is man's flight from himself; this is precisely the context that Montaigne intends, and he must have remembered a phrase earlier in the ode:

> Patriae quis exul
> Se quoque fugit?

Is leaving the country another attempt at self-delusion?

Montaigne is the first person in France to assert what later will be so universally accepted – that language in literary works is 'l'originel langage des Dieux'. A century later La Fontaine will say:

> C'est ainsi que ma muse, aux bords d'une onde pure,
> Traduisait en langue des dieux
> Tout ce que disent sous les cieux
> Tant d'êtres empruntants la voix de la nature.
> (Epilogue to book 11 of the *Fables*)

I have tried to convey the excitement, the strangeness and the profundity of Montaigne's writing. The fact that these essays are written in a highly self-conscious way, belying Montaigne's habitual attitude of looking down upon himself and his writings, tells us that the only way to enjoy the *Essais* is to read and reread it in much the same way that Montaigne himself read the classical writers. We, like Flaubert, chew his phrases which have so much 'jus' and 'chair' inside them.

CHAPTER 8

The Study of the Self: Psychology and Humanity

'th'intertraffique of the minde'
Samuel Daniel

There are only two important things in Montaigne's view: his mind and himself. In trying to write down himself he says in 'De la praesumption' (II.17):

> Le monde regarde tousjours vis à vis; moy, je replie ma veue au dedans, je la plante, je l'amuse là. Chacun regarde devant soy; moy, je regarde dedans moy: je n'ay affaire qu'à moy, je me considere sans cesse, je me contrerolle, je me gouste . . .
>
> (Villey-Saulnier, p. 657)

> The world lookes ever for right, I turne my sight inward, there I fix it, there I ammuse it. Every man lookes before himselfe, I looke within my selfe: I have no busines but with my selfe. I uncessantly consider, controle and taste my selfe.

This angle of vision can be wide; it can be ironical; it can be humorous. We can note the words Montaigne uses. Cotgrave gives as the meaning of *replie*: 'to redouble, to bow, fould, or plait into many doublings; to make to turne, or wind in and out verie often'. For *plante* Cotgrave gives 'to plant, set; settle, fix, ground'. For *amuse* he gives: 'to amuse; to make to muse, or think of; wonder or gaze at; to put into a dumpe; to stay, hold or delay from going forward by discourses, questions, or any other documents'. The 'try-outs' of an English meaning are interesting because they all have *movement* in common. Movement inwards, outwards, upwards, downwards, sideways, horizontally and vertically. For *contrerolle* Cotgrave gives: 'to controll; observe, oversee, spie faults in; also, to take and keepe a copie of a roll of accounts; to play the controller anyway'.

This internal angle involves ceaselessly 'controlling' oneself. Moreover, the word *controlleur* had specific meanings in the sixteenth century: 'an Officer, that takes notes, or keepes a roll, of another Officers accounts, thereby to discover him if he do amisse', Montaigne must have known this meaning. He is both the person who takes the notes and the person whose books are kept as a roll, in case he should be taken amiss. There were other subdivisions of the original meaning: there were *contrerolleurs des aides* – like tax-inspectors; *contrerolleur de l'Audience de France* – 'the controller of the Chancerie attendant on the king's person'; there were *contrerolleurs du Domaine* – administrators of the king's domain (for example, the *contrerolleur* would make up leases of farms, he would assist in the sale of wood, wine, corn, hay, fish, and so on). In 1581, Henri III established the post of *contrerolleur general du Domaine* and then abolished it in 1584. If Montaigne was aware of these things (and who would say that he was ever not aware?), then when he uses this verb all these associations must be borne in mind. For 'je me gouste', Cotgrave gives:

> to tast, or take an essay of; to tast, savor; touch upon; feele, or conceive a little; also, to admit of, digest indifferently, take a liking to, to begin to affect, or fancie; also, to have some experience, a little insight, meane knowledge in.

Thus, Montaigne's way is a concrete communication of the act of contemplating all; all that happens around him is sucked in – a truly voluptuous sensation. Here are some features of his mental landscape; he describes a 'poetic' world where all is a-shiver, where the *dedans* (repeated) is shifting sand and where the two personalities – the watcher and the watched – are constantly, unceasingly seeing each other from every possible angle.

Montaigne can say with Valéry:

> Notre *personnalité* elle-même, que nous prenons grossièrement pour notre plus intime et plus profonde *propriété*, pour notre souverain bien, n'est qu'une *chose*, et muable et accidentelle, auprès de ce *moi* le plus nu; puisque nous pouvons penser à elle, calculer ses intérêts, et meme les perdre un peu de vue, elle n'est donc qu'une divinité psychologique secondaire qui habite notre miroir et qui obéit à notre nom.
>
> (*Cahiers* (Paris: Imprimerie Nationale, 1957–61), Vol. 1, p. 1226: author's italics)

The two verbs that Montaigne uses – *gouster* and *je me roulle* – mean experience (in the English meaning of the word, and indeed in Montaigne's meaning in his last essay), understanding and evaluation. Cotgrave gives for *je me roulle* 'rowle, turne round, fould up or inwards; or to rowle along', and these are precisely the instruments for examining this *chose, et muable et accidentelle*. Montaigne is committed to an internal biography:

> Un auteur qui *compose* une biographie peut essayer de *vivre* son personnage, ou bien, de le *construire*. Et il y a opposition entre ces partis. *Vivre*, c'est se transformer dans l'incomplet. La *vie* en ce sens, est toute anecdotes, détails, instants.
>
> (*Cahiers*, Vol. 1, p. 1156: author's italics)

Montaigne's way of coming to terms with himself is much more difficult than our normal way precisely because our normal way is a way of distorting reality and we are never aware of the trap of finding justifications for ourselves. Montaigne rejects the way of having *idées fixes*; his way of proceeding is against the mechanism of abstract general ideas which make it impossible to describe an experience in its individuality. He breaks down abstract categories on every thing.

If my hypothesis that Montaigne was consciously aware of his desire to write a mixture of fiction and autobiography is granted, what we have in the early chapters in the 1580 edition is a series of meditations upon and experimentation with certain basic categories of his own mind: *ame, jugement, imagination, volonté, fantasie, memoire* and *intelligence*. The essays are an attempt to determine how these states of mind work – for instance, in facing death and life; in examining the rules of conduct for a man; in finding out what one means by *vertu, devoir, tranquillité*, and so on. Internal biography makes it important that psychological and ethical phenomena are seen in different situations, and thus the examples are situationalized very differently.

Montaigne rarely repeats himself. Where he appears to do so he is in fact pointing to a correspondence between two modes of thought. The composition is self-conscious from the start: for example, the first and last essays are on the same theme – man 'ondoyant et divers'; and the first essay of all is similar to the first essay in book II. He gives examples which on first reading hide the true subject – which is man. Let us take the first essay of book I: he lists all the different ways of softening the minds of victors in battle, some distinctly contrary to others. He plays with these opposites for three or four pages. Then he states the real subject; his attitude to it is clear and his expression of it precise: 'Certes c'est un subject merveilleusement vain, divers, ondoyant que l'homme. Il est malaisé d'y fonder jugement constant et uniforme' (Villey-Saulnier, p. 9). The adverb *merveilleusement* has a sense (now lost) of *étonnement* or *extraordinairement* (cf. Rabelais, who said Pantagruel 'estoit si merveilleusement grand'). The insinuations here are that we should 'wonder at'/'be astonished by'. Taken with *vain* the expression is almost a conceit: 'extraordinarily vain' or *merveilleusement vain* is to become a leitmotif throughout the essays whenever Montaigne deals with religious or metaphysical themes. *Divers* means everything that he is going to see in his study of man; *ondoyant* still retains the physical sense of 'undula'/'a little wave'; it marks the billowing, uncertain, variable and inconsistent nature of man. This assertion, however, is followed by a negative judgement on it: 'Il est malaisé d'y fonder jugement constant et uniforme.' From a glance at this whole sentence we can see how he is admiring the rich and complex reality of the fusion between man's body and man's mind. There is no break between the apparently physical phenomenon and the apparently intellectual judgement. From the viewpoint of immediate experience there is a constant interaction between the physiological and the psychological: they are really two sides of the same thing – the human condition.

The idea of *cheval eschappé* (I.8) entailing movement and agitation is transformed in the tenth essay, 'Du parler prompt ou tardif', into mind as opposed to judgement: 'Il semble que ce soit plus le propre de l'esprit, d'avoir son operation prompte et soudaine, et plus le propre du jugement de l'avoir lente et posée' (Villey-Saulnier, p. 39). The mind 'va gayment et librement' otherwise it is useless; this corresponds to the agitation of the mind (I.4 and I.8). Montaigne compares works that smell of the midnight oil with those which are not constrained in any way. And in this reflection there is a metaphor of the soul/mind like a donkey blindfold at his wheel: 'l'ame trop bandée et trop tenduë à son enterprise, la met au rouet, la rompt et l'empesche . . . '. Then there is a further simile: 'ainsi qu'il advient à l'eau qui, par force de se presser de sa violence et abondance, ne peut trouver issuë en un goulet ouvert' (Villey-Saulnier, p. 40). There is implicitly here a criticism of works that are too elaborated and too worked on with the skill of a rhetorician, and implicitly, too, a rejection of such writing on his own part. In the next paragraph the mind is neither *esbranlée* nor *piquée* if seen with its natural condition, nor even *secouée*, but *solicitée* – not by passion as in the example of

Cassius he had just given, but by a softer touch: 'elle veut estre
eschaufée et reveillée par les occasions estrangeres, presentes et
fortuites. Si elle va toute seule, elle ne fait que trainer et languir.
L'agitation est sa vie et sa grace' (ibid.).[1]

Already there are signs of non-premeditation and of allowing the
mind to wander towards the obscure depths of sleep/awakening,
voluntary and involuntary memory, the memory of the body as
opposed to the mind and its recollections. Immediately after
'L'agitation est sa vie et sa grace' we find this paragraph:

> Je ne me tiens pas bien en ma possession et disposition. Le hasard y
> a plus de droict que moy. L'occasion, la compaignie le branle
> mesme de ma voix, tire plus de mon esprit, que je n'y trouve lors
> que je le sonde, et employe à part moy. (ibid.)

> I cannot well containe myselfe in mine owne possession and
> disposition, chance hath more interest in it than myself; occasion,
> company, yea the change of my voice, drawes more from my minde
> than I can finde therein, when by myselfe I second and endevor to
> employ the same.

Here Montaigne takes the view that one's whole being is difficult to
keep unified. *Possession* – not only is it hard for him to exert control
over the mind; there is also the impression that he is not altogether in
possession of his mind. Very concrete, very tiny things – like the
ruffling of a breeze and perhaps, particularly, the act of speaking – do
solicite[2] his mind better than when he is voluntarily trying to make the
mind work *à part soy*. External stimuli are crucial to the kind of
internal meditation that he is engaged on.

We can say that Montaigne discovered the element of chance
working in terms of what is present at one moment, lost another
moment, found again by a chance encounter, perhaps found again by
another person. Montaigne implies here that intelligence and judgement have nothing to do with sensibility or the imagination:
impressions, reminiscences work on the mind gently, awaken it and
solicit its help. The work of intelligence and judgement comes *after*
experience – experience always comes first, as opposed to scientific
experimentation where the work of intelligence usually comes first.
This is exactly the same as Proust, who in the *Temps retrouvé*, finds
that intelligence and judgement 'n'avaient rien du tout en commun
avec la sensibilité' but 'des impressions obscures avaient quelquefois . . .

sollicité ma pensée' and made it discover not a new sensation but a new truth: 'comme si nos plus belles idées étaient comme des airs de musique qui nous reviendraient sans que nous les eussions jamais entendus, et que nous nous efforcerions d'écouter, de transcrire'.[3] The time element is there in Montaigne, too: his '[ame]' is 'reveillée par les occasions estrangeres, presentes et fortuites'. The experience is of the actual moment, living his life through the present; the past and the future have a bearing only on what he is doing or thinking now. The last sentence of the essay in the 1580 version, 'Ainsi les paroles en valent mieux que les escripts, s'il y peut avoir chois où il n'y a point de pris' (Villey-Saulnier, p. 40), refers to Montaigne's actual experience of being a lawyer, with words at his lips, and being a writer – the translation of Raimond Sebond and other works besides the *Essais*.

The imperious call to know himself, as we saw at the end of the 'Apologie' (Chapter 4), does take on an epistemological resonance. But this quest of self-knowledge is further complicated by the fact that it is in written rather than oral form. There is one moment in the *Essais* when, perhaps, this might have been shown: it is the erased passage in 'De la vanité' (III.9); it reads like this:

Ie sçay bien que ie ne lairray apres moy, aucun respondant, si affectionné de bien loing, & entendu en mon faict, comme i'ay esté au sien. Il n'y a personne à qui ie vousisse pleinement compromettre de ma peinture. Luy seul iouyssoit de ma vraye image, & l'emporta. C'est pourquoy ie me deschiffre moy-mesme, si curieusement.

(EP, pl. 895)

I know full well that I shall not leave when I die any person so beloved from far and well up in my character as I was for him. There is no one to whom I could fully commit my portrait. He alone enjoyed my true image and took it away when he died. That is the reason why I am analysing myself so precisely. (DGC)

Emotional? Very. The death of his friend La Boëtie is the real reason for writing? Maybe. The pressure of the emotion is great, and he puts an insertional mark which he then crosses out. Montaigne the artist – not Montaigne the man – thought it best to hide the reasons? Maybe. But for the critic it points to the fact that 'sincerity' is extremely difficult to prove or disprove in any writer. True sincerity is very far from autobiographical accuracy. The passage suggests that if

La Boëtie had lived there would not be any writing of the same kind. That might have been true in the early essays but, by 1588, Montaigne is discovering and recording things that never could have been talked about to anyone.[4] Thus he decided to cut out the passage. Montaigne sees that his own writing is an example of what he has been discovering:

> En mes escris mesmes je ne retrouve pas tousjours l'air de ma premiere imagination: je ne sçay ce que j'ay voulu dire, et m'eschaude souvent à corriger et y mettre un nouveau sens, pour avoir perdu le premier, qui vallait mieux. (Villey-Saulnier, p. 566)

> Even in my writings I shall not at all times finde the tracke or ayre of my first imaginations; I wot not my selfe what I would have said, and shall vexe and fret my selfe in correcting and giving a new sense to them, because I have peradventure forgotten or lost the former, which happily was better.

This is a basic trouble that affects all of us: our mind offers us something in a split second, but once we have got round to the pen that vision is lost, the colour and the light have vanished. Montaigne can say: 'Chacun à peu près en diroit autant de soy, s'il se regardoit comme moy' (ibid., p. 566). His own method of reading reaches a similar point: 'Si je m'y plantois, je m'y perdrois, et le temps: car j'ay un esprit primsautier. Ce que je ne voye de la premiere charge, je le voy moins en m'y obstinant' (ibid., p. 409). This shows clearly a creative rather than a critical intelligence: forcing oneself to concentrate entirely on something, logically trying to get at the meaning of it, any way that one might use to try to understand it – all these devices are useless for Montaigne's mind.

In the essay 'Comme nous pleurons et rions d'un mesme corps' (I.38) he suggests that there are muscles in the body which make one laugh and cry at the same time. Furthermore he asserts that it is simply a change in man's point of view:

> il n'y a rien de changé, mais nostre ame regarde la chose d'un autre oeil, et se la represente par un autre visage: *car chaque chose a plusieurs biais et plusieurs lustres.* La parenté, les anciennes accointances et amitiez saisissent nostre imagination et la passionnent pour l'heure, selon leur condition; mais le contour en est si brusque, qu'il nous eschappe.

> (ibid., p. 235: my italics)

there is nothing changed: But that our minde beholds the thing
with another eie, and under another shape, it self unto us. For
every thing hath divers faces, sundry byases, and severall lustres.
Aliance, kinred, old acquaintances, and long friendship seize on
our imagination, and at that instant passionate the same according
to their qualitie, but the turne or change of it is so violent that it
escapes us.

It is the way we look at things, the way they act, that determines a
personality; Montaigne is after that unknown personality, 'le mystère
de la personnalité', that makes all men wildly different from each
other.[5]

It is this multiplicity of time and space, this plurality of angles and
this multiformed perspective that make me think, in particular, of
Bergson, who published his *Essai sur les données immédiates de la
conscience* in 1888. In the essay he divides time into two categories:
mathematical time which is unreal and is an effect of the spatializing
tendency of the intellect, and *durée* – the multiplicity and flow of states
of consciousness. At the end of the 'Apologie' Montaigne comes to the
absolute conception of Time: we all think of nine o'clock in the
morning as something definite – the time when lectures begin, or we
start teaching, or we open our shop. This is mechanical; but there is
another way in which nine o'clock is not absolute or definite; there is
hardly a moment when it stands still 'car c'est chose mobile que le
temps et qui apparoit comme en ombre, avec la matiere coulante et
fluante tousiours, sans jamais demeurer stable ny permanente'. We
may look at the words 'present', 'future', 'past' – it is as if our
intelligence is making a structure for time to fit into, but of course
time will not ever fit: 'Et quant à ces mots: present, instant,
maintenant, par lesquels il semble que principalement nous soustenons
et fondons l'intelligence du temps . . . ' (Villey-Saulnier, p. 603).
This major breakthrough by Montaigne on the question of time will be
analysed by several different writers later, especially Bergson and
Proust. The dominant tense of the verb is the present throughout the
Essais: Montaigne's thought moves backwards and forwards and at
times catches the present moment acutely – 'A chaque minute il me
semble que je m'eschape . . . ' (ibid., p. 88). Similarly Bergson's view
of language:

Bref, le mot aux contours bien arrêtés, le mot brutal, qui
emmagasine ce qu'il y a de stable, de commun et par conséquent

d'impersonnel dans les impressions de l'humanité, écrase ou tout au
moins recouvre les impressions délicates et fugitives de notre
conscience individuelle . . .

(Edition of Paris: Presses Universitaires de France, 1976, p. 98)

Does it not recall the extremely penetrating critique of language in 'De
l'experience' (III.13) where Montaigne talks about the implications of
all human communication – nothing but commentary after commentary in order to speak intelligibly. The 'I' who is living his biography
is a mass of sensations and vague fragmentary thoughts: the flickering,
shifting, unstable moment-to-moment being of the consciousness.
Tackling words is the 'metaphysical', the 'real' Montaigne; the *Essais*
is the answer to life's questions; thus writing has become a total,
almost metaphysical enterprise with self-knowledge and self-revelation
paramount. Note how urgent his language becomes when he says: 'Je
suis affamé de me faire connoistre; et ne me chaut à combien, pourveu
que ce soit veritablement; ou, pour dire mieux, je n'ay faim de rien,
mais je crains mortellement d'estre pris en eschange par ceux à qui il
arrive de connoistre mon nom' (III.5; Villey-Saulnier, p. 847: 'I
greedily long to make my selfe knowne, nor care I at what rate, so it
be truly; or, to say better, I hunger for nothing; but I hate mortally to
be mistaken by such as shall happen to know my name'), or 'Je ne
laisse rien à desirer et deviner de moy. Si on doibt s'en entretenir, je
veus que ce soit veritablement et justement. Je reviendrois volontiers
de l'autre monde pour démentir celuy qui me formeroit autre que je
n'estois, fut ce pour m'honorer' (III.9; ibid., p. 983: 'I leave nothing
to be desired or divined of me. If one must entertaine himselfe with
them, I would have it to be truly and justly. I would willingly come
from the other world to give him the lie that should frame me other
then I had been; were it he meant to honour me'. Montaigne observes
the fabricated and shifting character of his own life. Meaning vanishes
and yet he must restore it.

Let us return to the essay 'De l'exercitation' (II.6) where, as we
saw, the notion of the subconscious appears, perhaps, for the first time
in European thought. We have discussed it partly in Chapter 3: his
own experience of the loss of consciousness when he fell off his horse.
Among the 1588–92 marginalia there are one little note and another
one which takes up to three and a half pages. The first one, 'Combien
facilement nous passons de veiller au dormir. Avec combien peu
d'interest nous perdons la connoissance de la lumiere et de nous'
(Villey-Saulnier, p. 372), is rather similar to a statement in the

'Apologie': 'Nous veillons dormans, et veillans dormons' (ibid., p. 596). This suggests that streaks of thought converge in two different essays, and both are in the 1588–92 marginalia. He used his thoughts to focus attention on different angles.[6] During the last four years of his life Montaigne was intensely creative. We can imagine him reading one essay and new thoughts developing in his mind; they provoked him to write marginal comments, and then he remembered another essay on roughly the same subject to which he could add quite different marginalia. In this way he is dealing with words in the manner of a poet: for instance, the facsimile of Eliot's 'The Waste Land' shows the creativity of mind that was engendered by the crossings-off of passages that were disapproved of by Pound. But unlike Eliot, who had a friend-poet to read his poems, Montaigne simply has Montaigne. The severe criticism of his writing is made by the creator himself.

Montaigne is exploring an unfamiliar area of psychological reality and he uses his own consciousness as his primary material, so he must articulate experience in such a way that the reader himself in turn recognizes in the *Essais* Montaigne's own movements of consciousness and sees that whatever he is going to get out of them must come from his own experience and his own movements of consciousness, not Montaigne's.

We as readers are following Ariadne's thread in the dense labyrinth of Montaigne's inner life. Literature depends on the reader for its existence and therefore it posits a demand: the reader is appealed upon to continue reading a work, to read it 'properly' and 'seriously'. The larger piece of the marginalia right at the end of 'De l'exercitation' begins the process of finding humanity in the *Essais* as a whole. It starts thus: 'Et ne me doibt on sçavoir mauvais gré pour tant, si je la communique. Ce qui me sert, peut aussi par accident servir à un autre. Au demeurant, je ne gaste rien, je n'use que du mien. Et, si je fay le fol, c'est à mes despends et sans l'interest de personne' (ibid., p. 377: 'Yet ought no man to blame me if I impart the same. What serves my turne may haply serve another mans: otherwise I marre nothing; what I make use of is mine owne'). This minute analysis of sensations – the sight of blood brings in the functioning of the brain, the soft sweetness and languor that accompanies sleep, the automatic functioning of a great part of our actions – this precision of detail, this depth of observation, this choice of metaphors to render his thought transparent and this Proustian interconnection of body and mind – *perhaps* someone else will one day use this discovery and go much further than Montaigne, I, the writer can go. This is the true beginning of the *moraliste* tradition in French literature: writers who are concerned with the nature of man. Montaigne presents us with a knowledge of the human mind, a vision of human life as it is in the universe. The fact that this is a non-metaphysical and a non-religious examination of man's behaviour with lucidity and human sympathy is important. It is through the psychological investigation of the *Essais* that Montaigne can attain a conception of self. He stresses the difficulty of the enterprise and the challenge of the task: 'C'est une espineuse entreprinse, et plus qu'il ne semble, de suyvre une alleure si vagabonde que celle de nostre esprit; de penetrer les profondeurs opaques de ses replis internes; de choisir et arrester tant de menus airs de ses agitations' (ibid., p. 378).

There is first of all the problem of language: language is based on the mechanism of abstract and general ideas and does not describe things in their individuality; the right word becomes a functional necessity; Montaigne's solution is to have a concrete terminology which attempts to communicate the 'thinginess' of things; thus imagery and metaphors break down the abstractions of categories. The *entreprinse* is *espineuse*, which Cotgrave gives as 'Thornie, brierie, full of brambles'; the depths of his flickering consciousness are *opaques* – 'Duskie, gloomie, obscure, thicke and darke, or thicke-shadowing, blacke'.

Now he tells us more of his method in edging inwards this psychological penetration: 'Il y a plusieurs années que je n'ay que moy pour visée à mes pensées, que je ne contrerolle et estudie que moy; et, si j'estudie autre chose, c'est pour soudain le coucher sur moy, ou en mov, pour mieux dire' (ibid., p. 378: 'Many yeares are past since I have no other aime whereto my thoughts bend, but my selfe, and that I controule and study nothing but my selfe. And if I study anything else, it is immediately to place it upon, or to say better in my selfe').

Everything he writes about is seen as on a line with his essays and assails to paint himself. The self-portrait is not progressing violently but slowly. Not only must the analysis be constant but he must also try to organize the bits and pieces of himself that he is studying: 'Encore se faut-il testoner, encore se faut-il ordonner et renger pour sortir en place.' 'Yet must a man handsomely trimme-up, yea and dispose and range himselfe to appear on the Theatre of this world'. We note that this sentence means that there is an aesthetic aim in this self-portrait which we shall examine in our next chapter. Imperfections must be recorded as well as qualities, in fact everything of the 'estre et branle de leur ame'. In a way, Montaigne says, his writings of himself are like confessions:

> Nous nous disons religieusement à Dieu, et à nostre confesseur, comme noz voisins à tout le peuple. Mais nous n'en disons, me respondra-on, que les accusations. Nous disons donc tout: car nostre vertu mesme est fautiere et repentable. (ibid., p. 379)[7]

> We religiously shrive our selves to God and our Confessor, as our neighbours to all the people. But will some answer me, we report but accusation; wee then report all: For even our virtue it self is faulty and repentable.

There are the two statements – 'Mon mestier et mon art, c'est vivre' and 'Ce ne sont mes gestes que j'escris, c'est moy, c'est mon essence' (ibid., p. 379) – which relay to his readers a sort of 'metaphysical' Montaigne, living, breathing, eating, writing, observing, scanning his life, thoughts, movements, sensations and emotions. Of this essay we can say with Proust:

> En réalité, chaque lecteur est, quand il lit, le propre lecteur de soi-même. L'ouvrage de l'écrivain n'est qu'une espèce d'instrument optique qu'il offre au lecteur afin de lui permettre de discerner ce que, sans ce livre, il n'eut peut-être pas vu en soi-même.[8]

This introspection and this attempt to capture moving reality are composed with further orchestrations, one of them being the constant fluctuation of the world and of self. In the first chapter of book II, 'De l'inconstance de nos actions', we can see Montaigne making concrete images and vocabulary break through conventions of abstract terminology and capturing in a better way aspects of our psychological make-up. Mankind is fluttering, floating, flying irresolutely at the puff of a wind

> aller apres les inclinations de nostre apetit, à gauche, à dextre, contre-mont, contre-bas, selon le vent des occasions nous emporte. Nous ne pensons ce que nous voulons, qu'à l'instant que nous le voulons . . . Ce que nous avons à cett'heure proposé, nous le changeons tantost, et tantost encore retournons sur nos pas: ce n'est que branle et inconstance.
>
> (Villey-Saulnier, p. 333)

to follow the inclination of our appetite this way and that way, on the left and on the right hand; upward and downeward, according as the winde of occasions doth transport us: we never thinke on what we would have, but at the instant we would have it . . . What we even now purposed we alter by and by, and presently returne to our former biase: all is but changing, motion, and inconstancy.

The fragmentation, the breaking up into smaller units are there, but also introspection depends not only on a *vent des occasions* but even on the angle of vision that Montaigne has chosen: 'mais en outre je me remue et trouble moy mesme par l'instabilité de ma posture . . . Je donne à mon ame tantost un visage, tantost un autre, selon le costé où je la couche' (ibid., p. 335). Here the dissolution of personality – just a congregation of diverse and multiple facets – makes us see that there is no single identity that we can pin down. And yet there is something permanent, as we shall see in a minute, but before that we are going to examine a famous passage from the beginning of 'Du repentir' (III.2; Villey-Saulnier, pp. 804–5).

(B) Les autres forment l'homme; je le recite et en represente un particulier bien mal formé, et lequel, si j'avoy à façonner de nouveau, je ferois vrayement bien autre qu'il n'est. Meshuy c'est fait. Or les traits de ma peinture ne forvoyent point, quoy qu'ils se changent et diversifient. Le monde n'est qu'une branloire perenne. Toutes choses y branlent sans cesse: la terre, les rochers du Caucase, les pyramides d'Ægypte, et du branle public et du leur. La constance mesme n'est autre chose qu'un branle plus languissant. Je ne puis asseurer mon object. Il va trouble et chancelant, d'une yvresse naturelle. Je le prens en ce point, comme il est, en l'instant que je m'amuse à luy. Je ne peints pas l'estre. Je peints le passage: non un passage d'aage en autre, ou, comme dict le peuple, de sept en sept ans, mais de jour en jour, de minute en minute. Il faut accommoder mon histoire à l'heure. Je pourray tantost changer, non de fortune seulement, mais aussi d'intention. C'est un contrerolle de divers et muables accidens et d'imaginations irresoluës et, quand il y eschet, contraires: soit que je sois autre moy-mesme, soit que je saisisse les subjects par autres circonstances et considerations. Tant y a que je me contredits bien à l'adventure, mais la verité, comme disoit Demades, je ne la contre-dy point. Si mon ame pouvoit prendre pied, je ne m'essaierois pas, je me resoudrois: elle est tousjours en apprentissage et en espreuve. Je propose une vie basse et sans lustre, c'est tout un. On attache aussi bien toute la philosophie morale à une vie populaire et privée que à une vie de plus riche estoffe: chaque homme porte la forme entiere de l'humaine condition.

(C) Les autheurs se communiquent au peuple par quelque marque particuliere et estrangere; moy le premier par mon estre universel, comme Michel de Montaigne, non comme grammairien ou poëte ou jurisconsulte. Si le monde se plaint de quoy je parle trop de moy, je me plains de quoy il ne pense seulement pas à soy.

Others fashion man, I repeat him; and represent a particular one, but ill made; and whom were I to forme anew, he should be far other than he is; but he is now made. And though the lines of my picture change and vary, yet lose they not themselves. The world runnes all on wheeles. All things therein moove without inter-mission; yea, the earth, the rockes of Caucasus, and the Pyramides of Ægypt, both with the publike and their own motion. Constancy itselfe is nothing but a languishing and wavering dance. I cannot settle my object; it goeth so unquietly and staggering, with a naturall drunkennesse; I take it in this plight, as it is at the instant I amuse myselfe about it. I describe not the essence but the passage; not a passage from age to age, or as the people reckon, from seaven yeares to seaven, but from day to day, from minute to minute. My history must be fitted to the present. I may soone change, not onely fortune, but intention. It is a counter-roule of divers and variable accidents and irresolute imaginations, and sometimes contrary; whether it be that myselfe am other, or that I apprehend subjects by other circumstances and considerations. Howsoever, I may perhaps gaine-say myselfe, but truth (as Demades said) I never gaine-say. Were my mind setled, I would not essay, but resolve myselfe. It is still a prentise and a probationer. I propose a meane life and without luster; 'tis all one. They fasten all morall Philosophy as well to a popular and private life as to one of richer stuffe. Every man beareth the whole stampe of humane condition. Authors communicate themselves unto the world by some special and strange marke; I the first, by my generall disposition; as Michael de Montaigne, not as a grammarian, or a poet, or a lawyer. If the world complaine, I speak too much of myselfe, I complaine it thinkes no more of itselfe.

Who are the others? Every writer who has written on man: this means all Greek and Roman writers and every author whom

Montaigne has read. They all mould, fashion, shape man: that is, they draw a circle round a man; biographies are books where one writer thinks he can see *exactly* and state *fully* the characteristics of another man. I, the writer Montaigne, recite him, rehearse him, repeat him and tell him over again and again. Other writers are external, moving horizontally along a path; I am internal, moving vertically along my route. Notice how this first antithesis is conveyed without conjunctions or indeed any connectives. It is an astounding claim and yet it is true. The last paragraph is a marginal comment and it helps us understand this antithesis: other writers are specialists – be they poets, grammarians or lawyers – whereas Montaigne is offering himself to the literary world simply as Michel de Montaigne, but it is a whole person as opposed to the particular form of a specialist.

The comic tone of this passage interrelates with vast figures like God and our cosmos, and is intersected by realist concretions and movement with an intensity which is piercing. The comment on himself as a particularly badly shaped man is in an amused, slightly mocking tone: 'meshuy c'est fait' – 'but now it's done'. I am not God the creator. I can never be him. No lament, no mature resignation. Simply a comic and wry acceptance that he is this way. The play between I and I, between Montaigne the author and Montaigne the theme, is the centre of the passage, and the original intellectual effort to probe the problem of self-analysis breaks through the style. It is not a logical argument going through points and proving right certain intellectual thoughts. It is more the association of ideas, the intuitive faculty of seeing different things from different viewpoints, joining thoughts together and grouping them on the trajectory of words. When Montaigne seems disorganized and chaotic it is because we, as active readers, have not grapsed the structures of his thought.

Basically, the passage is a syllogism: I describe myself; I am a creature who constantly changes; *ergo*, the description, too, must conform to this and constantly change. But it is encrusted with 'poetic' and imaginative passages which are astonishing in the light they shed. Take the theme of time and space beginning with 'Le monde n'est qu'une branloire perenne'. He has chosen the metaphor of swinging or dancing. Hear what Cotgrave says about *bransle*: 'also, a brawle, or daunce, wherein many men, and women holding by the hands sometimes in a ring, and otherwhiles at length, move all together'. This world picture in motion is reminiscent of Ronsard's fascination with the dance of the stars in, for example, 'Les Estoilles', where, as finely analysed by Odette de Mourgues,

Objects are not juxtaposed, but born out of each other and they change according to the will of stars. Our bodies have their germs in lumps of earth and dead trees, water originates from the sea. Centuries follow each other in endless succession; so do the seasons, cold, wet and warm in turn, and every year the earth yields its bounty of flowers and corn. And man's fate follows the same ineluctable course. There is no break in the sequence of events, no pause.[9]

To the suggestiveness of the *branloire* where our cosmos seems to dance, Montaigne adds 'branlent . . . du branle public' – and ends the sentence with 'un branle plus languissant', thus making us feel the jigging, swinging, dancing of all things moved by time. If we could visualize the pyramids of Egypt two thousand years ago they would have appeared very different from what they are today. So would whole countries as they, too, are geologically altered according to soil erosion or the sea taking away such apparently firm and fixed things as cliffs or rocks. Then Montaigne makes constancy also move and become a see-saw rolling slowly from inconstancy to inconstancy.

Between constancy and the next sentence, 'Je ne puis asseurer mon object', a clause is missing: it would say that I, the object I am studying, being a fragment of the world, must likewise be subject to the double change mentioned in the previous paragraph – the public and the private motions. 'Mon object va trouble' – the object is his self, an abstract concept, and so he chooses a metaphor – that of drunkenness – to make it visible and concrete. We are, so to speak, asked to visualize a drunken man tottering on a path, slipping from side to side and bumping into natural hazards such as fences or cows. No longer is consciousness a vague abstract thing; it is moving – 'va trouble et chancelant' ('it goeth so unquietly and staggering': Florio); there is the nebulousness of everything when we are drunk, and yet Montaigne seizes on the instant, the very precise moment when the self is tottering, and writes or, rather, pins down that moment. The elusive nature of momentary awareness, the shifts of awareness from one state to another, from one instant to the next, are acutely observed by Montaigne, and he states the workings of consciousness as 'Je ne peints pas l'estre. Je peints le passage'. It is essentially the *movement* of thought between instants that he wishes to describe; not a movement of one year to the next in a linear autobiography but 'de minute en minute'. Thus Montaigne stresses the microscopic nature of his thought and its mobility in time present, so that bits of statements like

'Moy à cette heure et moy tantost sommes bien deux . . . ' (III.9; Villey-Saulnier, p. 964) run through the *Essais* as leitmotifs. Although Montaigne as a man may disapprove of wild thought, disorganized and impressionistic as it is, Montaigne the artist, far from disapproving of the *fantasies*, wants to encourage them so that words like 'me plaisent le mieux . . . à l'improuveu . . . lors que je les cerche moins' are entirely approving terms. When he is on horseback having these conversations with himself, he is in the 'entretiens de suite' fully involved, but the time-gap between having the thoughts, the form, the question and answer and writing them down is disastrous; even the blinking of an eye is enough to make them disappear, and there remains in the memory, the voluntary memory, nothing but 'une vaine image'. The attempt to call up things through the reflective consciousness is useless for 'plus j'ahane à le trouver, plus je l'enfonce en oubliance' (III.5; Villey-Saulnier, p. 876). Willpower is therefore unable to pick what it wants from the storehouse of memory – 'elle me sert à son heure et non pas à la mienne' (II.17; Villey-Saulnier, p. 650). Involuntary memory is a kind of *moment privilégié* – the impulsion given by outside reality:

> L'occasion, la compaignie, le branle mesme de ma voix, tire plus de mon esprit que je n'y trouve lors que je le sonde et emploie à part moy . . . je ne me trouve pas où je me cherche; et me trouve plus par rencontre que par l'inquisition de mon jugement.
>
> (I.10; Villey-Saulnier, p. 40)

occasion, company, yea the change of my voice drawes more from my minde than I can finde therein, when by myselfe I second and endevor to employ the same . . . where I seeke myselfe, I finde not myselfe: and I finde myselfe more by chance, than by the search of mine owne judgement.

From all this fluctuation in time, space, personality, we acknowledge Montaigne's absolute honesty when he says in our passage that 'je me contredits bien à l'adventure' but truth he does not contradict, as Demades that brilliant orator and diplomat at Athens (350–319 BC) has it. What does this mean? Truth equals here: that every minute Montaigne records is his faithful honesty in trying to put over to his reader what he actually experiences. The reader can find him inconsistent, problematic and illogical, but he cannot find him insincere, deceptive or lacking in integrity, for he is only 'trying out' his experience, 'assailing' himself and the world or essaying his thoughts: 'elle [ame] est tousjours en apprentissage et en espreuve'. Montaigne's concern for intellectual honesty means that he must keep fidelity at the forefront of his mind in this sustained process of observation and self-criticism. His world was a 'lived', and not an 'explained' one.

The next paragraph beginning 'Je propose une vie basse' contains the biggest claim that Montaigne has made – and, indeed, any writer for the next few centuries: 'chaque homme porte la forme entiere de l'humaine condition'. 'Every man beareth the whole stamp of human condition' (Florio). *Condition* – the general disposition of human nature; *forme* – the outline or shape which marks humanity. This general and astonishing claim is just, for from the very beginning he has stated, 'en l'estude que je fay, duquel le subject c'est l'homme . . . ' or 'Certes, c'est un subject merveilleusement vain, divers, et ondoyant, que l'homme' (Villey-Saulnier, p. 9: an (A) passage). The claim is deepened by a sentence later in 'Du repentir'; 'il n'est personne, s'il s'escoute, qui ne descouvre en soy une forme sienne, une forme maistresse, qui luicte contre l'institution, et contre la tempeste des passions qui luy sont contraires' (ibid., p. 811 – a (B) passage: 'There is no man (if he listen to himselfe) that doth not discover in himselfe a peculiar forme of his, a swaying forme, which wrestleth against the institution, and against the tempests of passions, which are contrary unto him').

This central part of character which remains the same, this *forme maistresse* or 'master mould' as Screech would say, which every man has, is precisely the permanent force in mankind, and it means that we do know (at least half the time) what we are doing in the task of living. The self-portraiture grows so important in his mind that the marginalia in the *exemplaire* show that it is the only thing that he cares about. To give the reader the whole of himself needs prudence, conscientiousness, honesty, no illusions, no falling in love with himself nor excusing any act or behaviour that comes to the surface.

To the attraction of Montaigne as a writer is added now, for me, the inward fragrance of values which come from the interrelationship between life and literature: self-knowledge – the physical, moral and aesthetic values we work out in personal terms; attempts to discover the basic *me* – the *forme maistresse* – which is at the base of one's personal identity; the lesson of solitude, of having 'une arrière boutique' which is safe from external circumstances, the getting rid of all illusions like Christianity; the rejection of authority; the relying not on one's memory but on one's judgement; the desire to be supple and nimble and sharp in one's intellect; in literary criticism the rejection of topics like 'Victor Hugo's nightcap' or 'How many children had Lady Macbeth?'; the need to be honest with oneself and others; the knowledge that books are an exercise in judgement and a spur to action rather than a means of instruction; the accepting of the relativity of all things, including knowledge – everything has limits; the attempt to be adaptable to all external circumstances and the realization that one's role in life is to mould, form, pattern one's life in accordance with one's *forme maistresse*, that is, 'sçavoyr jouyr loiallement de son estre'. This list of values is to me the perfume exhaled by the *Essais*.

Montaigne gives us the first study of man based on introspection. How different it is from Barrès' archaeological excavations into the self in *Un Homme libre*. And how dissimilar it is in tone and attitude from that of Roquentin in Sartre's *La Nausée*, who exists, the past does not (something similar to Montaigne) but he is a gluey viscous self to which fragmentary thoughts occur and sensations happen, and if things exist with names, then they must exist to the point of degeneration and obscenity. Sartre seems to leave the solitary individual in his solipsistic centre capable only of a sort of Platonic solution – the Negress's song, a circle of purity, the pure work of art exists in another world – which does not fit the premisses.

By painting the *passage* from one state to another Montaigne does communicate with his 'essence', which is not a single metaphysical entity, but the action of thought on things, a continual movement between things and a judgement on each new thing as a new source of richness. The freedom from stiffness or rigidity, the flexibility of intelligence, the capacity for ready adaptation to various conditions, the fluid, pliant and nimble mind, the free, rapid and varied execution of tiny details – all make us see the direct expressions of personal substance.

The possibility of intense pleasure in this self-analysis – 'je me goûte moi-même' – is a double one, both for the writer and for the reader. For the writer, 'moi, je me roule en moi-même', the whole enterprise of breaking down abstract general ideas is mind-stretching, but he can see that it is only through words that he can catch the nuances of his psychological life. And the reader can watch the writer in 'De l'inconstance de nos actions' (Villey-Saulnier, p. 337) replacing the stilted vision of our actions by one that captures the coloured reality within us by constant metaphors: concrete terms for psychology. Take this metaphor, for example: 'Nous sommes tous de lopins et d'une contexture si informe et diverse, que chaque piece, chaque moment, faict son jeu' (Florio's translation: 'We are all framed of flaps and patches and of so shapelesse and diverse a contexture that every peece and every moment playeth his part'). We may note the frequency of words like *contexture* throughout the *Essais* – an emphasis on construction and coherence – but we may note, too, that this word is denied by the *lopins* image, suggesting that human personality is a jumble of heterogeneous elements with no unifying principle. It hints at the fact that our actions appear *inconstantes*, not because they have no underlying unity but because we do not perceive that unity. There is a tension between the *lopins* and the *contexture*.

How very modern and audacious Montaigne is when he approaches a taboo subject like sex.[10] He dares to say and to explore and elucidate a good deal more than sixteenth-century authors like Rabelais, Des Périers, Nicholas de Troyes or Brantôme. He realizes that the kinds of language that are most important for discussing copulation are unquotable and that language is at its poorest in this area. We remember his saying in the 'Au lecteur' (which he hardly touched up since its appearance in the first edition of 1580):

> Mes defauts s'y liront au vif, et ma forme naïfve, autant que la reverence publicque me l'a permis. Que si j'eusse esté entre ces nations qu'on dict vivre encore sous la douce liberté des premieres loix de nature, je t'asseure que je m'y fusse tres-volontiers peint tout entier, et tout nud.
>
> (Villey-Saulnier, p. 3)

> My imperfections shall therein be read to the life, and my naturall forme discerned, so farre-forth as publike reverence hath permitted me. For if my fortune had beene to have lived among those nations which yet are said to live under the sweet liberty of Nature's first and uncorrupted lawes, I assure thee, I would most willingly have pourtrayed myselfe fully and naked.

Towards the end of his essay 'Sur des vers de Virgile' (III.5) he asserts firmly that sex is central to his self-portrait; 'Chacune de mes pieces me faict esgalement moy que tout autre. Et nulle autre ne me faict plus proprement homme que cette cy. Je dois au publiq universellement mon pourtrait' (Villey-Saulnier, p. 887: 'Each of my pieces are equally mine, one as another: and no other doth more properly make me a man then this. My whole pourtraiture I universally owe unto the world').

As we saw in the last chapter, Montaigne had a sophisticated approach to sex: the extension of the pre-intercourse period, delaying tactics and secrecy. He accepts the humiliating reality to be found in the make-up of any human being. He is aware of his own temperament, his hypersensitive nervous system and his impetuous excitability. In 'Sur des vers de Virgile' the confession is boldly put: 'Chacun est discret en la confession, on le devoit estre en l'action; la hardiesse de faillir est auncunement [somewhat] compensée et bridée, par la hardiesse de le confesser' (ibid., p. 845). We read into this daring statement the fact that Montaigne has never been discreet in his actions: from the time he was being educated at the Collège de Guyenne to 1588, 'je ne suis pas de si long temps cassé de l'estat et suitte de ce Dieu [Cupid] que je n'aye la memoire informée de ses forces et valeurs' (ibid., p. 848), he has been over-virile *locis genitalibus*.

In this essay he gives a last and affectionate farewell to a well-loved theme – sex and lust.[11] A number of leitmotifs come in: sexual intercourse is a natural act and yet akin to the bestial; he condemns society for giving differing laws of chastity to both sexes. Montaigne knows (as did all writers – witness the whole theme of cuckoldry through the ages) that women are more lustful than men. Chastity is far more difficult than any other virtue: 'Il n'y a poinct de faire plus espineux qu'est ce non faire, ny plus actif.' Lust is violent, otherwise it would be unnatural; love is insatiable – 'elle va tousjours outre sa possession' (ibid., p. 885). Montaigne states the fact that men need clothing and outward ceremony to excite their desire: 'Apprenons aux dames à se faire valoir, à s'estimer, à nous amuser et à nous piper.' Eyes, speech, shifts of the body can be stimulating and sexually inviting. His own attitude to marriage is that the main purpose is to procreate; lasvicious lovemaking does not enter the question, and the relationship is more akin to friendship than to love. He nails the thesis in quite hard when he says 'un bon mariage, s'il en est' (ibid., p. 851), looking forward to the famous maxim 113 by La Rochefoucauld: 'Il y a de bons mariages, mais il n'y en a point de délicieux.' Montaigne's language is exceptionally concrete in this essay, and yet how universal his statements are: for instance, 'cet excez de ma licence' and 'ces vertus couardes et mineuses nées de nos imperfections'. The balance between the ills of the body and those of the mind is beautifully put through the imagery of light in the two verbs qualifying them; 'Les maus du cors s'esclercissent en augmentant . . . Les maus de lame s'obscurcissent en leur force . . . ' (EP, pl. 765). The imagery hovering around vice is so concrete that we almost 'see' an ulcer-like erosion in the human body which Montaigne is plucking out: 'Voila pourquoi il les faut souvent remanier au iour, d'une main impiteuse, [he had put *rude* at first, then crossed it out and wrote *impiteuse*] les ouurir et arracher du creus de nostre poitrine' (ibid.). It makes us think of Baudelaire's poem 'Au lecteur' where there is a similar (although much more Romantic than Montaigne) shuttle between abstract vices and concrete ulcers:

> La sottise, l'erreur, le péché, la lésine,
> Occupent nos esprits et travaillent nos corps,
> Et nous alimentons nos aimables remords,
> Comme les mendiants nourrissent leur vermine.

Montaigne's comments on his own vice (and therefore everyone's vice) are a preparation for La Rochefoucauld's *Maximes*. For example, 'Ceux qui le celent à autruy le celent à eus mesmes . . . ' can be matched by 'nous nous déguisons à nous-mêmes' (119) which 'also implies a constant struggle with a cunning antagonist who does his best to camouflage his true features. The climate of our inner life is that of self-deception.'[12] Or this statement, 'Les maus de lame s'obscurcissent en leur force: le plus malade les sent le moins . . . ' (EP, pl. 765), with the metaphoric light and darkness through the verb *s'obscurcissent*, is remarkably like the *moralisme* of La Rochefoucauld.

Sex, in 'Sur des vers de Virgile', is seen by readers as being one of the most human and humane points that Montaigne makes. The whole question of *lasciveté, l'amour, la concupiscence* is to be viewed in the context of life and literature, and the position of *la volupté* in the hierarchy of values around love is discussed firmly. The marginalia in the *Essais* also pose some problems. For instance, the deliberate alterations in using terms for passions. Thus, for example, in 'De la moderation' (EP, pl. 165) we find that it is 'L'amitié que nous portons à nos femmes': it is not *l'amour*. Lower down that page we find crossed out 'soit en l'amitié, soit aux effects de la iouïssance'. Intercourse in 1588 he had called 'cette accointance' (EP, pl. 167); he now changes it to 'l'embrassement'. There are deletions as well as alterations: for example, the question of homosexuality. In a marginal note (EP, pl. 803) there are signs of little alteration and it is finally deleted. Montaigne hesitated and finally crossed out 'L'amour des garçons' and put 'en toute espece d'amour'. I think that further research on homosexuality in the marginalia might bring forth interesting *trouvailles*. The marginalia make me feel that Montaigne is doing what Queneau does in writing novels. 'On peut faire rimer des situations ou des personnages comme on fait rimer les mots; on peut même se contenter d'allitérations' (*Bâtons, chiffres et lettres* (Paris: Gallimard, 1950, p. 42). Research on the marginalia would enable one to see the fruits clearly and sample them with care so that the results would be 'placed' not in a 'theoretical system or a system determined by abstract consideration' but in an 'organisation of similarly "placed" things'.[13]

Introspection goes hand in hand with general reflection on the *condition humaine*. Even if no one reads his *Essais* it will not have been in vain, for writing down events or thoughts Montaigne has made some thing 'de couleurs plus nettes' than merely the minute thought, sensation or behaviour as they were. 'Je n'ay pas plus faict mon livre que mon livre m'a faict, livre consubstantiel à son autheur, d'une occupation, membre de ma vie' ('Du Démentir', II.18; Villey-Saulnier, p. 665). There is a certain deep disquiet in Montaigne – which makes him very different from the serene man that literary labels call him – a disquiet which is rumbling beneath the *Essais*.

We are trying to recapture Montaigne in an imaginative way in order to project his mind and personality more exactly for twentieth-century readers. The tendency of both traditional scholarship and *la nouvelle critique* is to neglect the plain meaning of literary texts in favour of extraneous considerations. Quite simply, Montaigne in observing himself so scrupulously finds what is in each one of us. As an intelligent critic and creative artist he sends us back to the text and makes us read what is there a thousand times. Human make-up is merely a texture of contradictions, conscious and half-conscious aspects which are continually changing. Montaigne gives us a portrait of man, through a particular individual.

Finally we must answer several critics when they say that Montaigne cared little for men but was fond of mankind: a charge that his frequent use of 'le vulgaire' or 'le menu peuple' would lead one to suspect. But Donald Frame, in a fine article, looks at the *exemplaire* and shows convincingly that Montaigne had a 'vastly heightened sense of identification with all mankind'.[14] He argues that there is a change of attitude from a slight disdain of 'le vulgaire' to a rather more optimistic view in which even acute pain leaves life still worth living, for we are 'tous du vulgaire' (EP, pl. 509). I fully agree with this point and would go further in quoting another passage:

(C) Les paisans simples sont honnestes gens, et honnestes gens les philosphes, ou, selon nostre temps, des natures fortes et claires, enrichies d'une large instruction de sciences utiles. Les mestis qui ont dedaigné le premier siege d'ignorance de lettres, et n'ont peu joindre l'autre (le cul entre deux selles, desquels je suis, et tant d'autres), sont dangereux, ineptes, importuns: ceux icy troublent le monde. Pourtant de ma part je me recule tant que je puis dans le premier et naturel siege, d'où je me suis pour neant essayé de partir.

('Des vaines subtilitez', I.54; Villey-Saulnier, p. 313)

The simple peasants are honest men, so are philosophers (or as our time nameth them, strong and cleare natures), enriched with a large instruction of profitable sciences. The mongrell sort of husband-men, who have disdained the first forme of ignorance of letters, and could never reach unto the other (as they that sit betweene two stooles, of which besides so many others I am one) are dangerous, peevish, foolish, and importunate, and they which trouble the world most. Therefore doe I (as much as lieth in me withdraw my selfe into the first and naturall seat, whence I never assaied to depart.

The mature Montaigne depicts himself as a sort of mongrel sitting 'le cul entre deux selles', where the very analogy is rough, earthy and unspiritual. The sense of human dignity is clothed wrily with a garment of absurdity; the paradox is there, and Montaigne accepts it with a smile.

CHAPTER 9

The Art de Vivre: Experience and Aesthetics

> J'ay mis tous mes efforts à former ma vie. Voylà mon mestier et mon ouvrage. Je suis moins faiseur de livres que de nulle autre besoigne.

The most difficult thing about Montaigne is to find the core in the centre of an essay. As readers we analyse different aspects to emphasize different points; we decide which of an essay's various themes is the essential one and which are the 'digressions'. The essays in book III are a great deal richer in imagery; they are more clearly orchestrated, and leitmotifs link one essay to another. They are all about Montaigne's basic preoccupations: ethics, politics, personality, diversion, sex or lust, *le masque*, *la parole*, experience, old age, death, his own writing of himself and the way he chooses to express himself.

In many chapters of this book we have talked nonchalantly of Montaigne's experience, but are we sure that we know what Montaigne means by *expérience*? In classical Latin *experientia* meant three things; first, a trial, proof or experiment – 'experientia tentare quaedam' as Varro said; second, effort or endeavour; and, third, the knowledge gained by repeated trials, experimental knowledge, practice, experience. Montaigne takes over these three meanings and adds (what is the English meaning of 'experience') the something directly perceived or felt via the body and senses with the force of personal acquaintance or participation. Only after a sensuous contact with the phenomenon come deductions of the intellect, comparisons, analogies for explaining the phenomenon. It is opposed to speculation and to imagination. It is the most immediate, and the least intellectual, apprehension of life through the body.[1]

In one way experience provides the central theme to all the essays in book III (particularly 'Sur des vers de Virgile' and 'De la vanité') but it is crucial to the last essay, 'De l'experience' (III.13). All the apparently superficial traits of 'autobiography', the irrelevant air, the mock-affectation are recurrent themes of the *peinture du moi*; they are profound because Montaigne has discovered the one thing that reason or speculation cannot explore. 'Enfin toute cette fricassée que je barbouille icy' (Villey-Saulnier, p. 1079) means it is firsthand knowledge he records rather than a second hand knowledge gained by reading books. The themes of health, of eating and drinking, of sleeping – 'Le dormir a occupé une grande partie de ma vie' (ibid., p. 1096) – and of disease are closely textured in the essay, and it is the actual experiencing of, say, symptoms of a disease like gallstones that makes this essay so exciting and rewarding. Coupled with the themes of health and disease, there comes custom which frees us from bondage to routine, followed by the flexibility of Montaigne's own nature. The richness of the essay lies in the interweaving of threads of ideas with fibres from his actual experience to form a texture of splendid complexity. Let us take, for instance, the way the intellect works when it is uncontrolled by actual experience.

The attack against intellectual deduction takes on the major part of the beginning of the essay. Instead of seizing reality the intellect distorts it; it makes up general rules which are fixed and immovable, instead of seeing that diversity and variety of phenomena are perhaps the only things that can be seen. For instance, jurisdiction: laws can never cover all the variations of actions, and anyway actions are not fixed but continually moving. 'Il y a peu de relation de nos actions, qui sont en perpetuelle mutation, avec les loix fixes et immobiles' (ibid., p. 1066). Classification oversimplifies behaviour and, what is more, language, legal jargon makes one lose sight of what the words stand for: 'Pourquoy est-ce que nostre langage commun, si aisé à tout autre usage, devient obscur et non intelligible en un contract et testament . . . ? (ibid., p. 1066). Abstraction never fills the gaps between thousands of concrete facts: 'Au rebours, nous obscurcissons et ensevelissons l'intelligence; nous ne la descouvrons plus qu'à la mercy de tant de clostures et barrieres' (ibid., p. 1068). Montaigne uses fine concrete phrases to suggest that man is forever chasing after the right subtlety and forever falls into obscurity. The multitude of commentaries and interpretations makes one see that Montaigne was seeing clear-sightedly the end of the Renaissance, 'd'un subjet nous en faisons mille, et retombons en multipliant et subdivisant, à l'infinité des atomes d'Epicurus' (ibid., p. 1067). But he goes much further than merely giving a criticism of the Renaissance; he suggests that secondhand material, that is, the printed word, the value of predigested material, is inherently in the workings of our intelligence: 'il ne faict que fureter et quester, et va sans cesse tournoiant, bastissant et s'empestrant en sa besongne, comme nos vers de soye et s'y estouffe' (ibid., p. 1068). We are trapped by the way our mind works; we see truth from a distance; once we approach it, we are strangled in the difficulty and obscurity of it so that we are in an eternal *chasse de connaissance*. We can see that words take us further and further away from the core of truth. Language is inadequate as a psychological and metaphysical instrument, 'on eschange un mot pour un autre mot, et souvent plus incogneu' (ibid., p. 1069). We interpret the interpretations: 'il y a plus affaire à interpreter les interpretations qu'à interpreter les choses, et plus de livres sur les livres que sur autre subject: nous ne faisons que nous entregloser'. At which point in the argument Montaigne realizes his writing is involved: '(B) Combien souvent et sottement à l'avanture ay-je estandu mon livre à parler de soy?' In reading what he had said, he is urged to make it much clearer; he glosses the adverb *sottement*: 'Foolishly, if it were but for this reason, that I should have remembered that what I speake of others they doe the like of me' (Florio). Montaigne perceives full well that he is caught in the same trap – that for all his honesty, his frenetic thirst for being truly and properly understood, his attempt to portray himself from every point of view, his urgent desire to give the essence of himself, complete sincerity is impossible because of the reader in the text: 'à poinct nommé j'escry de moy et de mes escrits comme de mes autres actions, que mon theme se renverse en soy, je ne sçay si chacun la prendra' (ibid., p. 1069). In living his biography, in offering complete self-manifestation, Montaigne can see himself becoming a different Montaigne, can see the interconnections between the man who lives and the man who writes: 'Je n'ay pas plus faict mon livre que mon livre m'a faict, livre consubstantiel à son autheur, d'une occupation propre, membre de ma vie; non d'une occupation et fin tierce et estrangière comme tous autres livres' (II.18; Villey-Saulnier, p. 665: 'I have no more made my booke then my booke hath made me. A booke consubstantiall to his author: of a peculiar and fit occupation. A member of my life. Not of an occupation and end strange and forraine, as all other bookes'). The multiplicity of selves is quite clearly known by him.

Montaigne returns to justice in this denigration of man's intellect; we must see that justice is a social institution divorced from experience; the authority of law is rather a social power than an authority of right or reason: 'les loix se maintiennent en credit, non par ce qu'elles sont justes, mais par ce qu'elles sont loix' (ibid., p. 1072). As part of his attack on intellectual deduction Montaigne uses personal experience to denounce medicine: 'L'experience est proprement sur son fumier au subject de la medecine, où la raison luy quite toute la place' (ibid., p. 1079). All the negative points about man's intellect are explored very acutely by Montaigne. But he knows how much we need intelligence, if only for the reason that we must know how little we know.

We shall pause on, perhaps, the most subtle of all the essays – 'De la diversion' (III.4) – to perceive how Montaigne organizes his intellect, coupled with his sensibility, in order to create a fine psychological painting around the emotion of grief. He launches straight away with a personal experience: he had to visit a grieving lady, show his compassion and yet cause a little diminution of her grief. Declining any of the arguments from philosophy and any of the devices offered by that grandiloquent rhetoric *à la cicéronienne*, Montaigne starts by 'declinant tout mollement noz propos et les gauchissant peu à peu aus subjects plus voisins, et puis un peu plus esloingnez, selon qu'elle se prestoit plus à moy, je luy desrobay imperceptiblement cette pensée doulereuse' (Villey-Saulnier, p. 831). In this way, Montaigne made the real grief of the lady turn from its ordinary course and, through distraction or diversion, he appeased its sad occupation of her thoughts and made her, so to speak, forget herself. From this event Montaigne moves to give us a personal example where he used distraction for his own grief:

> Je fus autrefois touché d'un puissant desplaisir, selon ma complexion, et encores plus juste que puissant: je m'y fusse perdu à l'avanture si je m'en fusse simplement fié à mes forces. Ayant besoing d'une vehemente diversion pour m'en distraire, je me fis, par art, amoureux, et par estude, à quoy l'aage m'aidoit. L'amour me soulagea et retira du mal qui m'estoit causé par l'amitié.
>
> (ibid., p. 835)

> I was once neerely touched with a heavy displeasure, according to my complexion, and yet more just then heavie: I had peradventure lost my selfe in it, had I only relied upon mine owne strength. Needing a vehement diversion to with-draw me from it, I did by arte and studie make my selfe a lover, whereto my age assissted me: love discharged and diverted me from the inconvenience which good will and amitie had caused in me.

This *desplaisir* was, of course, the death of his friend La Boëtie, of whom he wrote the fine essay 'De l'amitié' (I.28).[2] The friendship between these two marks an early emotional phase in Montaigne's youth; it is the one personal tie that appears in his life. He reveals that in his life 'Aux amitiés communes je suis aucunement stérile et froid' (Villey-Saulnier, p. 821) and gives as the reason 'm'ayant duit et affriandé dès jeunesse à une amitié seule et parfaicte, m'a à la verité aucunement desgouté des autres' (ibid., p. 821). And so in spite of being sociable and capable of 'me porter allegrement aux grandes compaignies' (ibid., p. 823) he likes society only 'par intervalles et à mon poinct'. The fact that he made an almost metaphysical marriage with La Boëtie, that he was profoundly shocked at his death in 1563, that almost eighteen years later he remarked in his *Journal de voyage* (p. 1270), 'Et ce mesme matin escrivant à M. Ossat, je tumbe en un pancement si penible de M. de la Boëtie, et y fus si longtemps sans me raviser que cela me fit grand mal' – all this points to an emotional crisis in his life. How he manages to make the grief lighter is precisely again diversion: he started a love-affair quite honestly in order to be rid of thoughts of his lost friend. His tactic is not to try to suppress thoughts, not to aim at vanquishing them, but to change, diversify, alter course, occupation, company or place: this he finds useful – 'Tousjours la variation soulage, dissout et dissipe' (Villey-Saulnier, p. 836). We do not find abstractions influencing man emotionally but tiny things such as 'Le souvenir d'un adieu, d'une action, d'une grace particuliere, d'une recommandation derniere, nous afflige . . . Le son mesmes des noms, qui nous tintoüine aux oreilles' (ibid., p. 837). The gestures and lamentations of man Montaigne finds that 'c'est une plainte grammairienne et voyelle'. The distress of his illness keeps death and the thought of death quite close and yet 'Je voyois nonchalamment la mort, quand je la voyois universellement, comme fin de la vie; je la gourmande en bloc; par le menu, elle me pille' (ibid., p. 837). So by taking La Boëtie's death as the centre of his essay Montaigne makes the reader see as valuable the 'trick' of diverting any emotion.

Another essay where there is a positive role given to intellect is 'De trois commerces' (III.3). At the beginning we hear him say 'Nostre principalle suffisance, c'est sçavoir s'appliquer à divers usages' (ibid., p. 818): this suppleness of body and mind and this adaptability mean that man has the power to develop other potentialities, rather than following a fixed and rigid logical line in life: 'C'est estre, mais ce n'est pas vivre, que se tenir attaché et obligé par necessité à un seul train' (ibid., p. 818). The quality of intellectual flexibility is primordial in Montaigne's evaluation of a man's life: 'Je louerois un'ame à divers estages qui sçache et se tendre et se desmonter . . . ' (ibid., p. 821). This suppleness of mind means that Montaigne is as happy to talk with his servants as he is to entertain Henri de Navarre. In this essay we have hints of the feeling of disponibility that Gide and Sartre take up in the twentieth century. It is a state of mind where actions, feelings and sentiments are not constrained by previous agreements, by previous actions; it is in fact the flexibility of one's intelligence again: 'La vie est un mouvement inegal, irregulier et multiforme. Ce n'est pas estre amy de soy, et moins encore maistre, c'est en estre esclave, de se suivre incessamment, et estre si pris à ses inclinations qu'on n'en puisse fourvoyer, qu'on ne les puisse tordre' (ibid., p. 819). Life is an experiment, and Montaigne's art is a reverberation of his existence. His is the attempt to live a life free of commitments to anything or anyone but himself.

There is another positive role of the intellect unveiled for us in the essay 'De l'art de conferer' (III.8). The art of conversation is so important to Montaigne that he would choose to lose his sight than his tongue or ear. What kind of conversation does he like? It is particularly an intellectual kind: 'Nulles propositions m'estonnent, nulle creance me blesse, quelque contrarieté qu'elle ayt à la mienne' (Villey-Saulnier, p. 923). A person will propose something, and immediately Montaigne suggests the opposite. In other words, it does not matter what the subject is, the form remains the only thing that is important: 'Et me semble estre excusable si j'accepte plustost le nombre impair; le jeudy au pris du vendredi; si je m'aime mieux douziesme ou quatorziesme que treziesme à table' (ibid., p. 923). Contradictions 'm'esveillent seulement et m'exercent'; the rapid reply, the ready response, the comparing of two things, the making of analogies, the humour and wit involved in conversation are there 'Si je confere avec une ame forte et un roide jousteur, il me presse les flancs, me pique à gauche et à dextre, ses imaginations eslancent les miennes' (ibid., p. 923). This is the kind of High Table conversation in Oxford or Cambridge that one would like to witness: a company of intelligent human beings – if possible, intellectuals – arguing over American policy, *bouillabaisse*, ways of bringing up vegetables and children, a word in a Shakespearian sonnet, Catullus' or Sappho's verse, Jane Grigson's book on fruit, world-circling by air or sea or even a donkey, and so on. The cut and thrust of debate would be keen and amusing if they were all Montaignes. This is perhaps the 'commerce particulier que les honnêtes gens doivent avoir ensemble' described by La Rochefoucauld. It is Montaigne's influence on the seventeenth century that the intellectually inclined salons lifted conversation to the level of a minor art with elegance, accuracy, wit, humour and conciseness. However, Montaigne brings in a few personal reservations on this art of conversation: first, 'J'ayme à contester et à discourir, mais *c'est avec peu d'hommes et pour moy*' (ibid., p. 923: my italics). Second, Montaigne does not suffer fools willingly. He notes that 'La sottise est une mauvaise qualité; mais de ne la pouvoir supporter, et s'en despiter et ronger, comme il m'advient, c'est une autre sorte de maladie qui ne doit guere à la sottise en importunité; et est ce qu'à present je veux accuser du mien' (ibid., p. 923). Or the later comment, 'Il est impossible de traitter de bonne foy avec un sot' (ibid., p. 925), or 'Et cettuy-cy, qui vous assourdit de prefaces et digressions inutiles' (ibid., p. 926), or 'j'accuse mon impatience' (ibid., p. 928) – all this means that it is only a small circle who would pass Montaigne's very rigorous standards. Third, his way of arguing is sometimes too pig-headed, 'et me jette à une façon de debattre testue, malicieuse et imperieuse, dequoy j'ay à rougir apres' (ibid., p. 925). None the less, with no reservation, he praises 'une societé et familiarité forte et virile, une amitié qui se flatte en l'aspreté et vigueur de son commerce, comme l'amour, es morsures et esgratigneures sanglantes' (ibid., p. 924). This is very high praise indeed, when we think of what he has told us of his amorous behaviour.

Although the intellect is seen as a high priority in 'De l'art de conferer', it is not found alone. For aesthetic values enter very properly in his argument: 'Tout homme peut dire veritablement; mais dire ordonnéement, prudemment et suffisamment, peu d'hommes le peuvent' (ibid., p. 928) and 'Ce n'est pas tant la force et la subtilité que je demande, comme l'ordre' (ibid., p. 925). This idea of order ties up with a handsome, full and orderly conversation which is similar to the talk of shepherds or children: in other words it is a *natural* rather than a sophisticated order. We shall be coming back to this aesthetic value in a moment. But let us see first what the leitmotif of illness and of old age brings to his meditation.

The theme of old age takes on rather a different turn in the marginalia of 1588–92: the attitude is, sometimes, less that of a wise man than that of a slightly bitter man. This leads me on to question the role of death or thinking about death in the last few years of his life. In 'Sur des vers de Virgile' the value of health is recognized but he can talk about it without sharing it, '[la santé] telle qu'autrefois la

verdeur des ans et la securité me la fournissoient par veneuës' (ibid.,
p. 844). The effect of illness is noted – 'affesse mon esprit, le clouë et
faict un effect contraire – and he comes back again and again to it with
little marginal comments like 'et le mauvais estat de nostre santé'. In
an essay celebrating sexuality, life and health, is not the one thing that
matters to a man denied now to Montaigne? 'Les seuls vrais plaisirs de
la vie' have now disappeared, and he feels impotent.

Another example may be taken from 'De l'experience'. In the 1588
version he is talking about pleasure; he takes a particular event – a
dinner party – and develops this through the opinion of Alcibiades
and Varro. The former would not allow music to divert diners from
the pleasures of eating and talking. The latter (through Aulus Gellius,
13.9) wanted the people, the menu, the place and the climate to be
just right. There is just one correction to it: as he writes 'en bien
divers temps' he decides that this is the wrong spot for such a phrase
and so he crosses it out and writes instead: 'la fortune me rendit de
principale douceur en divers temps de mon aage . . . '. The passage is
expressed in personal terms: it draws upon the memory of several fine
dinner-parties he himself had given. His imagination aids his memory:
the *douceur*, the fitness in body and mind that each of his guests
shares, and his own *fleurissant* age are all brought in. Then, with an
abruptness that makes it rather emotional, he ends the passage with
'Mon estat m'en forclose' (Villey-Saulnier, p. 1106). The years since
1588 have not been cloudless: his health is deteriorating fast; he has
fewer chances for scintillating conversation; solitude is his fate:

> La decrepitude est qualité solitaire. Je suis sociable jusques à excez.
> Si me semble il raisonnable que meshuy je soustraye de la veue du
> monde mon importunité, et la couve à moy seul, que *je m'appile et
> me recueille en ma coque, comme les tortues.* J'apprens à veoir les
> hommes sans m'y tenir: ce seroit outrage en un pas si pendant. *Il
> est temps de tourner le dos à la compagnie.*
>
>   (ibid., p. 982: a (C) passage; my italics)[3]

> Decrepitude is a solitary quality. I am sociable even unto excesse,
> yet doe I thinke it reasonable at last to subtract my opportunity
> from the sight of the world, and hatch it in myselfe. Let me shrowd
> and shrugge myselfe into my shell as a tortoise, and learne to see
> men without taking hold of them. I should outrage them in so
> steepe a passage. It is now high time to turne from the company.

This is Montaigne at his most mature, accepting the facts of ageing and dying, and accepting, too, the unsociableness of old age, decayed and enfeebled with infirmities – 'So do our minutes hasten to their end'. And yet his imagination, his wit and humour vibrate, and he makes a simile – comparing his retreat to that of a tortoise in its shell – which is entrancingly witty and most humane. We may compare this passage with the way that the theme of age and death is treated at the beginning of 'Sur des vers de Virgile' (III.5): irony about himself and about other men, a calm statement that before he considered 'les jours poisans et tenebreux' as extraordinary, while now in old age it is a fine day that becomes extraordinary. Note the humorous statement, 'Que je me chatouille, je ne puis tantost plus arracher un pauvre rire de ce meschant corps' (Villey-Saulnier, p. 842). Or this one: 'Les ans m'entrainent s'ils veulent, mais à reculons' (ibid., pp. 841–2).

Illness, the disease of the gall bladder, and old age play a rich and final role in showing us the positive points about life in 'De l'experience'. We are given precise points of his experience of illness: for example, 'Car depuis quelques années, aux courvées de la guerre, quand toute la nuict y court, comme il advient communéement, apres cinq ou six heures l'estomac me commence à troubler, avec vehemente douleur de teste, et n'arrive poinct au jour sans vomir' (ibid., p. 1084: 'For some yeares since, in the out-roades or night-services that happen in times of warre, which many times continue all night, five or sixe houres after my stomache beginnes to qualme, my head feeleth a violent aking, so that I can hardly hold out till morning without vomiting'). Against this example we could put an opposite one, or at least show the extent that this one had to be meditated about: 'J'argumente que les vomissemens extremes et frequens que je souffre me purgent' (ibid., p. 1094). Humour and wit come in when he talks of his stones: 'Et sain et malade, je me suis volontiers laissé aller aux appetits qui me pressoient. Je donne grande authorité à mes desirs et propensions. D'estre subject à la cholique et subject à m'abstenir du plaisir de manger des huitres, ce sont deux maux pour un' (ibid., p. 1086: 'Both in health and in sicknesse I have willingly seconded and given my selfe over to those appetites that pressed me. I allow great authority to my desires and propensions. I love not to cure one evill by another mischiefe. I hate those remedies that importune more than sickness. To be subject to the cholike, and to be tied to abstaine from the pleasure I have in eating of oysters, are two mischiefes for one'). He states firmly that 'Il faut apprendre à souffrir ce qu'on ne peut eviter. Nostre vie est composée, comme l'armonie du monde, de choses contraires, aussi de divers tons, doux et aspres, aigus et plats, mols et graves' (ibid., p. 1089). We may notice the adjectives here: *douz* seems to come from taste – smooth, sweet, delicious; *aspres* – tart, sharp, unpleasant in taste; *aigus* – piercing and strident; *plats* – flat, plain, low; *mols* – soft, supple and tender; and *graves* – stately, solemn and heavy. Montaigne is working with different, opposite terms in order to make the reader think of a texture of his own life. Life is a tapestry woven around our individual personality; it hides good and bad parts, and we must accept the good and better with the bad and worse. A serene resignation. But if it is resignation it has only been reached after difficulties; it is the triumph of sacrifice. We may remember him saying in the *Journal de voyage* (p. 1306): 'J'étudiois quand je voulois . . . Je sentois seulement un peu le défaut de compaignie telle que je l'aurois désirée, etant forcé de jouir seul et sans communication des plaisirs que je goûtois' or the confession that 'Je n'ai rien si enemi à ma santé, que l'ennui et oisifveté' (p. 1234). Or 'Mais il vaut mieux encore estre seul qu'en compaignie ennuyeuse et inepte' (p. 987).

Montaigne loathes monotony; he sees in talking about the pleasure in travelling ('De la vanité, II.9) that this is a sign of disquiet in himself; it is an escape from domestic commitment – 'ces espines domestiques sont drues et desliées, elles nous mordent plus aigu et sans menace' (Villey-Saulnier, p. 950), and it is partly cowardice; it is an omen of 'inquietude et irresolution – nos maistresses qualités et predominantes'. How does Montaigne face up to the fact that the imperfections he views in himself as well as illness, old age and death are to be accepted wisely and intelligently? He has put his finger on the solution: 'Ce n'est pas assez de compter les experiences, il les faut poisir et assortir; et les faut avoir digerées et alambiquées, pour en tirer les raisons et conclusions qu'elles portent' ('De l'art de conferer', III.8; Villey-Saulnier, p. 931). The act of experiencing, and of experimenting, is judged by the intellect and sensibility and becomes the fruit of experiences, made from a long life. Thus Montaigne comes to a conclusion:

J'ose non seulement parler de moy, mais parler seulement de moy: je fourvoye quand j'escry d'autre chose et me desrobe à mon subject. Je ne m'ayme pas si indiscretement et ne suis si attaché et meslé à moy que je ne puisse distinguer et considerer à quartier: comme un voisin, comme un arbre. C'est pareillement faillir de ne

veoir pas jusques où on vaut, ou d'en dire plus qu'on n'en void.
(ibid., p. 942: a (C) passage)

I dare not onely speake of my selfe, but speake alone of my selfe. I
stragle when I write of any other matter, and digresse from my
subject. I doe not so discreetly love my selfe, and am so tied and
commixt to my selfe as that I cannot distinguish and consider my
selfe apart, as a neighbour, as a tree; it is an equall error either not
to see how farre a man's worth stretcheth, or to say more of it then
one seeth good cause.

This is an authoritarian statement. He makes it with assurance, with
affirmation and with conviction. And so when we turn to the positive
things he says about life and death we are not surprised to hear in 'De
l'experience': 'comme en general j'apprens ma debilité et la trahison
de mon entendement; d'où je tire la reformation de toute la masse. En
toutes mes autres erreurs je faits de mesme, et sens de cette reigle
grande utilité à la vie' (ibid., p. 1074). After this statement there is a
marginalia which reasserts it more firmly and more wrily: '(C)
D'apprendre qu'on a dict ou faict une sottise, ce n'est rien que cela; il
faut apprendre qu'on n'est qu'un sot, instruction bien plus ample et
importante' (ibid., p. 1074). His memory has always been atrocious,
and so when today she promises to remember 'elle a beau me jurer à
cette heure et m'asseurer, je secouë les oreilles' (ibid., p. 1074). A
similar stance is seen in 'Sur des vers de Virgile' where Montaigne
refers to the difficulty of expressing faults in oneself. *Je me suis
ordonné*: the tone here is 'military'; one part of Montaigne being
commanded by another part; beneath this, there is the grim facing
up to the worst features of himself. Here is a man who likes
communicating everything about himself and who is applying
moral/aesthetic terms to thoughts and actions: *laid et lache*, the first
coming from aesthetics and the second one from a moral line (cf.
emotional tones of Stoicism here – look at the way *vice/laideur/
incommodité* are treated in 'Du repentir', III.2).
   The attitude to death/life in 'De l'experience' is acceptance of the
first – 'Nous sommes pour vieillir, pour affoiblir, pour estre malades
en despit de toute medecine' (Villey-Saulnier, p. 1089) and 'Voilà une
dent qui me vient de choir, sans douleur, sans effort' (ibid.,
p. 1101) – and positive activity over the other:

Les plus belles vies, sont à mon gré celles, qui se rangent au

modelle commun, [then he crosses out] sans merueille [and writes
above it] et humain: aueq ordre: mais sans miracle.

(ibid., p. 1116)

It is important to Montaigne nearing death that his/everyman's life
should be human: not superhuman, not ascetic, not divine, but
human above all else. But it has to have another layer before it can be
'une belle vie': it must be 'aveq ordre'. He envisages an aesthetic
pattern round all our thoughts, activities and feelings. Immediately
following this sentence he comes to the last pronouncement he makes
about himself – on the subject of his old age. There are four adverbs
that he plays with here. First: 'Or la vieillesse a un peu besoin d'estre
traictée plus doucement et plus delicatement.' These he crosses out in
favour of 'bassement . . . facilement': but they do not convey his
feelings about old age and they seem inferior to the first two. He
crosses them out and in the space between them writes *the* adverb,
'tendrement'; this adverb is the most sensitive of the five.[4] The flavour
of delicate tenderness is caught here and communicated subtly to the
reader; it is part of Montaigne's sensibility which makes personal
emotion of immense value in the study of other men. Here we can
'feel' that the gap between 'je suis moy-mesmes la matiere de mon
livre' and 'chaque homme porte la forme entiere de l'humaine
condition' has closed. Montaigne wants man to stretch gently,
delicately and kindly to other men in their closing years; sympathy
and tenderness are desired in love and friendship. In this 'vivre
coliqueux' (ibid., p. 759) 'Je ne vise pas de ce costé là, je m'ayme trop'
(ibid., p. 916), he fears, and yet 'Quand je pourray me faire craindre,
j'aimeroy encore mieux me faire aymer' (ibid., p. 393).

The judgement on man is stated concretely in this phrase: 'Cette
longue attention que j'employe à me considerer me dresse à juger aussi
passablement des autres, et est peu de choses dequoy je parle plus
heureusement et excusablement' (ibid., p. 1076). The nature of this
self-criticism is 'J'estudie tout: ce qu'il me faut fuyr, ce qu'il me faut
suyvre' (ibid., p. 1076). Every tiny thing in his life is studied, and he
is attentive to anything that he comes across, physically; he needs to
know his body thoroughly with all its idiosyncrasies in order to give
shape to his *train de vie*. The *art de vivre* of Montaigne can never be
expected to be a model; what he wants to convey to his readers is
precisely that every human being must do the same thing; everyone
will find his *own forme maistresse* which conditions his life in
accordance with his own physical make-up and his own mental,

intellectual and emotional landscape. Reading the *Essais* must make a
capable reader aware of himself and so, as Terence Cave has so
brilliantly argued, 'the coherence of an individual's reading materials
lies ultimately in their application to his own character and
circumstances, rather than to those of the defunct author'.[5] All that
Montaigne can do is to offer himself as an example; after that, it must
be up to the reader.

'Je ne me juge que par vray sentiment, non par discours' (ibid.,
p. 1095), and so we are forewarned that concrete experience rather
than secondhand knowledge gained by reading is going to be
extremely important in Montaigne's *art de vivre*: 'J'aymerois mieux
m'entendre bien en moy qu'en Ciceron' (ibid., p. 1073). Habit and
good sense coupled with experience underline his attitude. For
example:

> ne puis ny dormir sur jour, ny faire collation entre les repas, ny
> desjeuner, ny m'aller coucher sans grand intervalle, (C) comme de
> trois heures, (B) apres le soupper, ny faire des enfans qu'avant le
> sommeil, ny les faire debout, ny porter ma sueur, ny m'abreuver
> d'eau pure ou de vin pur, ny me tenir nud teste long temps, ny me
> faire tondre apres disner . . . Moy je me laisse aller aussi à certaine
> forme de verres . . . Tout métail m'y desplait au pris d'une matiere
> claire et transparente. (C) Que mes yeux y tastent aussi, selon leur
> capacité.
>
> (ibid., pp. 1083–4)

> I can neither sleepe by day, nor eate betweene meales, nor break
> my fast, nor goe to bed without some entermission (as of three
> hours after supper), nor get children but before I fall asleepe, and
> that never standing, nor beare mine owne sweate, nor quench my
> thirst either with cleere water or wine alone, nor continue long
> bare-headed, nor having mine hair cut after dinner . . . As for me,
> I observe a kinde of like methode in glasses, and of one certaine
> forme . . . I mislike all manner of metall in regard of a bright
> transparent matter: let mine eyes also have taste of what I drinke
> according to their capacity.

This entrancing picture makes us know more about his personal
habits – such as being unable to create children standing up – and
they appear not as trivia but as essential features of Montaigne's
behaviour. He describes the ecstatic pleasure after passing a stone

(ibid., p. 1093), a pleasure like 'la belle lumiere de la santé'; he humorously places the 'use' of his wife between eating melons and drinking wine; he likes a good night's sleep – eight or nine hours – without a woman; he cannot face three meals a day but always has wind when he only eats once; he can dine without a tablecloth but cannot bear to be without a clean napkin, and he seldom uses a fork or a spoon. His taste in food and drink changes:

> En plusieurs choses je sens mon estomac et mon appetit aller ainsi diversifiant: j'ay rechangé du blanc au clairet, et puis du clairet au blanc. Je suis friant de poisson et fais mes jours gras des maigres, et mes festes des jours de jeusne; je croy ce qu'aucuns disent, qu'il est de plus aisée digestion que la chair.
>
> (ibid., pp. 1102–3)

In divers other things I feele my appetit to change, and my stomacke to diversifie from time to time. I have altred my course of drinking, sometimes from white to claret wine, and then from claret to white againe. I am very friand and gluttonous of fish, and keepe my shroving dayes upon fish dayes, and my feasts upon fasting-dayes. I believe as some others doe, that fish is of lighter digestion than flesh.

But he states that 'l'extreme fruict de ma santé c'est la volupté: tenons nous à la premiere presente et cogneuë' (ibid., p. 1103).

Montaigne realizes that he appreciates life better if he treats his body and mind well. This means working on that deep power of imagination: 'Or je trete mon imagination le plus doucement que je puis et la deschargerois, si je pouvois, de toute peine et contestation. Il la faut secourir, et flatter et piper qui peut' (ibid., p. 1090). His mind teaches him the necessity of maladies in old age, and his is not the worst one; anyway, everybody is in the same boat, and that is a consolation. His illness does not disturb his intellectual activities, and gives him the opportunity for patience and heroism, for which he would *not* have volunteered. The idea of a natural way of living is a leitmotif of this essay: 'Quoy que je reçoive desagreablement me nuit, et rien ne me nuit que je face avec faim et allegresse' (ibid., p. 1086). He even makes a dialogue between himself and nature: 'Laissons faire un peu à nature: elle entend mieux ses affaires que nous. – Mais un tel en mourut. – Si fairés vous, sinon de ce mal là, d'un autre. Et combien n'ont pas laissé d'en mourir, ayant trois medecins à leur cul?'

(ibid., p. 1088) where the quirky joke is put in nature's mouth not in his. The many marginalia reinforce the ideas of nature and order; for instance, in the statement that appalled someone like Pascal: 'Le plus simplement se commettre à nature, c'est s'y commettre le plus sagement. O que c'est un doux et mol chevet, et sain, que l'ignorance et l'incuriosité, à reposer une teste bien faicto' (ibid., p. 1073). Here we see waiting for a final stage-call the ideas that we met in Chapter 3: *savant/sage/ignorant/docta ignorantia* – well beloved by 'The Brethren of the Common Life' but refashioned and restructured by Montaigne.

His whole *art de vivre* is an intellectualization of the present; how to suck all the enjoyments of the moment and be able to double-enjoy them in poetry. Pleasures are called 'intellectuellement sensibles' and 'sensiblement intellectuels'. Before analysing these phrases let us look at another containing the word *plaisirs*. It occurs in the paragraph that I omitted from the critical commentary in Chapter 2. It is a comment introduced from the field of philosophy. What do the philosophers like Aristotle, Zeno, Pythagoras and Socrates have to say on pleasure (ibid., p. 1107)?

The 1588 version starts, 'Il en est de nostre ieunesse, qui protestent ambitieusement de les fouler aux pieds,' which is rather flat. It is then almost totally crossed out, and in 1592 we have the following statement written in tiny handwriting above it: 'Il en est qui d'une farouche stupidite come dict Aristote en sont desgoutez. J'en conois qui par ambition ~~protest~~ . . . le front' (EP, pl. 1012). The idea of *ieunesse* is lost; the ambitiousness of the protest is also cut out. But this time we have instead 'une farouche stupidite' – a very strong phrase, bringing in 'wild, savage, untamed, fierce, untractable, fell, cruell, shrewd, forward, curst' (Cotgrave) around the *farouche*, coupled with 'stupiditie, sencelesnesse, dullnesse, blockishnesse' (Cotgrave) around *stupiditie*. This strong emotive and harsh attitude is 'softened' by Aristotle – at least it has a convincing classical authority behind it. The second part of the sentence reads in 1588: 'que ne renoncent ils encores au respirer; que ne viuent-ils du leur et ne refusent la lumiere de ce qu'elle est gratuite et ne leur couste ny inuantion ny uigur'. The tone is beginning to be sarcastic now and leads much more aptly into the next sentence with its list of mythological figures. That is left intact. He offers the philosophers whom he is attacking Mars, Pallas and Mercury instead of Venus, Ceres and Bacchus. The point is an easy one: three gods connected with war as opposed to love, earth and wine. The whole of the next sentence is crossed out:

Ces humeurs vanteuses [a first correction was *farouches* but that was eventually crossed off the same time as the whole sentence], se peuuent forger quelque contentement, car que ne peut sur nous la fantasie, mais de sagesse, [and above another correction *non pas aux sages*, ultimately crossed off] elles n'en tiennent tache.

This rather staid sentence was put out of joint by the author's humour and wit: 'Chercheront ils pas, le quadrature du cercle iuchez sur leurs fames . . .'[6]

The rest of the text contains only two changes of word, and the phrase 'plaisirs humains & corporels' becomes 'plaisirs naturels par consequent necessaires et iustes' – which maintains the balance between what is natural and what therefore is just and necessary for man. The first change of word is '& qu'il s'y croupisse' becomes 'ny qu'il s'y ueautre'. *Croupir* as Cotgrave defines it is 'to crooch, bow, stoope, grow or goe double', already a metaphor but the change is still very inventive. Florio translated this sentence perfectly: 'yet would I not have the minde to be fastned thereunto, nor *wallow* upon it nor lie along thereon, but apply it selfe and sit at it' (my italics).[7] The verbal fabric is quite acute here: the personification of *esprit*, the giving to it of movement and shape, helps the reader grasp the new and almost tactile image through which he is to understand the working of man's mind.

The next change of phrase concerns the pleasures of Caesar and Alexander. The 1588 version makes the 'plaisirs humains & corporels'; the alteration makes it stylistically more apt – 'plaisirs naturels, et par consequent necessaires et iustes' (EP, pl. 1012). And finally he changes 'la vie commune' into 'la vie ordinaire'. Though the text itself has undergone many significant changes the marginalia bring us still more surely to the heart of the *Essais*. 'Qu'il s'y see non qu'il s'y couche. Artistippus ne defandoit que le corps come si nous n'auions d'ame: Zenon n'embrassoit que l'ame come si n'auions pas de corps. Tous deux vicieusement' (ibid.). We understand *vicieusement* as 'Viciously, lewdly, corruptly, faultily' (Cotgrave). Montaigne does not use it as a Christian – the ethics are not Christian; he means us to look at Aristippus and Zeno as philosophers who were faulty; they are wrongly out of step with Socrates' way of living, which is, as we are immediately told, the best way:

Pythagoras disent-ils a suivy une philosophie toute en contemplation; Socrates toute en meurs et en action: Platon en a trouve le temperament entre les deux. Mais ils le disent pour en conter. Et le vrey temperament se trouve en Socrates et Platon est bien plus Socratique que Pythagorique et luy siet mieux.

(ibid.)

Pythagoras (say they) hath followed a philosophie all in contemplation; Socrates altogether in manners and in action; Plato hath found a mediocrity between both. But they say so by way of discourse, for the true temperature is found in Socrates, and Plato is more Socratical than Pythagorical, and it becomes him best.

This is Montaigne's most mature thinking; he embraces the Socratic way of living and perhaps sees Plato as being essentially Socratic rather than Pythagorian (suggested by St Augustine or Ficino?).

Now we can see what lies behind these phrases 'intellectuellement sensibles' and 'sensiblement intellectuels': there is no separation between the intellect and sensibility. Montaigne glories in being ordinary, earthy and unintellectual. But the apparently simple rules for living are rendered extremely intellectual: the cult of moderation in everything means that he leaves temperance aside and moves to an intense harmonization of opposing forces which were inherent in him. The balance of forces is viewed as something ethical and aesthetic; the moral consciousness controls the feeling that animates the *Essais*. His way of life is far more difficult to achieve: 'Le peuple se trompe: on va bien plus facilement par les bouts, où l'extremité sert de borne d'arrest et de guide, que par la voye du millieu, large et ouverte, et selon l'art que selon nature, mais bien moins noblement aussi, et moins recommandablement' (Villey-Saulnier, p. 1110). On rereading this sentence Montaigne feels that his own position is not too clear and so he adds: 'La grandeur de l'ame n'est pas tant tirer à mont et tirer avant comme sçavoir se ranger et circonscrire. Elle tient pour grand tout ce qui est assez, et montre sa hauteur à aimer mieux les choses moyennes que les eminentes' (ibid., p. 1110). The middle way is not an easy one; much easier is it to go to extremities, for there are guides, goals, stopping-places, stopovers and stoplights for us there. This other Montaigne path puts terrific responsibility on oneself. The need for constant discipline and checking of body and mind is implicit in the phrase 'sçavoir se ranger et circonscrire'. Then we have the 1588 version, reading: '(B) Il n'est rien si beau et legitime que de faire bien l'homme et deuëment, ny science si ardue que de bien sçavoir vivre cette vie.'

There is one addition in the text itself that I should like to consider briefly: the words 'et naturellement' added above 'sçavoir viure cette vie'. On rereading the whole of 'De l'experience' it struck Montaigne that his whole *art de vivre* was based on what a wise man thought of nature. The ultimate way of looking at life and death is to accept a tooth falling out, as one grows older, as part of nature's pattern. From this point of view we can see that adding 'naturellement' was significant:

> Disdain not death, but be well satisfied with it, because this, too, is one of the things which Nature wills. For as are adolescence and old age, growth and maturity, development of teeth and beard and grey hair, begetting, conception and childbearing and the rest of the natural functions which life's seasons bring, such also is actual dissolution. This, therefore, is like a man of trained reason, not to be rash or violent or disdainful in the face of death, but to wait for it as one of the natural functions; and as you now wait for the unborn child to come forth from your wife's womb, so expect the hour in which your soul will drop from this shell.
>
> (*The Meditations of Marcus Aurelius Antoninus*,
> ed. A. S. L. Farquharson, Oxford: Clarendon Press, 1944, 9.3)

There is a deep resemblance between the two writers; again Montaigne echoes the Stoic thought of Marcus Aurelius in a register which is his own; he redigests it 'en sang et nourriture'; the skeleton may be Stoic but the whole flesh and blood are Montaigne's.

Virtue is now for Montaigne a harmonious system of impulses, balanced by adaptability, order, moderation and consistency. Ethics are subsumed into an aesthetic view of life. Life takes on a larger importance for him: 'Principallement à cette heure que j'aperçoy la mienne si briefve en temps, je la veux estendre en pois' (Villey-Saulnier, p. 1111). He wants to draw it out, to deepen and enrich it: 'Je veux arrester la promptitude de sa fuite par la promptitude de ma sesie, et par la vigueur de l'usage compenser la hastiveté de son escoulement: à mesure que la possession du vivre est plus courte, il me la faut rendre plus profonde et pleine' (ibid., pp. 1111–12). There is an intense *joie de vivre* in the dying pages of 'De l'experience'. He has a dictionary for himself ('J'ay un dictionnaire tout à part moy') where the phrase 'passe-temps' occurs:

> Cette fraze ordinaire de passe-temps et de passer le temps

represente l'usage de ces prudentes gens, qui ne pensent point avoir meilleur compte de leur vie que de la couler et eschapper, de la passer, gauchir et, autant qu'il est en eux, ignorer et fuir, comme chose de qualité ennuyeuse et desdaignable. Mais je la cognois autre, et la trouve et prisable et commode, voyre en son dernier decours, où je la tiens.

(ibid., p. 1111)

This vulgar phrase of passe time and to pass the time, represents the custome of those wise men who thinke to have no better account of their life then to passe it over and bawke it, and so much as in them lyeth to ignore and aveyd it, as a thing of an yrkesome, tedious, and to bee disdained quality. But I know it to bee otherwise, and finde it to be both priseable and commodious, yea in her last declination, where I hold it.

So that in his failing years he admires nature's gift to him; he wants to double the pleasure of life; he wants to be woken when asleep so that he can know the joy of having been asleep. Every pleasure associates his mind, 'je ne la [volupté] laisse pas friponer aux sens, j'y associe mon ame, non pas pour s'y engager, mais pour s'y agreer' (ibid., p. 1112). There is a continual interaction between body and mind, and there is a sophistication of pleasure. But he had a strong sense of his own conscience, and he curbed his pleasures by reflection and self-control. In following Nature he was indeed following his own nature, and that meant not merely giving in to his instincts; he was following a Nature which had been strengthened and improved by conscious effort. Nature has rendered acts necessary and pleasurable, and we are violating her rules if we cut out the pleasure. 'Composer nos mœurs' is the most basic thing a human can do and living life fully is primordial: 'Nostre grand et glorieux chef-d'œuvre c'est vivre à propos' (ibid., p. 1108).

To the question 'Quoy, avez vous pas vescu?' Montaigne gives this resounding answer: 'C'est non seulement la fondamentale mais la plus illustre de vos occupations' (ibid., p. 1108). We feel the vigour of being alive; this 'homme languagier comme je suis' (ibid., p. 870) is living the whole drama of human life. Leitmotifs like *ordonnéement*, *sçavoir vivre*, *vivre*, and so on, lay stress on the sense of aesthetic appeal being much stronger than a moral one in the *art de vivre*. Montaigne shows a firm grasp of human experience; even in the last pages he shows that his world included children: 'je m'adonne volontiers aux petits, soit pour ce qu'il y a plus de gloire, soit par naturelle compassion, qui peut infiniement en moy' (ibid., p. 1100). His vision comprises all mankind, 'cette marmaille d'hommes que nous sommes' (ibid., p. 1114) or 'nous autres hommenetz' (ibid., p. 1114) or 'nous mesmes, qui sommes de la voirie du peuple' (p. 1040). The intimate delight of reading that he gives us is following him actualizing in words his particularized vision of humanity.

Eliot states in 'Tradition and the individual talent' that by 1600 the French had already a more mature prose than the English had, and the Greek and Latin classics were read as living authors. This is largely due to Montaigne, who was trying to awaken in France the audience of intellectual and emotional awareness that had existed in Rome in the first century BC. In II.17 he had this comment on the audience: 'Et puis, pour qui escrivez vous?' He answers this *vous* voice by dividing people into three categories: the 'sçavants', the 'ames communes et populaires' and 'La tierce, à qui vous tombez en partage, des ames reglées et fortes d'elles-mesmes . . .'. This is what Montaigne means by *honnetes hommes*, and very significantly he gives La Boëtie as an example: 'je di des parties naturelles de l'ame et le mieux né . . . c'etoit vrayment un'ame pleine et qui montroit un beau visage à tout sens; un'ame à la vieille marque . . .'. Montaigne is a civilized and mature gentleman. He admires above all the Gascon dialect, and we may chuckle as we remember that his *Essais* for four hundred years has been faulted by some people for having too many Gasconisms in it.[8] He states that the dialect is 'à la verité un langage masle et militaire plus qu'autre que j'entende . . .'. He compares it with French, to the latter's delicate floweriness, 'autant nerveux puissant et pertinant, comme le François est gratieus, delicat et abondant'. But Montaigne's language is both sinewy, manly, fleshy and delicate, full and gracious. Claude Expilly writing a sonnet to praise the great man starts with the line, 'Que tu es admirable en ce masle langage . . . ,' and ends with:

> Les siècles à venir chanteront à bon droit,
> Montaigne par lui-mesme ensigna comme on doit
> Et bien dire et bien vivre, et bien mourir encore.
> (Appeared for the first time in the 1595 edition of the *Essais*)

How admirable you are in this manly tongue . . . Future ages will rightly sing how Montaigne through himself taught how man must speak well, live well and above all die well. (DGC)

CHAPTER 10

Montaigne through the Ages

J'escris mon livre à peu d'hommes et à peu d'années. (III.9; Villey-Saulnier, p. 982)

This chapter will not attempt to describe chronologically the fortunes of Montaigne in the reading world.[1] I want to kindle a little curiosity and pleasurableness in seeing how reading him has made some French and English authors more intelligent and humorous.

(i)

Montaigne was famous years before his death. In 1584, La Croix du Maine described how Montaigne published the essays in 1580 and 1582 in Bordeaux and Rouen and several other towns 'tant cet ouvrage a été bien reçu de tous hommes de lettres'.[2] The learned Dutch philosopher Justus Lipsius called him a French Thales and wrote in April 1588: 'Ego te [Montaigne] talem censeo, qualem publice descripsi uno verbo.'[3] His many friends such as Pierre de Brach, Estienne Pasquier, Jacques Auguste de Thou, Duplessis-Mornay, Pierre Charron, d'Aubigné, and so on, would agree with Tabourot des Accords when he said in 1588: 'tout ravi de sa simplicité,/Reconnaissant ton style intimitable,/T'adore ainsi qu'une divinité/Te voyant seul à toi-même semblable'. In Lambeth Palace Library there is a letter (which has been published) dated 10 October 1592 written by Pierre de Brach telling Anthony Bacon (the older brother of Francis) of Montaigne's death. He had obviously been in a personal relationship with Montaigne when he was in Bordeaux in 1583 and 1585. The older Bacon (1558–1618), a diplomatist of some repute, had recognized something interesting about the *Essais* and taken a copy with him back to England. Since we know the date of Anthony Bacon's stay in Bordeaux we can suggest, hypothetically, that the copy of Montaigne's *Essais* that he bought was either the first edition printed by Simon Millanges in 1580 or the second edition (which was, apart from the moving account of his meeting the 'mad' poet Tasso in Ferrara and many Italian quotations, really a reprint of the 1580) of 1582. This is confirmed by Francis Bacon's publication in 1597 of his *Essays* where there is no mention of the third book of Montaigne's *Essais* and little attempt to interpret his thoughts. However, it was with Bacon's *Essays* that the influence of Montaigne in England began – although it must be said there was nothing of Montaigne in Bacon; the new genre of essays was quickly famous in both England and France. In 1603, Florio brought out his famous translation and it was this, much more than Bacon's *Essays*, that gave Gonzalo a speech in *The Tempest* and that inspired several aphorisms in Jonson's *Timber, or Discoveries Made upon Men and Matters* (posthumously printed in 1640). Montaigne was admired immediately in England: authors used adverbs and adjectives such as 'prettily' (Bacon), '[he] speaks nobly, honestly and wisely' (Cornwallis) 'colourably and wittily' (Walton).

We can see how early was the reaction to Florio by looking briefly at drama in the first two decades of the seventeenth century. Webster, in *The White Devil* (1612), pillages Montaigne on the question of marriage, passion and satiety, suicide and the inner self. For example, Flamineo says in Act I, scene 2: ' 'tis just like a summer bird-cage in a garden, the birds that are without, despaire to get in, and the birds that are within despaire and are in a consumption for feare they shall never get out' (Montaigne, III.5); or in the same scene: 'They know our desire is increas'd by the difficultie of injoying; whereas satiety is a blunt, weary and drowsie passion' (III.5), where the whole of Montaigne's attitude on sex and lust is 'copied'. But we are, perhaps, more troubled when there is a complete change of key, as when Webster in Act III, scene 1, lines 43–5, makes use of Montaigne's splendid simile of trying to grasp water in the 'Apologie' (II.12) to get at man's inability to know anything: 'it would be even as if one should go about to graspe the water: for, how much the more he shall close and presse that which by its owne nature is ever gliding, so much the more he shall loose what he would hold and fasten' (Florio). Or the point of language where Montaigne makes acute remarks such as 'When such like repetitions pinch me, and that I looke more nearly to them, I find them but grammaticall laments, the word and the tune wound me. Even as Preachers exclamations do often move their auditory more than their reasons' (III.4: Florio) and Webster simply has:

> Leave your prating,
> For these are but grammatical laments,
> Feminine arguments . . .

There are several pillages of Montaigne in Marston's *The Dutch Courtezan* (1605) and in the *Parasitaster, or The Fawne* (1606); for instance, Florio's words in 'De l'amitié' (I.28) on heterosexual love, 'enjoying doth lose it, as having a corporall end subject to satietie', are merely repeated by Marston:

> To kill a friend
> To gain a woman! To lose a virtuous self
> For appetite and sensual end, whose very having
> Loseth all appetite, and gives satiety!
> That corporal end . . .
> (*The Dutch Courtezan*, Act II, sc. 2, ll.221–5)

Or again, in 'We taste nothing purely' (II.20) Florio says: 'When I imagine man fraught with all the commodities may be wished, let us suppose all his severall members were for ever possessed with a pleasure like unto that of generation, even in the highest point that may be; I finde him to sinke under the burden of his ease, and perceive him altogether unable to beare so pure, so constant, and so universall a sensuality'; Marston says: 'Imagine all a man possess'd with a perpetuall pleasure, like that of generation, even in the highest lusciousness, he straight sinkes as unable to bear so continuall, so pure, so universall a sensuality' (*Parasitaster*, Act IV, sc. 1). The concrete, idiomatic and racy language of Florio makes his translation live so that the concrete nature of Jacobean drama is imbued with the *Essais*.

Meanwhile in France our attention is caught by Montaigne's adopted daughter's work in editing the *Essais*. In 1595 she produced an edition which was regarded as the 'standard' version by the seventeenth, eighteenth and nineteeenth centuries. As mentioned in my first chapter, there is a need to collate this text with the *exemplaire*. Mademoiselle de Gournay lived long into the seventeenth century and re-edited the version in 1625 and in 1635, cutting out several archaic words and warning readers in her prefaces that she had done so. Her letter to Lipsius dated 2 May 1596 says that 'J'estois sa fille, ie suis son sepulcre; i'estois son second estre, ie suis ses cendres', which may be honest but it shows the highly emotional and heavily exaggerated attitude she had to Montaigne.[4] Her prefaces are in the same style, and in another letter to Lipsius she admits that 'mon gibbier n'est pas la poésie', which makes one a little hesitant to eulogize her editorship.[5] Indeed, when she published in 1626 *L'Ombre de Mademoiselle de Gournay* attacking the Malherbian poets, and in particular Malherbe himself, calling them 'poètes grammairiens' and 'docteurs en négative' the poets riddled her with harsh satirical epigrams and she never recovered her reputation. The other French woman who was concerned with Montaigne in the early seventeenth century was Jeanne de Lestonnac. Her mother was a sister of Montaigne; she was a Protestant, and Montaigne supervised the upbringing of the daughter in the true Catholic faith. After her marriage, the upbringing of her family and her widowhood she became a nun and in 1607 founded the Compagnie de Marie Notre-Dame in Bordeaux. A recent article brings forth many similarities in education between Montaigne and his niece: for example, the formation of a person with mind and body interlocked; physical exercises which would give the mind a 'stretching'; knowledge of others and, above all, knowledge of oneself.[6] The house in Bordeaux had close connections with the Jesuits (who, as we have seen, were admired by Montaigne), and their optimism is already an opposite to the growing pessimism of the Jansenists.

The neurotic emotional bursts of indignation given to the *Essais* by Pascal, Bossuet, the Port-Royalists, and so on, do not hide the fact that Montaignian doubt set a powerful example for sceptical thinkers for the next two centuries and for inquiring minds today. Pascal owed practically all to Montaigne, whilst Descartes, in his highly subjective and personal works, changed the *nescio* of Montaigne into an active methodic doubt – *nolo credere*.

(ii)

That there was an eclipse in publishing the *Essais* between 1669 and 1724 is true,[7] but does this mean that the *honnêtes hommes* of the Golden Age in French literature had not read Montaigne? To explain the apparent rejection of the sixteenth century let us turn to Marcel Raymond, who said: 'On peut d'abord, et très justement, faire le départ entre la théorie des humanistes et des docteurs et les œuvres des artistes.'[8] And he cites La Fontaine as an example of someone who is both an admirer of ancient literature and a lover of Boccaccio and Montaigne.

In the first half of the century Montaigne was avidly read, admired and loved in France: for instance, Racan called him 'mon cher ami', for Pierre Camus, Bishop of Belley, he was the 'agréable Montaigne', for Regnier he was *the* master and he tries in his *Satires* to put into poetry many of the arguments of the 'Apologie'. For the *libertin* (in the wide sense it has nothing to do with impiety) writers Montaigne's love of solitude, his fervent cult of friendship, his refusal to accept anything that smacked of social prejudice and his disdain for richness and honour were important factors in their use of him. For instance, Théophile de Viau in his famous ode –

> Dans ce parc un valon secret
> Tout voilé de ramages sombres,
> Où le soleil est si discret
> Qu'il n'y force jamais les ombres,
> Presse d'un cours si diligent
> Les flots de deux ruisseaux d'argent
> Et donne une fraischeur si vive
> A tous les objets d'alentour,
> Que mesme les martyrs d'Amour
> Y trouvent leur douleur captive . . .

– is depicting with concrete precision a landscape with certain Montaignian qualities: solitude, freshness and imagination. Montaigne's essay 'De l'inconstance de nos actions' (II.1), with the floating, wavering, fleeting images of time, seems to be the background for the constant fluctuation and half-shade of:

> Parfois, dans une claire nuit . . .
> Diane quitte son Berger
> Et s'en va là-dedans nager
> Avecque ses étoiles nues.
>
> Les ondes, qui leur font l'amour,
> Se refrisent sur leurs épaules,
> Et font danser tout à l'entour
> L'ombre des roseaux et des saules.
>   ('La Maison de Silvie')

The primacy of the intellect in Montaigne gives Corneille's frequent quotation of him in his *Examens* and prefaces to his plays a surety of authority: thus, for instance, the sentence in I.37, 'Qu'on me donne l'action la plus excellente et pure, je m'en vais y fournir vraisemblable-ment cinquante vicieuses intentions', is cited in the 'Lettre-préface' to *La Suivante*. Many of Corneille's favourite leitmotifs such as *être* and *paraître* or dissimulation have deep roots in Montaigne's thoughts on the human condition.

The doubleness of everything in this universe so often discussed by Montaigne can be seen as the dramatist's experimentation with tragedy and comedy – seeing everything from a double point of view. While Montaigne's 'Apologie' is at once attacked by the church (and his *Essais* put on the Index in 1676) and praised by philosophers such as Gassendi, two currents of his thought stand out in the seventeenth century: his art of conversation and his study of man. *L'art de plaire* becomes the one rule that dominated life in the salons and literature: in 1625, Voiture was presented to Madame de Rambouillet and worldly elegance was translated into literary *galanterie*. Madame de Sévigné calls Montaigne an 'ancien ami', whilst Madame de La Fayette would like to have him as a neighbour. Huet said that one could scarcely find a gentleman of discernment in all France who did not possess Montaigne in his library. To lead us on to the great authors let us have a look at what Huet said of Montaigne's style:

> Son style . . . est d'un tour véritablement singulier et d'un caractère original. Son imagination vive lui fournit sur toutes sortes de sujets une grande variété d'images dont il compose cette abondance d'agréables métaphores, dans lesquelles aucun écrivain ne l'a jamais égalé. C'est sa figure favorite, figure qui . . . est la marque d'un bon esprit, parce qu'elle vient de la fécondité du fonds qui produit ces images, de la vivacité qui les découvre facilement et à propos, et du discernement qui fait choisir les plus convenables.[9]

How extraordinary that this Bishop d'Avranches, the editor of Origen's *Commentary on St Matthew* (1668), brilliant in mathematics and anatomy, writer of Latin verse, haunter of the salon of Mademoiselle de Scudéry and author of the *Demonstratio evangelica* (1674), should have made a judgement on Montaigne which stresses his imagination, his imagery and above all his metaphors. Is this a hint towards the second side of the classical coin? One side that lies in the poor resources available in seventeenth-century language has been brilliantly argued by Odette de Mourgues in her 1980 Zaharoff Lecture in the University of Oxford entitled 'Quelques paradoxes sur le classicisme'. The other side, I would like to suggest tentatively, is in the reading of Montaigne by authors such as Molière, La Fontaine, Perrault, Madame de Sévigné and La Bruyère. I take La Fontaine as my example. He quotes Montaigne on the structure and style of what one is writing:

> Sans m'arreter à aucun arrangement, *non plus que faisait Montaigne*, je passe de l'hôtel de Conti aux affaires de delà les monts, c'est-à-dire d'une princesse extrêment vive à un pape: qui va mourir. (My italics)[10]

Is this not choosing as a direct predecessor a man whose uttermost nonchalance is cleverly feigned? This choice shows the feeling La Fontaine has for Montaigne, for the supple shape and structures of his *Essais* and for the extremely concrete language he has made his own. He has this to say on heroic poetry:

> c'est assurément le plus beau de tous, le plus fleuri, le plus susceptible d'ornement et de ces figures nobles et hardies qui font une langue à part, une langue assez charmante pour qu'on l'appelle la langue des dieux.[11]

Or when he is discussing the reading of one of Plato's dialogues:

> on se laisse amuser insensiblement comme par une espèce de charme. Voilà ce qu'il faut considérer là-dessus: laissons-nous entraîner à notre plaisir, et ne cherchons pas matière de critiquer; c'est une chose trop aisée à faire.[12]

Do these two quotations not bring to our memory what Montaigne was saying in Chapter 6 of this book? La Fontaine knows his Longinus well, although *Les Amours de Psyché* was published in 1669, five years before the first French translation by Boileau came out in 1674. He must have read Longinus in one of the Latin translations. When he discusses tragedy and comedy he says:

> La tragédie a encore cela au-dessus de la comédie, que le style dont elle se sert est sublime; et les beautés du sublime, si nous en croyons Longin et la vérité, sont bien plus grandes et ont tout un autre que celles du médiocre. Elles enlèvent l'âme, et se font sentir à tout le monde avec la soudaineté des éclairs.[13]

The very language here, for instance, 'enlèvent l'âme' and 'la soudaineté des éclairs', is reminiscent of Montaigne's language in passages of literary criticism.

In his masterpiece the *Fables* he can skip from *tendresse* to irony, from mock-heroic to fantasy, from erudite words to legal terms, from archaic language to a simple one, and his command of every known prosodic experimentation enables him to write *vers libres* or *irréguliers* with supreme confidence. Montaigne would approve his use of Aesop (note his nine occurrences in the *Essais*, and he is called 'ce grand homme' – III.13; Villey-Saulnier, p. 1115 – and an 'autheur de tres-rare excellence' – II.37; Villey-Saulnier, p. 769), his use of *ordre* together with the absolute knowledge that man does not know anything:

> [on the three dialogues of Plato that are translated by Maucroix] ils faisaient avouer au moins qu'on ne peut connaître parfaitement la moindre chose qui soit au monde . . . nous ne cherchons qu'à nous amuser; les Athéniens cherchaient aussi à s'instruire. En cela il faut procéder avec quelque ordre.[14]

And finally there is deep down in both authors this melancholy and eternal *ennui*. La Fontaine writes to Maucroix, 'Je mourrais d'ennui, si je ne composais plus,' and when he is almost 70 years old he writes to Madame d'Hervart the letter which is a nice illustration of what Montaigne wanted in 'De l'art de conferer':

> Je voudrais bien le voir aussi . . .
> Mais pour varier son ennui.
> Car vous savez, Madame, qu'il s'ennuie partout . . .

It is mainly in the *Journal de voyage en Italie* that we can see, explicitly, Montaigne's feelings as regards *ennui*:

> Je n'ai rien si enemi à ma santé, que l'ennui et oisifveté: là, j'avois tousjours quelque occupation, sinon plesante que j'usse peu desirer, au moins suffisante à me desennuier: comme à visiter les antiquités, les vignes, qui sont des jardins et lieus de plesir, de beauté singuliere . . .[15]

He goes on to say: 'Tous ces amusemans m'embesouignoint assez: de melancholie, qui èst ma mort, et de chagrin, je n'en avois nul' occasion, ny dedans ny hors la maison.'

(iii)

That there was no eclipse in England is due, mainly, to the translation of Charles Cotton which came out in 1685–6, reprinted in 1693 and in 1700; since that time it has been often reprinted. It does not have Florio's Renaissance style but it is more correct. Many writers have recorded the affinity of English and Guyenne taste – an affinity which means that Montaigne is much loved. His fund of quiet humour made it almost a humour *à l'anglaise.* In eighteenth-century England the genre of essay knew no bounds from George Berkeley (1685–1753) with his *An Essay towards a New Theory of Vision* to David Hume (1711–76), who spent the years 1734–7 in France and wrote *Essays.* But I want to concentrate on one writer – Alexander Pope (1688–1744) – to whom Montaigne spelled out humaneness and wisdom.

We find him mentioning Montaigne in one of his imitations of Horace where he is trying to establish a camaraderie between himself as author and his reader:

> I love to pour out all myself, as plain
> As downright Shippen, or as old Montagne.
> In them, as certain to be lov'd as seen,
> The Soul stood forth, nor kept a Thought within.[16]

Here the frankness and the wholehearted way Montaigne has of analysing himself are of prime importance. Pope is interested in human nature, in the potentialities of man, in the limitations of human destiny and the duties, dignity, crimes and pleasures of human life. Hence his *Essay on Man* (1733–4), consisting of four Epistles. Now, it is known that Pope acquired Cotton's translation in 1706 when he was 18 and read it, as Maynard Mack says,

> I suspect, many times before he died, but at any rate all the way through, at least once, with the greatest thoroughness. There is hardly a page that is not starred up and down with his marginal commas, and there are also far more explicit verbal comments in this than in any other book of his with which I am acquainted.[17]

Pope's deep affection for Montaigne is revealed in the marginal comments in his copy of Cotton's translations. (Incidentally, he also owned a French edition, a folio copy of the 1652 Paris edition from the press of Augustin Courbe.) Thus he approves thoroughly of Montaigne's account of his education in I.26; Pope's own formal education stopped by about 12 or 13 years of age and then he spent five years reading English, French, Italian, Latin and Greek poets, so that he writes in the margin 'mutato nomine de me Fabula narratur' and 'Alter ego'. Or the famous phrase that Montaigne utters (III.5) as regards his own writing – 'I am vex'd that my *Essays* only serve the Ladies for a common moveable, a Book to lie in the Parlour Window; this Chapter shall preferr me to the Closet; I love to traffick with them a little in private . . . ' – and Pope comments: 'For ye Ladies.' A final comment on the whole book is made on the last page: 'This is (in my Opinion) the very best Book for Information of Manners, that has been writ; This Author says nothing but what every one feels att the Heart. Whoever deny it, are not more wise than Montaigne, but less honest.'

Pope's marginal comments show a truly evaluative mind: for example, Montaigne's view on medicine is 'the most excellent extant' and his discourse on old age and death is approved of as is his attitude towards the cruelty of the Spaniards towards the natives in South America – Pope, who was a Roman Catholic, notes 'Tantum Relligio potuit suadere malorum'. His knowledge of the *Essais* is extensive from the correction of the source of an anecdote, to the witty noting of the famous legend about Cicero who 'lying with a Wench, found he had discharged his Stone in the Sheets' (Pope asks where did Montaigne get the story from) and to the arousal properties of weavers in their task (Pope asks the question 'Had our Chaucer this in his Eye, when he made his Wife of Bath a Weaver?').

In his rejection of all doctrinaire and rigid opinions Pope can affirm:

> But ask not, to what Doctors I apply?
> Sworn to no Master, of no Sect am I:
> As drives the storm, at any door I knock:
> And house with Montaigne now, or now with Locke.[18]

To his estate in Twickenham there came, in 1726, Voltaire to pay his respects to the British Homer, and no doubt they would have heartily agreed on their affection for Montaigne.

Voltaire is, as is well known, an enemy of Pascal, and we cannot find two men in French literature more antipathetic to each other than these two. But the interesting thing is the way Voltaire chooses to defend Montaigne in his *Lettres philosophiques* on two extremely different occasions in his attack on Pascal.[19] The language that Pascal uses is, as ever, very emotional: 'Les défauts de Montagne [sic] sont grands. Il est plein de mots sales et déshonnêtes. Cela ne vaut rien. Ses sentiments sur l'homicide volontaire et sur la mort sont horribles.'[20] Voltaire's answer is finely humane and reasonable:

Montagne [sic] parle en philosophe, non en chrétien. Il dit le pour et le contre de l'homicide volontaire. Philosophiquement parlant, quel mal fait à la société un homme qui la quitte quand il ne peut plus la servir? Un vieillard a la pierre et souffre des douleurs insupportables. On lui dit: 'Si vous ne vous faites tailler, vous allez mourir; si l'on vous taille, vous pourrez, encore radoter, baver et traîner pendant un an, à charge à vous-même et aux vôtres.' Je suppose que le bonhomme prenne alors le parti de n'être plus à charge à personne. Voilà à peu près le cas que Montagne expose.[21]

The second occasion reaches the fibre of the *Essais*, for we can still argue over religion or suicide on moral grounds but what we cannot argue about is the content and the aim of Montaigne; where Pascal has indignantly said 'le sot projet que Montaigne a eu de se peindre . . . Car, de dire des sottises par hasard et par faiblesse, c'est un mal ordinaire; mais d'en dire à dessein, c'est ce qui n'est pas supportable, et d'en dire de telles que celle-là', Voltaire answers: 'Le charmant projet que Montagne a eu de se peindre naïvement, comme il a fait! Car il a peint la nature humaine. Et le pauvre projet de Nicole, de Malebranche, de Pascal, de décrier Montagne'.[22]

(iv)

Napoleon carried a copy of Montaigne with him throughout his Russian campaign, but we may surmise that the Caesar he also travelled with was rather more to his taste than Montaigne. Montaigne's *peinture du moi* attracted, among others, Senancour, Chateaubriand, Madame de Staël, Nodier and Sainte-Beuve. Some others like Marceline Desbordes-Valmore, George Sand and Lamartine reacted emotionally to many aspects of Montaigne's thought, including his notion of women and society.[23] Eulogy and detraction continued in France throughout the century, although it must be said that there were far more who admired than castigated him. The amount of Montaigne in Flaubert has recently been shown in a fine article by Alison Fairlie.[24] She shows how Montaigne's clarity, humanity and consciousness of style make him 'un père nourricier' of Flaubert and also how he reads him as a *livre de chevet* during the night he watches by the body of his dead sister. Like Montaigne himself, who loved to pick out gastronomic figures when describing his reading, Flaubert has a delight for images such as 'En littérature, en gastronomie, il est certains fruits qu'on mange à pleine bouche, dont on a le gosier plein, et si succulents que le jus vous entre jusqu'au coeur' (p. 345). But it was the psychological penetration, the minute observation of the self, the fine discriminations of feeling and the knowledge that one is one's main subject when writing that made Flaubert see in Montaigne his own self. Flaubert's own influence as a novelist of fine distinction crossed the Atlantic and made him a forerunner of the American novel particularly of Henry James. But it is in Emerson (1803–82) that we can feel strongly the attraction of Montaigne for Americans. One of Emerson's strange and weird essays entitled 'Circles' makes us see that it is almost a translation of Montaigne:

> Our moods do not believe in each other. Today I am full of thoughts and can write what I please. I see no reason why I should not have the same thought, the same power of expression, tomorrow. What I write, whilst I write it, seems the most natural thing in the world; but yesterday I saw a dreary vacuity in this direction in which now I see so much; and a month hence, I doubt not, I shall wonder who he was that wrote so many continuous pages. Alas for this infirm faith, this will not strenuous, this vast ebb of a vast flow! I am God in nature; I am a weed by the wall.[25]

In the twentieth century we are relieved and delighted by E. M. Forster's choice of guides in the shape of Erasmus and Montaigne. In France there is, of course, Proust, who says, 'Un livre est un grand cimetière où sur la plupart des tombes on ne peut plus lire les noms effacés',[26] and who has been referred to often in this book. But the really fascinating couple around Montaigne are Gide and Valéry. Gide had a strong condescending, even patronizing, attitude towards Montaigne, whom he used as a cover under which he could air his own hedonism.[27] Valéry whispered once in his *Cahiers* the *aveu* 'C'est l'an dernier, au lit, à Montrozier que j'ai ouvert un

Montaigne. En peu de minutes, je l'ai renvoyé. Il m'assommait. Tout le monde peut écrire de ces choses',[28] and elsewhere says: 'Montaigne ni Pascal ne font presque plus figure de *penseurs*' (*Cahiers* (Paris: Imprimerie Nationale, 1957–61), Vol. 2, p. 1186).

Does this mean a complete rejection of the *Essais* as they are so overridden with clichés? Not exactly. For Valéry takes Montaigne very seriously in this statement, 'Montaigne, Pascal, Rousseau sont universellement un peu plus que des auteurs: ils sont des exemplaires très divers d'attitudes significatives dans la vie, tellement que nous ne pouvons penser à leur œuvre que nous ne pensions à leur être'.[29] And in 1941 (four years before he died) he is ill at the château of Montrozier and he has as a comfort 'Dans ce vaste lit, la radio; les remèdes, un Montaigne, un Diderot, un Balzac . . .'.[30] However, there is a more fascinating point behind this, and it is perhaps a point not seen by either Gide or Valéry. If we remember Montaigne's unique experience of friendship/love with La Boëtie which he expresses thus in 'De l'amitié' (I.28) – 'Ce n'est pas une speciale consideration, ny deux, ny trois, ny quatre, ny mille: c'est je ne sçay quelle quinte essence de tout ce meslange, qui, ayant saisi toute ma volonté, l'amena se plonger et se perdre dans la sienne' (Villey-Saulnier, p. 189) – and turn to examine the friendship between Valéry and Gide, we find the former puzzling over this relationship. Gide comes back from his holiday in Egypt and calls to see his friend on 21 April 1939.

> Finalement, il y a de la tendresse entre nous. Je lui dis qu'il n'y a pas d'êtres plus différents que lui et moi. Oui (dit-il), nous sommes aux antipodes. Et moi: Et nous nous aimons bien . . . Sur quoi, il se penche et nous nous baisons, et je lui dis: Nous sommes de bien vieux amis . . .
>
> (*Cahiers*, Vol. 1, p. 165)

Valéry ponders this fact: 'Il a voulu séduire les gens, les jeunes surtout; et les charmer, avec des manières qui mélangent le genre Evangile au genre du séducteur d'enfants . . . Je suis excessivement séparatif' (p. 169). For forty-eight years they have been friends and have not known one another, and Valéry proceeds to sort out this relationship: 'Mon idée était que cette "amitié" fut une expérience vitale, presque "métaphysique" puisque la volonté d'approximation de Deux Moi-c'est-à-dire de deux UNique-par voie d'échanges de plus en plus précis s'y développât aux dépens de tout' (ibid.). When

Montaigne characterizes the friendship with La Boëtie he says: 'Si on me presse de dire pourquoy je l'aymais, je sens que cela ne se peut exprimer, qu'en respondant: Par ce que c'estoit luy; par ce que c'estoit moy.' Valéry says something like him:

> Je l'aime, je ne sais pourquoi, ni en quoi, car il n'est pas de natures plus opposées, moins conformes en goûts et en directions de l'esprit. Mais enfin, il en est ainsi, et rien de plus certain qu'une inclination qui existe par soi-même, sans le moindre argument, sans communauté de sentiments ni d'idées, – et comme sans cause.
>
> (p. 179)

The picture of friendship between Gide and Valéry comes as a fitting tribute to the genius of Montaigne. As Eliot said, 'of all authors Montaigne is one of the least destructible . . . It is hardly too much to say that Montaigne is the most essential author to know, if we would understand the course of French thought during the last three hundred years.'[31] The firm grasp of human experience, the kind of toughness of body and mind, the peculiar honesty and the refined sensibility shown by Montaigne make the *Essais* 'le seul livre au monde de son espece' (II.8).

(v)

The Montaigne of the scholarly world is a monster. Is he a Christian, pagan, sceptic, stoic, an epicurean, a fideist, a rationalistic man, a positivist, an optimist, a pessimist, an eclectic, an emotive man, an indifferent man . . . ? By his diversity, his outright self-contradictions, and continual evasions he is impossible to pin down to any doctrine. Montaigne's own words – 'On couche volontiers le sens des escris d'autrui à la faveur des opinions qu'on a préjugées en soi' (I.12; Villey-Saulnier, p. 448) – are warning signs for the scholar or critic. So much has been written on the *Essais* this century that I am forced to be selective in choosing what I think are important works.

The textual problem – what weight is placed on the 1595 edition, the urgent need to collate it with the *exemplaire* and the bringing into question major ideas Montaigne had on religion, friendship, politics and so on – is complex. Strowski's immense scholarship did produce the Edition Municipale, and the Villey edition (first produced in 1924, and reprinted in 1965 and 1978) still holds head position in the textual field. But there are problems of interpretation which suggest acutely that there is a need for another text. One example clarifies this point. In 1939, Maurice Riveline wrote a most moving, scholarly and intimate book called *Montaigne et l'amitié* (Paris: Presses Universitaires de France). He argued that friendship for Montaigne was not *un coup de foudre* and not a *passion* but was intellectual rather than sentimental. And he uses a passage as 'proof' of this phenomenon:

> O mon amy! En vaux-je mieux d'en avoir le goust, ou si j'en vaux moins? J'en vaux certes bien mieux. Son regret me console et m'honore. *Est-ce pas un pieux et plaisant office de ma vie, d'en faire à tout jamais les obseques?* Est-il jouyissance qui vaille cette privation?
> (cited on p. 72 of his book: Riveline's italics)

This is a crucial problem: in the *exemplaire* there is no mention of 'O mon amy!' and it seems to me doubtful that Montaigne would have added the exclamation mark. (In many other cases it is the editor that has added the mark, and not Montaigne.) The 1595 edition has the phrase as Riveline quotes it. Furthermore the rest of the passage is crossed out quite heavily in the *exemplaire*, and both Armaingaud and Strowski think that the erasure is not in the hand of Montaigne. Since it is quite important for Riveline's main argument he ought to mention the problem before going on to say: 'Quand il n'y aurait, en tout et pour tout, que ces mots pour nous renseigner, ils seraient bien probants; ils suffiraient pour autoriser et même pour requérir la recherche détaillée de l'influence de l'amitié sur la pensée de Montaigne.' This he does with matchless skill, thereby forecasting Butor's little book, which does the same thing but much less well.[32] However Strowski's assurance – that it was not erased by Montaigne himself, for his erasures are normally done in fine strokes instead of the heavy double crossings-out here – is questionable. In fact it seems that of all the crossings-out the most revealing is the one in 'De la vanité', which is so thick and double-marked that it has smudged the following page as well. It concerns La Boëtie's death, and I have quoted it before (see p. 119). There is a marginal comment (which one can almost not read): 'Et si en y a qu Il m . . . que je recuse, pour le . . . conoistre trop excessivement proclives e . . . ma faveur.' Riveline discusses this (p. 110) and again he accepts that the crossing-out was not by Montaigne's hand. This is almost impossible to say, for there are numerous passages knocked off the *Essais* between 1588 and 1592 and we have no evidence of what caution Pierre de Brach,

Madame de Montaigne or Marie de Gournay took as editors. Therefore, the judgement is highly subjective and hypothetical, and one cannot pronounce on it in the light of present-day knowledge.

The splendid appearance of Leake's *Concordance des Essais de Montaigne* (Geneva: Droz, 1981) is very valuable, for it enables us to see the author *mis à nu* with all the traceries and verbal patterns catalogued and numbered. Readers can now obtain a better sense of the *Essais* in its linguistic control, in thematic continuity, in semantic levels, and so on. The superb appendix I contains a word-frequency table, arranged numerically and in descending order of usage. No one will be surprised at the 17,694 uses of *et* nor the 1180 times of *homme/hommes*, but I was intrigued to discover the single entry of *abhorrée*, *Enfer* and *Purgatoire*; delighted at the comic *Déboutonné*, *Grandissime*, *Fricassée* and *Appendicules*; amazed at the entry of *Masturbation*, *Catze* and *Titillation*; and very warmly satisfied by *Branloire*, *Entregloser*, *Gambades*, *Primsautier*, *Sensiblement*, *Tendresse* and *Tissue*. This *Concordance* provides the serious and active reader with an indispensable tool for studying Montaigne. Absent, unfortunately, are the many Latin, Greek and Italian quotations. This is an unhappy choice, for the subject of quotation has in recent years received a good deal of critical attention.

Sayce's thorough book came out in 1972, and in his third chapter he investigates Montaigne's reading habits and makes certain evaluatory remarks: for instance, he remarks on 'the great disproportion between classical and Christian sources has a clear bearing on Montaigne's religious position' (p. 33) or the way in which a quotation may slip in subversive thoughts or the manner of adaptation of direct quotation. His investigation has been followed by Lino Pertile, Coleman, Mary B. McKinley, Antoine Compagnon and Cave.[33] Cave's study of Montaigne's habit of reading not only other persons' texts but his own book is crucial:

> He discusses his preferences and deficiencies as a reader, the difficulty of discovering the correct meaning of a text, the dangers of over-interpretation, the question of authorial intention and many other aspects of the topic which are still debated in our own day. (p. 133)

Indeed, in Cave's book, *The Cornucopian Text: Problems of Writing in the French Renaissance* (Oxford: Clarendon Press, 1979), he writes sensitively on Erasmus, Rabelais, Ronsard and Montaigne. The central argument óf the book is that imaginative literature may 'enact its own problematic nature'. The notion of intertextuality is important in the Renaissance, and Cave shows the plenitude/emptiness in all writing where pre-existing texts pre-form the writing of a text. 'Multiplicity of meaning is a fundamental element in the definition of "literature"' (p. 326). I would not agree with some of Cave's 'philosophical' arguments, but his perceptiveness has given all readers much to think about. Cave alerts all readers of the *Essais* and, indeed, of all literary texts to ironies, undertones, echoes between one passage and another and juxtaposition of sub-effects and intertexts.

The monumental and scrupulously scholarly biography of Trinquet unearths factual details, corrects the views of earlier scholars and presents Montaigne's childhood and adolescence in a true perspective. There remain as general studies the one by Hugo Friedrich, a professor in Freibourg, first written in German in 1949 and translated into French in 1968, and the posthumous study of Thibaudet.

Other studies are written from a particular viewpoint or with a particular object: such is the brilliant one by Michaël Baraz, *L'Etre et la connaissance selon Montaigne* (Paris: Corti, 1968), the well-argued one by Raymond C. La Charité, *The Concept of Judgment in Montaigne* (The Hague: Nijhoff, 1968), or the dazzling one by Jean Starobinski, *Montaigne en mouvement* (Paris: Gallimard, 1982), where the philosophical, the psychological, the literary and aesthetic approaches dance before the reader's eye. The theoretical tendency of recent years means that structuralism, post-structuralism, deconstruction and intertextuality are being applied to the *Essais*. But Montaigne, thank goodness, is not a theorist. May he have what he really wants: a sympathetic and active reader 'chewing' his *Essais*, 'un suffisant lecteur descouvre souvant és escrits d'autruy des perfections autres que celles que l'autheur y a mises et apperceües et y preste des sens et des visages plus riches' (I.xxiv).

NOTES

CHAPTER 1   INTRODUCTION

1   Several critics say that he overcame this hatred of Cicero later on in life (e.g.
F. P. Bowman, *Montaigne: Essays* (London: Edward Arnold, 1965), p. 13), but he
never gave up his dislike of the rhetorical works such as *De oratore*, his contempt
for Cicero's published poetry and, as we shall see later, his refusal to be a
Ciceronian. In the third book of his *Essais* he borrows much from the moral works
such as *De senectute* or *De natura deorum*: 'Quant à Cicero, les ouvrages qui me
peuvent servir chez-luy à mon desseing, ce sont ceux qui traitent de la philosophie
morale' (II.10).

2   Elie Vinet, *In schola aquitanica*, Burdigalae, apud S. Millangium, Typographium
regium, 1583.

3   ibid., p. 21.

4   ibid., pp. 25 ff: my italics. We know from the *Essais* (particularly I.26) that
Montaigne read in solitude (with the permission of Andrea de Gouvéa, principal of
the Collège de Guyenne) the classical writers and so was, partly, rid of the
allegorizing and commenting which were heavily present in all sixteenth-century
editions, and obviously in the teaching (see Vinet, *In schola aquitanica*). For further
documentation of this period of Montaigne's life, see the excellent account given in
Roger Trinquet, *La Jeunesse de Montaigne* (Paris: Nizet, 1972). Vinet's remark (*In
schola aquitanica*, p. 47) as regards religion – 'ils rendront un culte très religieux à
Dieu et aux saints' – is rather naïve. For further details, see Trinquet, *Jeunesse*,
pp. 492 ff. This factual account by Elie Vinet makes Pierre Villey's statements (*Les
Sources et l'évolution des Essais de Montaigne*, 2nd edn revised, 2 vols (Paris:
Hachette, 1933), Vol. 1, p. 170) seem very odd; for instance, apropos of Juvenal:
'C'est dire que c'est surtout entre 1580 et 1588 que Montaigne a lu cet auteur.' For
an excellent account of Vinet, see Louis Desgraves, *Elie Vinet, humaniste de
Bordeaux (1509–1587): vie, bibliographie, correspondance, bibliothèque*, Travaux
d'Humanisme et Renaissance 156 (Geneva, 1977).

5   We must remember that the praise, published in the 1588 edition, was very high,
for Montaigne had been to Venice, Rome, Florence, as well as Lyons – 'La ville me
pleut beaucoup': *Journal de voyage en Italie*, in *Montaigne: Oeuvres complètes*, ed.
Maurice Rat (Paris: Gallimard, 1962), p. 1339.

6   Trinquet, *Jeunesse*, pp. 509–55, has destroyed the myth of Montaigne's studies in
Toulouse which baffled critics like Strowski, Plattard and all others.

7   Here are a few books from Turnebus' press that were in Montaigne's library:
Apollinaire, Ex bibliotheca regia, Parisiis, 1552, apud Adr. Turnebum,
Typographium regium.
*Philon. Philonis Judaei in libros Mosis de mundi opificio, historicos, de legibus. Eiusdem
libri singulares.* Ex bibliotheca regia, Parisiis, ex officina Adriani Turnebi
typographi regiis typis, 1552.
Synesius. Parisiis, 1553. Ex officina Adriani Turnebi, typographi Regii, Regiis
typis.

8   The full title is: *La Theologie naturelle de Raymond Sebon Docteur excellent entre les
modernes, en laquelle part l'ordre de Nature, est demonstrée la verité de la Foy*

Chrestienne & Catholique, traduicte nouvellement de Latin en François. A Paris, chez Gilles Courbin, 1569. In 1581, Montaigne had it published for the second time. This time it revealed who was the translator. Montaigne's self-confidence had grown in strength.

9 For instance: *La mesnagerie de Xenophon. Les regles de mariage, de Plutarque. Lettre de consolation de Plutarque à sa femme. Le tout traduict de Grec en François par feu M. Estienne de La Boetie Conseiller du Roy en sa court de Parlement à Bordeaux. Ensemble quelques Vers Latins & François, de son invention. Item, un Discours sur la mort dudict Seigneur de La Boetie, par M. de Montaigne.* A Paris. De l'imprimerie de Federic Morel, rue S. Ian de Beauvais, au Franc Meurier, M.D.LXXI. Avec privilege.

10 There exists a story that his heart was buried in the parish church of St-Michel de Montaigne, and indeed, in June 1980 – which was the celebration in Bordeaux of the quatercentenary of the *Essais* – a plaque was unveiled in the church commemorating the event in the presence of those who attended the Colloquium.

11 See 'Montaigne: the living text', *French Studies*, vol. 40, no. 4 (October 1986).

12 The 1588 edition which appeared from the press of Abel L'Angelier has on its frontispiece 'Cinquiesme edition', but in fact we know only three editions prior to this 1588 edition – 1580, 1582 and 1587. The lost edition has been discussed by scholars, but until proof of the contrary appears we must regard the 1588 edition as the fourth. On the *exemplaire* Montaigne writes in his own hand 'Sixiesme edition', having crossed out the 'wrong' 'Cinquiesme edition'.

13 David Maskell, 'Quel est le dernier état authentique des *Essais* de Montaigne?', *Bibliothèque d'Humanisme et Renaissance*, Vol. 40 (Geneva: Droz, 1978), pp. 85–103).

14 R. A. Sayce, *The Essays of Montaigne: A Critical Exploration* (London: Weidenfeld & Nicolson, 1972), p. 57.

15 The fact that this phrase is not in the 1595 edition opens up two hypotheses. Either Mademoiselle de Gournay's transcription did not contain it or, if it did, she herself did not want it to be published. As the 'other' copy is not extant, either hypothesis is possible. For further details, see R. A. Sayce and David Maskell, *A Descriptive Bibliography of Montaigne's Essais, 1580–1700* (London: Bibliographical Society, 1984).

16 Maskell ('Quel est le dernier état authentique des *Essais* de Montaigne?', p. 23) comments also on the obsession of Montaigne after 1588 with the 'physical' appearance of his book.

17 Vol. 1, pp. xvii–xviii: 'Seule la ponctuation de Montaigne ne sera pas reproduite ici. Elle est certes curieuse et significative, mais tellement éloignée de notre usage que nous avons cru devoir en traduire les indications dans une ponctuation plus moderne.' Strowski puts the punctuation variants in an appendix.

CHAPTER 2
HOW TO READ A PAGE OF MONTAIGNE:
ACTIVE PARTICIPATION OF THE READER

1 Terence Cave, *The Cornucopian Text: Problems of Writing in the French Renaissance* (Oxford: Clarendon Press, 1979), p. 315. Another way of saying this absolute truth is: 'A centrifugal movement is established. Interpretation is destruction and dissipation: the murdered text reverts to its anonymous particles' (p. 315).

2 L. C. Knights, *Explorations: Essays in Criticism mainly on the Literature of the Seventeenth Century* (London: Chatto & Windus, 1963), p. ix.

3 For a brilliant article on Montaigne and reading, see Terence Cave, 'Problems of

reading in the *Essais*', in I. D. McFarlane and Ian Maclean (eds), *Montaigne: Essays in memory of Richard Sayce* (Oxford: Clarendon Press, 1982), pp. 133–68.

4 Michael Riffaterre, *La Production du texte* (Paris: Editions du Seuil, 1979), p. 12. He goes on to say: 'Ainsi limitée, l'explication diffère de l'interprétation structuraliste ordinaire qui cherche à tout intégrer à son modèle, mais qui ne parvient à intégrer que le texte comme matériau linguistique, pas le texte comme texte.'

5 Northrop Frye argues in *Anatomy of Criticism* (Princeton, NJ: Princeton University Press, 1957), p. 307, that 'Montaigne's *livre de bonne foi* is a confession made up of essays in which only the continuous narrative of the longer form is missing'. I prefer to regard them as a series of meditations similar to improvisations upon themes in a variety of keys.

6 10.2.18: 'Noveram quosdam qui se pulchre expressisse genus illud caelestis huius in dicendo viri sibi viderentur, si in clausula posuissent "esse videatur". Ergo primum est ut quod imitaturus est quisque intellegat, et quare bonum sit sciat.'

7 I have omitted one paragraph as it involves references to philosophy, which will be treated in a later chapter.

8 *The Confessions of Augustine*, ed. John Gibb and William Montgomery (Cambridge: Cambridge University Press, 1927). Written about the year 400, they are an account of Augustine's conversion.

9 Marcel Proust, *A la recherche du temps perdu*, Bibliothèque de la Pléiade (Paris: NRF, 1954), Vol. 3, p. 899.

10 For further details about quotations, see Lino Pertile, 'Paper and ink: the structure of unpredictability', in Raymond La Charité (ed.), *'O un Amy!' Essays on Montaigne in Honor of Donald M. Frame*, French Forum Monographs 5 (Lexington, Ky: French Forum Publications, 1977), pp. 190–218; Mary McKinley, *Words in a Corner: Studies in Montaigne's Latin Quotations* (Lexington, Ky: French Forum Publications, 1981); Antoine Compagnon, *La seconde main ou le travail de la citation* (Paris: Niyet, 1979); and my *The Gallo-Roman Muse: Aspects of Roman Literary Tradition in Sixteenth-Century France* (Cambridge: Cambridge University Press, 1979), ch. 7.

11 cf. 'Composer nos meurs est nostre office, non pas composer des livres, et gaigner, non pas des batailles et provinces, mais l'ordre et tranquillité à nostre conduite' (Villey-Saulnier, p. 1108). The 'ordre' and the 'tranquillité' are far from pointing in an ethical direction; they are aesthetic pointers; the 'composer' is the 'artful' (in the sense of 'full of art'/'full of learning') writer. We shall come back to this point in Chapter 9.

12 Blaise Pascal, *Pensées*, ed. L. Lafuma (Paris: Delmas, 1951), p. 217.

13 Paul Valéry, *Les Cahiers*, published in facsimile by the Centre National de Recherche Scientifique in 29 vols (Paris: Imprimerie Nationale, 1957–61).

CHAPTER 3
INTELLECTUAL AND PHILOSOPHICAL BACKGROUND

1 Rabelais, *Oeuvres complètes*, ed. Pierre Jourda (Paris: Garnier, 1962), Vol. 1, p. 259.

2 *Horace on Poetry: The 'Ars Poetica'* (Cambridge: Cambridge University Press, 1971), p. v.

3 *Q. Horatius Flaccus. Ex fide, atque auctoritate decem librorum manu scriptorum, opera Diony. Lambini Monstroliensis emendatus: ab eodemque commentarijs copiosissimis illustratus, nunc primum in lucem editus. Lugduni apud Ioann. Tornaesium. M.D.LXI.*, p. 480.

4　*Adriani Turnebi Regii philosophiae graecae professoris adversariorum. Tomus primus duodecim libros continens. Cum Indice copiosissimo.* Parisiis, Ex officina Gabrielis Buonij, in clauso Brunello, sub signo D. Claudij. 1564.

5　Jean Jehasse, *La Renaissance de la critique: l'essor de l'humanisme érudit de 1560 à 1614* (Saint-Etienne: Presses Universitaires, 1976).

6　For instance, Henri Estienne in his *De criticis vet. Gr. et Latinis, eorumque variis apud poetas potissimum reprehensionibus, Dissertatio Henrici Stephani. Lectori. Ex criticis monitis criticum tibi contrahe callum. Ut criticas sapiant callida scripta notas. Restitutionis Comment. Servii in Virgil & magnae ad eos accessionis Specimen.* Parisiis excudebatur, Anno MDLXXXVII.

7　*Dionysii Lambini monstroliensis graecarum litterarum doctoris Regij oratio postridie Idus Dec. pridie quam Phillippicarum Demosthenis explicationem orsus est.* Paris, 1563, pp. 6 ff.

8　See Roy E. Leake, *Concordance des Essais de Montaigne*, 2 vols (Geneva: Droz, 1981).

9　Many of these terms are to be found in Cicero and Quintilian: for instance, *textum* when they are talking about literary composition, texture, tissue and style – e.g. Quintilian (9.4.17), 'dicendi textum tenue'; *nervus* meaning vigour, force, strength, or *nervosus* meaning vigorous, energetic, as in Cicero (*De oratore*, 36.127): 'nervosus dicere'.

10　Turnebus' treatise on Cicero in *La meilleure forme d'orateurs* is translated into French by Vigenère (Paris, 1575) where you find that Caesar 'se desrobant de nos oreilles par sa grande facilité & douceur, pleine neantmoins de nerfs, & de majesté qui n'abandonne iamais le fil de la narration . . . ' (p. 3) or Tacitus is 'espois, moilleux, floride, hautain, & magnifique, mais plus entrecouppé qu'il ne devroit, hardi en sentences, en paroles encore plus, dont il est fort subtil ouvrier, voire un peu hazardeux & excessif en translations & figures, ne s'approchant que trop prez de la hardiesse & liberté poëtique, si le tout n'estoit accompagné de beaucoup d'invention, & d'une diligence merveilleuse'.

11　E. Gilson, *Les Idées et les lettres* (Paris: Vrin, 1932), p. 231.

12　Rabelais, *Oeuvres complètes*, ed. Pierre Jourda (Paris: Garnier, 1962), Vol. 1, pp. 261–2.

13　Marcel Proust, *A la recherche du temps perdu*, Bibliothèque de la Pléiade (Paris: NRF, 1954), Vol. 1, p. 864.

14　Pierre Villey, *Les Sources et l'évolution des Essais de Montaigne*, 2 vols (Paris: Hachette, 1908; revised edn 1933).

15　In the first issue of the *Bulletin de la Société des Amis de Montaigne* (1913–21) came the violent attack of Dr Armaingaud against the evolution-from-Stoicism thesis of Villey: 'M. Villey semble avoir senti la fragilité de sa thèse . . . elle répand une confusion fâcheuse sur l'ouvrage entier' (p. 157). In his edition of the *Essais* (1930) Villey has partly redrawn his position. In the last two decades many scholars have criticized Villey: for instance, Hugo Friedrich, *Montaigne* (Paris: Gallimard, 1968); M. Baraz, *L'Etre et la connaissance chez Montaigne* (Paris: Corti, 1968); and articles by J. P. Boon such as 'Evolution et esthétique dans les *Essais de Montaigne*', *Philological Quarterly*, vol. 47, no. 1 (1968), pp. 526 ff. Three recent writers are also highly critical of Villey: Zbigniew Gierczynski, 'Le rationalisme de Montaigne et l'unité de sa pensée', in Pierre Michel (ed.), *Montaigne et les Essais, 1580–1980: actes du Congrès de Bordeaux (Juin 1980)* (Paris/Geneva: Champion-Slatkine, 1983), pp. 135–53; Jules Brody, *Lectures de Montaigne* (Lexington, Ky: French Forum Publishers, 1981); and Donald Stone, 'Montaigne and Epicurus: a lesson in originality', R. Aulotte and others (eds), *Mélanges Saulnier* (Geneva: Droz, 1984), pp. 465–71.

16　I give one example, taken from the essay 'De la tristesse' (I.2). The 1588 edition starts with 'Je suis des plus exempts de ceste passion' and ends with 'Je suis peu en prise de ces violentes passions: j'ay l'apprehension naturellement dure; Et l'encrouste et espessis tous les jours par discours' (Villey-Saulnier, p. 14). Montaigne is trying to 'control' his passion by the enormous drive of his willpower. The *exemplaire* adds to the first sentence three and a half sentences which bring in Stoicism – 'les Stoiciens en defendent le sentiment à leurs sages'. A surprising progress in Montaigne? Maybe. It is interesting to note that Villey's tripartite division of Montaigne's evolution runs quite contrary to this example: here the Stoic position is only manifest in the 1588 edition.

17 For a discussion of the relevant Stoic doctrines, see E. Vernon Arnold, *Roman Stoicism* (London: Routledge & Kegan Paul, 1958), esp. pp. 281 and 291–300.

18 Montaigne's own copy of Diogenes Laertius is now in the Municipal Library of Libourne. For further details, see my article, 'Notes sur l'édition grecque de Diogène Laërce que possédait Montaigne', *Bulletin de la Société des Amis de Montaigne*, 6e série, no. 1 (1979), pp. 24–7.

19 This and the following three examples are all (A) passages.

20 Examples of either *apprentissage* or *apprenti* in other essays are: I.9, I.20, I.23, I.24, I.25, I.30, I.40, II.10, II.11, II.17, II.37, III.6, III.8, III.9, III.11 and III.12. Analyses of all the examples would be worthwhile.

21 The sentence which immediately follows this has a true Christian flavour about it: 'Mon cathedrant, c'est l'authorité de la volonté divine, qui nous reigle sans contredit et qui a son rang au dessus de ces humaines et vaines contestations' (an (A) passage).

22 The Oxford text reads: 'primitiae iuuenis miserae bellique propinqui/dura rudimenta'.

23 The *Concordance* gives *nonchalant* as an adjective five times and as a substantive once; *nonchalamment* six times; *nonchalance* fourteen times; *nonchallante* twice; *nonchallantes* once; and *nonchaloir* six times.

24 Montaigne's own copy is now in Chantilly. This Plantine 1570 Anvers edition of Caesar in the Musée Condé not only has the signature of Montaigne, but is also heavily annotated by him to such an extent that Paul Courteault could say in 'Le César de Montaigne au Musée Condé à Chantilly', *Bulletin de la Société des Amis de Montaigne*, 2nd series, vol. 11 (October 1941), pp. 9 ff.:

> Il porte 600 annotations de la main de Montaigne . . . On y surprend l'usage qu'il fait de ses lectures, les idées des auteurs qui se sont mêlées à sa pensée personnelle pour stimuler et mettre en mouvement son esprit . . . Il ne s'agit plus de réflexions sur une longue série d'événements, mais de jugements plus précis sur un court moment de l'histoire et sur un seul héros auquel il a consacré de très nombreuses pages dans son livre.

25 The *Concordance* gives *gaillard* five times; *gaillarde* five times; *gaillardement* twice; *gaillardes* four times; *gaillardise* five times; *gaillairds* twice; *nerveuse* twice; *nerveux* three times; *robuste* three times and one in the plural; *virile* seven times; *virilement* three times; *virilité* twice; *virils* once; *fluide* once and once in the plural; *fluidité* once and *caduque* four times.

CHAPTER 4
THE 'APOLOGIE DE RAIMOND SEBOND':
RELIGION AND SCEPTICISM

1 See F. A. Yates, *French Academies of the Sixteenth Century* (London: Warburg Institute, 1947), for a description of these academies.

2 H. Busson, *Le Rationalisme dans la littérature française de la Renaissance (1533–1601)* (Paris: Vrin, 1971).

3 *Journal de voyage en Italie*, in *Montaigne: Oeuvres complètes*, ed. Maurice Rat (Paris: Gallimard, 1962), pp. 1115–1342.

4 e.g. M. Dréano, *La Pensée religeuse de Montaigne* (Paris: Nizet, 1936; 2nd edn 1969), and A. Müller, *Montaigne*, Les Ecrivains devant Dieu (Paris: Desclée De Brouwer, 1965).

5 Blaise Pascal, *Pensées*, ed. L. Lafuma (Paris: Delmas, 1951), Vol. 1, p. 240.

6 For a full discussion of this, see A. Levi, *French Moralists* (Oxford: Clarendon Press, 1964), esp. pp. 51–63.

7 Sextus Empiricus, the late-classical philosopher, is clearly one of the sceptics whom Montaigne had read, for painted on the beams in his study was 'all that is certain is that nothing is certain' and 'I suspend judgement'. The *Hypotyposes pyrrhoniennes* had been translated in 1562 by Henri Estienne. For fuller details of Sextus, see Peter Burke's penetrating little book, *Montaigne* (Oxford: Oxford University Press, 1981), ch. 3.

8 For a different interpretation, see M. A. Screech, *Montaigne and Melancholy: The Wisdom of the Essays* (London: Duckworth, 1983), p. 46.

9 For fuller details, see Franck Lestringant, 'Le cannibalisme des "cannibales"', in *Bulletin de la Société des Amis de Montaigne*, 6e série, no. 11–12 (1982), pp. 19–38.

10 Pascal, though he stole so much from Montaigne, does have the obsessive emotional, metaphysical push towards faith. Examples of this neurotic quality abound, but I give only a few: 'Le *moi* est haïssable'; 'Que je haïs ces sottises, de ne pas croire l'Eucharistie, etc.' and 'J'admire avec quelle hardiesse ces personnes entreprennent de parler de Dieu'. He accuses Montaigne of *confusion*, of always talking about himself and of 'mourir lâchement et mollement par tout son livre'. In fact he has not seen the point of the *Essais*. *Sottise* is a favourite word with Pascal. For a full and fascinating treatment of European scepticism, see Richard H. Popkin, *The History of Scepticism from Erasmus to Descartes* (Assen: Royal Van Gorcum, 1968).

11 Marcel Proust, *A la recherche du temps perdu*, Bibliothèque de la Pléiade (Paris: NRF, 1954), Vol. 3, p. 912.

CHAPTER 5
POLITICAL AND ETHICAL IDEAS

1 For further details on the religious wars, see: J. H. M. Salmon, *Society in Crisis: France in the Sixteenth Century* (London: Benn, 1975), and J. H. Elliott, *Europe Divided, 1559–1598* (London: Collins, 1968).

2 For the influence of Borromeo on Henri III, see F. A. Yates, *The French Academies of the Sixteenth Century* (London: Warburg Institute, 1947), esp. chs 8 and 10.

3 Cotgrave gives as possible meanings of *saillies*: 'A sallie, eruption, violent issue, or breaking out upon; also, a leape, sault, bound, skip, iert.' But Florio goes further

when he translates Montaigne's phrase as 'The Poeticall furies, which ravish and transport their Author beyond himselfe . . . '. The spark of divine fire, the gift of poetry are sometimes in Montaigne as they are in Du Bellay or Ronsard. The *saillies poëtiques* are of much the same kind as Valéry's *trouvailles*, and they get to the fibrous centre of Montaigne's writing as we shall see later.

4   Pascal and the Jansenists objected quite strongly to this statement as they did to 'Si j'avois à revivre, je revivrois comme j'ay vecu; ni je ne pleins le passé ny je ne crains l'avenir'. But Montaigne is only giving his personal reaction, not laying down a general rule.

5   Professor Screech in his *Montaigne and Melancholy: The Wisdom of the Essays* (London: Duckworth, 1983) interprets this differently (p. 49) as for him 'Montaigne's religious world is a world of grace – though reason has to manage without it in the *Essays*' (p. 46).

6   See the fine article by Nicole Trèves, 'Beyond "l'utile" and "l'honnête": on some pioneering aspects of Machiavelli and Montaigne', *Bulletin de la Société des Amis de Montaigne*, 6e série, no. 15–16 (1983), pp. 45–60.

CHAPTER 6
THE CLASSICAL LITERARY BACKGROUND:
KNOWLEDGE AND IMAGINATION

1   I. D. McFarlane, 'Montaigne and the concept of imagination', in D. R. Haggis and others (eds), *The French Renaissance and Its Heritage: Essays presented to Alan M. Boase* (London: Methuen, 1968), pp. 117–37.

2   William Blount, *Glossographia; or, A Dictionary Interpreting the Hard Words of Whatsoever Language, Now Used in Our Refined English Tongue.*

3   Florio reads thus: 'What availes it us to have our bellies full of meat, if it be not digested? If it be not transchanged in us? except it nourish, augment, and strengthen us.'

4   *Scripta Selecta* (Leipzig, 1871), Vol. 1, p. 162.

5   *Montaigne: Oeuvres complètes*, ed. Maurice Rat (Paris: Gallimard, 1962), pp. 1223–4.

6   Cited by George Williamson, *The Senecan Amble* (London: Faber & Faber, 1951), p. 111.

7   See Terence Cave, *The Cornucopian Text: Problems of Writing in the French Renaissance* (Oxford: Clarendon Press, 1979), pp. 284–97.

8   Almost eighty years ago Pierre Villey put down his reconstruction of Montaigne's library in his *Les Sources et l'évolution des Essais de Montaigne*, 2 vols (Paris: Hachette, 1908; 2nd edn 1933). Others include: R. R. Bolgar, *The Classical Heritage and Its Beneficiaries* (Cambridge: Cambridge University Press, 1954), and R. R. Bolgar (ed.), *Classical Influences in European Culture, AD 1500–1700* (Cambridge: Cambridge University Press, 1976); Robert Aulotte, *Amyot et Plutarque: la tradition des 'moralia' au XVIe siècle* (Geneva: Droz, 1965); R. A. Sayce, *The Essays of Montaigne: A Critical Exploration* (London: Weidenfeld & Nicolson, 1972); Carol Clark, 'Seneca's letters to Lucilius as a source of some of Montaigne's imagery', *Bibliothèque d'Humanisme et Renaissance*, vol. 30 (1968), and her book *The Web of Metaphor: Studies in the Imagery of Montaigne's Essais*, French Forum Monographs 7 (Lexington, Ky: French Forum Publications, 1978); and my *The Gallo-Roman Muse: Aspects of Roman Literary Tradition in Sixteenth-Century France* (Cambridge: Cambridge University Press, 1979).

9   In Roy E. Leake, *Concordance to des Essais de Montaigne*, 2 vols (Geneva: Droz, 1981), we can see that Virgil is the favourite with thirteen quotations, then Catullus

with seven, Lucretius with six, Martial with five, and Horace with four.

10 In my article 'Longinus and Montaigne', *Bibliothèque d'Humanisme et Renaissance*, vol. 47, no. 2 (1985), pp. 405–13.

11 Muret was translating the treatise around 1554, but it never appeared in print and is regarded as lost. It is referred to by Andreas Dudith, a Hungarian humanist, in 1560. The Latin translation by Domenico Pizzimenti appeared in 1566. Franciscus Portus, a Cretan, edited the text in 1569 and had written a commentary on Longinus which was not published (but was mentioned by his son Aemilius in 1584) until the eighteenth century by Zacharias Pearce. In 1572 there appeared another Latin translation by Petrus Paganus. For further details, see B. Weinberg, 'Translations and commentaries of Longinus, *On the Sublime*, to 1600: a bibliography', in *Modern Philology*, vol. 47 (1950), pp. 145–51.

12 See my article, 'Catullus in Montaigne's 1580 version of "De la tristesse" (I.2)', *Bibliothèque d'Humanisme et Renaissance*, vol. 42 (1980), pp. 139–44.

13 *Longinus on the Sublime*, ed. W. Rhys Roberts (Cambridge: Cambridge University Press, 1907).

CHAPTER 7
THE AMBIGUOUS FRONTIER BETWEEN PROSE AND POETRY

1 The *editio princeps* came out in Brescia in 1473. Lambin edited it in 1563, had seen the readings of the St-Bertin manuscript, and with his fine scholarship had emended the text so that several of his corrections stand today. Villey suggested, rightly in my opinion, that Montaigne was using the Lambin edition. The admiration of Lucretius as a great Latin poet was shared by many scholars in the 1560s, including Scaliger. It was his use of metaphor that marked him for Renaissance scholars and poets. See the use made of him in Ronsard's *Hymnes*. For the influence of Lucretius on Montaigne, and for a fuller bibliography in this respect, see S. Fraisse, *L'Influence de Lucrèce en France au seizième siècle* (Paris: Nizet, 1962).

2 Cotgrave gives for *esguillette nouée*: 'a charming of a man's codpeece point so, as he shall not be able to use his owne wife, or woman (though he may use any other;): Hence *avoir l'esguillette nouée* signifies to want erection: (This impotencie is supposed to come by the force of certaine words utterred by the Charmer, while he ties a knot on the parties codpeece-point.)'

3 In 'De la tristesse' he opens in 1580 with 'Le conte dit' and then in 1588 claims 'je suis des plus exempts de cette passion'. The power of imagination and passion in Montaigne is paramount in 1580, and the disclaimer he introduces in 1588 is clearly to show them as 'controllable' – or at least it is his intention that they be 'controlled'; cf. 'De la peur' (I.18) where the opening is by way of a quotation from Virgil:

> Obstupui, steteruntque comae et vox faucibus haesit.

> I remained stupefied, my hair bristled and my voice was caught in the throat.
>
> > (*Aeneid*, 2.774)

Here the opening is in Latin as is the meaning and opening of 'De la force de l'imagination'.

4 A Plautus quotation before Martial is translated by Montaigne:

> Mulier tum benè olet, ubi nihil olet.

> la plus parfaicte senteur d'une femme, c'est ne sentir à rien.

5 He makes this confession in III.3 (Villey-Saulnier, p. 826):

> je diray cecy des erreurs de ma jeunesse. Non seulement pour le danger qu'il y a (C) de la santé (si n'ay je sceu si bien faire que je n'en aye eu deux atteintes, legeres toutesfois et preambulaires), (B) mais encores par mespris, je ne me suis guere adonné aux accointances venales et publiques: j'ay voulu esguiser ce plaisir par la difficulté, par le desir et par quelque gloire . . .

La difficulté vaincue is, of course, one leitmotif that runs through 'Sur des vers de Virgile'.

6 Roger Trinquet, *La Jeunesse de Montaigne* (Paris: Nizet, 1972), p. 573.
7 J. Petter, *Horace*, trans. B. Humez (London: Macmillan, 1964), p. 34.

CHAPTER 8
THE STUDY OF THE SELF: PSYCHOLOGY AND HUMANITY

1 Note the word *solicitée* and compare it with the use of exactly the same word in Proust:

> Cependant, je m'avisai au bout d'un moment, après avoir pensé à ces résurrections de la mémoire, que, d'une autre façon, des impressions obscures avaient quelquefois, et déjà à Combray du côté de Guermantes, solicité ma pensée . . .
> (*A la recherche du temps perdu*, Bibliothèque de la Pléiade, Paris: NRF, 1954, Vol. 3, p. 878)

2 Cotgrave gives for *soliciter*: 'To solicite, move, importune, intreat instantly, pursue earnestly, follow hard; also, to heed seriously, looke verie carefully unto.'
3 Proust, *A la recherche du temps perdu*, Vol. 3, p. 878.
4 It is fairly generally agreed that Montaigne at first merely gathered anecdotes, 'sententiae' and reflections on the human condition. See, for fuller details, Pierre Villey, *Les Sources et l'évolution des Essais de Montaigne*, 2nd edn revised, 2 vols (Paris: Hachette, 1933).
5 Compare Proust's idea that our social person is the creation of oneself by other people's thought:

> Mais même au point de vue des plus insignifiantes choses de la vie, nous ne sommes pas un tout matériellement constitué, identique pour tout le monde et dont chacun n'a qu'à aller prendre connaissance comme d'un cahier des charges ou d'un testament; notre personnalité sociale est une création de la pensée des autres.
> (Proust, *A la recherche du temps perdu*, Vol. 1, p. 19)

Sartre and others have taken the idea further.

6 See Lino Pertile, 'Paper and ink: the structure of unpredictability', in Raymond C. La Charité (ed.), *'O un Amy!' Essays on Montaigne in Honor of Donald M. Frame*, French Forum Monographs 5 (Lexington, Ky: French Forum Publications, 1977); Marianne S. Meijer, 'L'ordre des *Essais* dans les deux premiers volumes', in Pierre Michel (ed.), *Montaigne et les Essais, 1580–1980: actes du Congrès de Bordeaux (Juin 1980)* (Paris/Geneva: Champion-Slatkine, 1983), pp. 17–27.

7 Other uses of *confession/confesser* are, for instance: II.17, 'quant aux bransles de l'ame, je veux confesser ce que je sens'; II.20, 'Quand je me confesse à moy religieusement je trouve'; II.10, 'Mais, à confesser hardiment la verité'; II.12, 'Or j'accepte cette naifve et franche confession'.

8 Proust, *A la recherche du temps perdu*, Vol. 3, p. 911.

9 See the essay 'Ronsard's later poetry', in Terence Cave (ed.), *Ronsard the Poet* (London: Methuen, 1973), pp. 287–318.

10 The subject of sex has been largely avoided in Montaigne criticism. Writers who have dealt with sex are, for example: R. A. Sayce, *The Essays of Montaigne: A Critical Exploration* (London: Weidenfeld & Nicolson, 1972), pp. 127–33; Donald M. Frame, *Montaigne's Essais: A Study* (Englewood Cliffs, NJ: Prentice-Hall, 1969); P. Hallie, *The Scar of Montaigne: An Essay in Personal Philosophy* (Middletown, Conn.: Wesleyan University Press, 1966); and Géralde Nakam, 'Eros et les Muses dans "Sur des vers de Virgile"', in *Etudes seiziémistes offertes à Monsieur le Professeur V.-L. Saulnier* (Geneva: Droz, 1980), pp. 395–403.

11 A very broad range of human sexuality is covered by Montaigne. With a basic human curiosity he is almost an anthropologist in telling us of the sexual behaviour of Amerindians (Villey-Saulnier, p. 212), a sexologist in relating how Diogenes 'exerçant en publicq sa masturbation' (ibid., p. 535) or discussing impotence (ibid., p. 13: 'cette glace qui les saisit par la force d'une ardeur extreme, au giron mesme de la joüyssance' – the 1588 edition contained 'accident qui ne m'est pas incogneu', but he erased it finally), a frank gazer at himself 'Pour n'estre continent' (ibid., p. 229) and a hearty confessor of his own sexuality 'et notamment ceux en qui le corps peut beaucoup, comme en moy' (ibid., p. 824). The list of strange customs in 'De la coustume' (I.23), for instance, does not, in my opinion, point at the moralism of Montaigne; rather, the sheer fascination of finding that women 'pissent debout, les hommes accroupis' or countries where 'on faict circoncire les femmes' (Villey-Saulnier, p. 114) comes rather from a Herodotus of the Renaissance.

12 For further details, see Odette de Mourgues, *Two French Moralists: La Rochefoucauld and La Bruyère* (Cambridge: Cambridge University Press, 1978), esp. ch. 2, 'Psychological investigations'.

13 F. R. Leavis, *The Common Pursuit* (London: Chatto & Windus, 1952), p. 210.

14 Donald M. Frame, 'To "rise above humanity" and to "escape from the man": two moments in Montaigne's thought', *Romanic Review*, vol. 62 (1971), pp. 28–35.

CHAPTER 9
THE *ART DE VIVRE*:
EXPERIENCE AND AESTHETICS

1 See the fine article by W. G. Moore, 'Montaigne's notion of experience', in W. G. Moore and others (eds), *The French Mind: Studies in Honour of Gustave Rudler* (Oxford: Clarendon Press, 1952).

2 For a detailed comment on 'De l'amitié', see my *The Gallo-Roman Muse: Aspects of Roman Literary Tradition in Sixteenth-Century France* (Cambridge: Cambridge University Press, 1979), ch. 7.

3 The sentence immediately preceding this passage is a (B) version: 'Je me conseillerois volontiers Venise pour la retraicte d'une telle condition et foiblesse.' It is omitted by the 1595 Gournay edition and, of course, by Florio. It is a clear example of the need to collate the texts of the *exemplaire* and the 1595 edition.

4 cf. 'C'est chose tendre que la vie et aysée à troubler'; his views on the love he conceives and nurtures for Paris – 'Je l'ayme tendrement, jusques à ses verrues et à ses taches'; 'J'ay l'esprit tendre et facile à prendre l'essor' – all in the chapter 'De la vanité'.

5 Terence Cave, 'Problems of reading in the *Essais*', in I. D. McFarlane and Ian Maclean (eds), *Montaigne: Essays in Memory of Richard Sayce* (Oxford: Clarendon Press, 1982), p. 143.

6 cf. the same kind of humour in the marginalia of the last page, presumably written about the same time: 'Si auons nous beau monter sur des eschasses car sur des eschasses encore faut marcher de nos james. Et au plus esleue trhone du monde si ne somes assis que sur nostre cul' (EP, pl. 1019); cf. the substitution of 'cul' for 'costé' in EP, pl. 993.

7 Cotgrave gives 'L'esprit se veautre' as 'the mind revolves, casts about, or is diligently imployed', which does not get the right meaning. Guy Miège, in his *New Dictionary French and English* (London: Printed by Tho. Dawks for Thomas Bassett, 1677), gives 'se veautrer dans la boue' a merely literal translation 'to wallow in the mire' in the French-into-English part. But in the English-into-French part we have: 'To wallow in the mire, *se veautrer (se rouler) dans la bouë*. A puddle, where Swine wallow, *Bourbier où les pourceaux se veautrent*.' And then a metaphorical use: 'To wallow in pleasures, *nager dans les plaisirs*.' *OED* gives as a third meaning 'To roll about, or lie prostrate and relaxed in or upon some liquid, viscous, or yielding substance (e.g. mire, blood, water, dust, sand)'. The word often implied sensual enjoyment or indifference to defilement, and this is close to the sense in which Montaigne uses it. Florio understood the metaphor well.

8 For example, Guez de Balzac said: 'il estoit Gascon. Par conséquent, il ne se peut pas que son langage ne se sente des vices de son siecle et de son pays.'

CHAPTER 10
MONTAIGNE THROUGH THE AGES

1 For a chronological survey, see Alan M. Boase, *The Fortunes of Montaigne: A History of the Essays in France, 1580–1669* (London: Methuen, 1935); M. Dréano, *La Renommée de Montaigne en France au XVIIIe siècle, 1677–1802* (Angers: Editions de l'Ouest, 1953); Charles Dédeyan, *Montaigne chez ses amis anglo-saxons, 1760–1900*, 2 vols (Paris: Boivin, 1946); Donald M. Frame, *Montaigne in France, 1812–1852* (New York: Columbia University Press, 1940).

2 Villey-Saulnier, p. 1201.

3 ibid., p. 1202.

4 In the preface to her 1595 edition she says, for example, 'C'est à moy d'en parler: car moy seulle auois la parfaicte cognoissance de cette grand ame', admits to being 'la creature du grand Montaigne', and is of the opinion that 'ny l'amitié n'est plus ioincture ny liaison; c'est une double vie: estre amy c'est estre deux fois. Estre seul c'est n'estre que demy'; and without hesitation she follows this pillage from 'De l'amitié' (I.28) with 'ie croy que mon Pere eust esté d'opinion . . . '. Her piousness, her arrogance and her temerity mingle with her tone throughout of 'Entre nous femmelettes'.

5 As David Maskell in his essay seems to do. See his 'The evolution of the *Essais*', in

I. D. McFarlane and Ian Maclean (eds), *Montaigne: Essays in Memory of Richard Sayce* (Oxford: Clarendon Press, 1982), pp. 13–34.

6   F. Soury-Lavergne, ODN, 'Pédagogie de la nièce de Montaigne', in Pierre Michel (ed.), *Montaigne et les Essais, 1580–1980: actes du Congrès de Bordeaux (Juin 1980)* (Paris/Geneva: Champion-Slatkine, 1983), pp. 77–99.

7   Though we must not forget that there appeared in 1700 a fragmentation of the *Pensées . . . propres à former l'esprit*, nor the abridgement of 1677 called *L'Esprit des Essais*.

8   Marcel Raymond, *Génies de France* (Neuchâtel: L'Atre, 1942), p. 27.

9   Cited by Maurice Rat in his article on *Montaigne écrivain* in *Bulletin de la Société des Amis de Montaigne*, no. 17 (1968), p. 23.

10 Jean de La Fontaine, *Oeuvres diverses*, ed. Pierre Clarac (Paris: Pléiade, 1968), p. 707.

11 ibid., p. 3.

12 ibid., p. 655.

13 ibid., p. 184.

14 ibid., p. 653.

15 *Montaigne: Oeuvres complètes*, ed. Maurice Rat (Paris: Gallimard, 1962), pp. 1234–5.

16 Alexander Pope, *Poetical Works* (Oxford: Oxford University Press, 1983), p. 342.

17 Maynard Mack, *Collected in Himself* (London/Toronto: Associated University Press, 1982), p. 318.

18 Pope, *Poetical Works*, p. 351.

19 Voltaire, *Lettres philosophiques*, ed. F. A. Taylor (Oxford: Blackwell, 1946), p. 84.

20 Blaise Pascal, *Pensées*, ed. L. Lafuma (Paris: Delmas, 1951).

21 Voltaire, *Lettres philosophiques*, p. 111.

22 ibid., p. 115.

23 This was a misreading of Montaigne, particularly of 'Sur des vers de Virgile' (III.5) where his enlightened view of women stood out in the sixteenth century.

24 Alison Fairlie, 'Flaubert and the authors of the French Renaissance', in *Imagination and Language: Collected Essays on Constant, Baudelaire, Nerval and Flaubert* (Cambridge: Cambridge University Press, 1981), pp. 338–54.

25 R. W. Emerson, *Essays and Lectures* (New York: The Library of America, 1983), p. 401.

26 Marcel Proust, *A la recherche du temps perdu*, Bibliotèque de la Pléiade (Paris: NRF, 1954), Vol. 3, p. 903.

27 For a counter-argument, see W. M. L. Bell, 'Gide's *Essai sur Montaigne*: an assessment', in D. R. Haggis and others (eds), *The French Renaissance and Its Heritage: Essays Presented to Alan M. Boase* (London: Methuen, 1968), pp. 1–28.

28 Paul Valéry, *Les Cahiers*, ed. Judith Robinson (Paris: Gallimard, 1973), Vol. 1, p. 206.

29 Paul Valéry, *Oeuvres*, ed. Jean Hytier, Bibliothèque de la Pléiade (Paris: NRF, 1957), Vol. 1, p. 518.

30 ibid., Vol. 1, p. 68.

31 T. S. Eliot, *Selected Essays* (London: Faber & Faber, 1953), p. 409.

32 Maurice Riveline, *Essai sur les Essais* (Paris: Gallimard, 1968).

33 Lino Pertile, 'Paper and ink: the structure of unpredictability', in Raymond C. La Charité (ed.), *'O un Amy! Essays on Montaigne in Honor of Donald M. Frame*, French Forum Monographs 5 (Lexington, Ky: French Forum Publications, 1977); Dorothy Gabe Coleman, *The Gallo-Roman Muse: Aspects of Roman Literary Tradition in Sixteenth-Century France* (Cambridge: Cambridge University Press, 1979); Mary B. McKinley, *Words in a Corner: Studies in Montaigne's Latin Quotations* (Lexington, Ky: French Forum Publications, 1981); Antoine Compagnon, *La seconde main ou le travail de la citation* (Paris: Seuil, 1980); and Terence Cave, 'Problems of reading in the *Essais*', in I. D. McFarlane and Ian Maclean (eds), *Montaigne: Essays in Memory of Richard Sayce* (Oxford: Clarendon Press, 1982), pp. 133–66.

SELECT BIBLIOGRAPHY

(i) EDITIONS OF MONTAIGNE'S *ESSAIS*

Essais, ed. Alexandre Micha, 3 vols (Paris: Garnier-Flammarion, 1969).
Michel de Montaigne, *Essais*, ed. Jean Plattard, 6 vols (Paris: Société des Belles Lettres, 1959).
Les Essais de Montaigne, ed. Pierre Villey, with a preface by V.-L. Saulnier, 2 vols (Paris: Presses Universitaires de France, 1978).
The Essays of Montaigne, trans. and ed. Jacob Zeitlin, 3 vols (New York: Columbia University Press, 1934–6).

(ii) CLASSICAL LITERATURE

Bolgar, R. R., *The Classical Heritage and Its Beneficiaries* (Cambridge: Cambridge University Press, 1954).
Bolgar, R. R. (ed.), *Classical Influences in European Culture, AD 1500–1700* (Cambridge: Cambridge University Press, 1976).
Catullus, *Opera*, ed. R. Mynors (Oxford: Clarendon Press, 1958).
Fraisse, S., *L'Influence de Lucrèce en France au seizième siècle* (Paris: Nizet, 1962).
Horace, *Opera*, ed. F. Klingner (Leipzig: Teubner, 1959).
Longinus on the Sublime, ed. and trans. W. Rhys Roberts (Cambridge: Cambridge University Press, 1907).
Lucretius, *De rerum natura*, ed. and trans. C. Bailey (Oxford: Clarendon Press, 1947).
Martial, *Epigrams*, ed. and trans. Walter C. A. Ker (London: Heinemann, 1961).
Ovid, *Amores*, trans. Guy Lee (London: John Murray, 1968).
Ovid, *Metamorphoses*, trans. Frank Justus Miller (London: Heinemann, 1966).
Propertius, *Opera*, ed. M. Schuster (Leipzig: Teubner, 1954).
Virgil, *Opera*, ed. R. Mynors (Oxford: Clarendon Press, 1969).

(iii) BOOKS ON MONTAIGNE'S *ESSAIS*

Baraz, Michaël, *L'Etre et la connaissance selon Montaigne* (Paris: Corti, 1968).
Boase, Alan M., *The Fortunes of Montaigne: A History of the Essays in France, 1580–1669* (London: Methuen, 1935).
Dédeyan, Charles, *Montaigne chez ses amis anglo-saxons, 1760–1900*, 2 vols (Paris: Boivin, 1946).

Dréano, M., *La Renommée de Montaigne en France au XVIIIe siècle, 1677–1802* (Angers: Editions de l'Ouest, 1953).

Frame, Donald M., *Montaigne in France, 1812–1852* (New York: Columbia University Press, 1940).

Friedrich, Hugo, *Montaigne*, trans. Robert Rovini (Paris: Gallimard, 1968).

Joukovsky, Françoise, Montaigne et le problème du temps (Paris: Nizet, 1972).

La Charité, Raymond C. (ed.), *'O un Amy!' Essays on Montaigne in Honor of Donald M. Frame*, French Forum Monographs 5 (Lexington, Ky: French Forum Publications, 1977).

Michel, Pierre (ed.), *Montaigne et les Essais, 1580–1980: actes du Congrès de Bordeaux (Juin 1980)* (Paris/Geneva: Champion-Slatkine, 1983).

Nakam, Géralde, *Montaigne et son temps: les événements et les Essais* (Paris: Nizet, 1982).

Sayce, R. A., *The Essays of Montaigne: A Critical Exploration* (London: Weidenfeld & Nicolson, 1972).

Starobinski, Jean, *Montaigne en mouvement* (Paris: Gallimard, 1982).

Thibaudet, Albert, *Montaigne* (Paris: Gallimard, 1963).

Villey, Pierre, *Les Sources et l'évolution des Essais de Montaigne*, 2nd edn, 2 vols (Paris: Hachette, 1933).

(iv)   CHAPTERS AND ARTICLES

Baraz, Michaël, 'Les images dans les *Essais* de Montaigne', *Bibliothèque d'Humanisme et Renaissance*, vol. 27 (Geneva: Droz, 1965), pp. 361–94.

Cave, Terence, 'Problems of reading in the *Essais*', in I. D. McFarlane and Ian Maclean (eds), *Montaigne: Essays in Memory of Richard Sayce* (Oxford: Clarendon Press, 1982), pp. 133–68.

Maskell, David, 'Quel est le dernier état authentique des *Essais* de Montaigne?', *Bibliothèque d'Humanisme et Renaissance*, vol. 40 (Geneva: Droz, 1978), pp. 85–103.

Moore, W. G., 'Montaigne's notion of experience', in W. G. Moore and others (eds), *The French Mind: Studies in Honour of Gustave Rudler* (Oxford: Clarendon Press, 1952).

Nakam, Géralde, 'Eros et les Muses dans "Sur des vers de Virgile"', in *Etudes seiziémistes offertes à Monsieur le Professeur V.-L. Saulnier* (Geneva: Droz, 1980), pp. 395–403.

Trèves, Nicole, 'Beyond "l'utile" and "l'honnête": on some pioneering aspects of Machiavelli and Montaigne', *Bulletin de la Société des Amis de Montaigne*, 6e série, no. 15–16 (1983), pp. 45–60.

(v)   GENERAL BOOKS

Arnold, E. Vernon, *Roman Stoicism* (London: Routledge & Kegan Paul, 1958).

Cave, Terence, *The Cornucopian Text: Problems of Writing in the French Renaissance* (Oxford: Clarendon Press, 1979).

Coleman, Dorothy Gabe, *The Gallo-Roman Muse: Aspects of Roman Literary Tradition in Sixteenth-Century France* (Cambridge: Cambridge University Press, 1979).

Eliot, T. S., *Selected Essays* (London: Faber & Faber, 1953).

Eliott, J. H., *Europe Divided, 1559–1598* (London: Collins, 1968).

Frye, Northrop, *Anatomy of Criticism* (Princeton, NJ: Princeton University Press, 1957).

Jehasse, Jean, *La Renaissance de la critique: l'essor de l'humanisme érudit de 1560 à 1614* (Saint-Etienne: Presses Universitaires, 1976).

Proust, Marcel, *A la recherche du temps perdu*, Bibliothèque de la Pléiade (Paris: NRF, 1954).

Riffaterre, Michael, *La Production du texte* (Paris: Editions du Seuil, 1979).

Salmon, J. H. M., *Society in Crisis: France in the Sixteenth Century* (London: Benn, 1975).

(vi) BIOGRAPHY

Frame, Donald M., *Montaigne: A Biography* (New York: Harcourt, Brace & World, 1965).

Montaigne, Michel de, *Journal de voyage en Italie*, in *Montaigne: Oeuvres complètes*, ed. Maurice Rat (Paris: Gallimard, 1962).

Trinquet, Roger, *La Jeunesse de Montaigne* (Paris: Nizet, 1972).

INDEX